EQUAL PAY FOR WOMEN

Equal Pay for Women

Progress and Problems in Seven Countries

Edited by Barrie O. Pettman

with the assistance of John Fyfe

HEMISPHERE PUBLISHING CORPORATION

Washington   London

McGRAW-HILL BOOK COMPANY

New York   St. Louis   San Francisco   Auckland   Bogotá
Düsseldorf   Johannesburg   London   Madrid   Mexico
Montreal   New Delhi   Panama   Paris   São Paulo
Singapore   Sydney   Tokyo   Toronto

EQUAL PAY FOR WOMEN: Progress and Problems in Seven Countries

1 2 3 4 5 6 7 8 9 0   D O D O   7 8 3 2 1 0 9 8 7

Published in the United States under license from MCB (Management Decision) Limited.

Library of Congress Cataloging in Publication Data

Main entry under title:

Equal pay for women.

  Includes index.
  1. Equal pay for equal work—Case studies.
I. Pettman, B. O. II. Fyfe, John.
HD6061.E65 1977   331.4'2   77-7335
ISBN 0-07-049735-4

Contents

Preface

The impetus for bringing together studies of the progress and problems of implementing the concept of equal pay for women in seven industrialised countries stemmed from a personal research project financed by the Bank of England's Houblon-Norman Fund to which this volume is gratefully dedicated.

Initially, two articles appeared on the progress of equal pay in Australia and America in the *International Journal of Social Economics*, a journal initiated by the International Institute of Social Economics. These articles were subsequently updated and expanded by the authors and other chapters on the United Kingdom, Germany, Canada and Japan were commissioned to provide this volume designed to coincide with the ending of International Women's Year.

Dr. Barrie O. Pettman

Notes on the Contributors

Addison, John T.
Educated at the London School of Economics, 1964-71. Obtained Ph.D. in 1971, which examined the external spillover effects of productivity bargaining within the Southampton/Fawley local labour market, 1960-1970. Senior Assistant Economic Adviser with the Office of Manpower Economics, 1971-72, and since August 1972 Lecturer in Political Economy at the University of Aberdeen. One-time consultant to the Commission on Industrial Relations, National Board for Prices and Incomes and the Institute of Manpower Studies. Currently, part-time labour economics adviser to Deloitte, Robson, Morrow and Co. Publications include *Wage Drift* (H.M.S.O. for the O.M.E., 1973) and numerous labour economics articles. Visiting Professor of Economics, Temple University 1975-76.

Buckley, John E.
Mr. Buckley is a labour economist with the US Department of Labor, Bureau of Labor Statistics. For the past decade he has been associated with the Bureau's Area Wage Survey Program. He has authored or co-authored numerous articles and reports on wages and related benefits within metropolitan areas.

Mr. Buckley is a member of the Council of the International Institute of Social Economics. He is a graduate of George Washington University, Washington, D.C.

Chiplin, Brian
Brian Chiplin has been a lecturer in the Department of Industrial Economics at the University of Nottingham since 1967. He has published widely on a number of topics including equal pay and discrimination, industrial training, the textile industry and the economics of crime. He is author of a forthcoming book on "Mergers and the State in the UK". He has also undertaken consultancy work for the Prices and Incomes Board, Office of Manpower Economics Bolton Committee on Small Firms, and a number of other organisations and industrial companies.

Brian Chiplin and Peter Sloane were jointly awarded a research grant in 1974 by the Social Science Research Council to undertake a major investigation into Discrimination and Female Employment in Great Britain.

John Fyfe
Was educated at the University of Wales and the Graduate Business Centre. He was a full-time trade union official and subsequently an Economic Adviser to the Department of Employment, the Office of Manpower Economics, the Pay Board, and currently the Manpower Services Commission.

John Fyfe is also a Council Member of the International Institute of Social Economics and on the Editorial Board of the *International Journal of Social Economics*.

Gunderson, Morley
Morley Gunderson is an Associate Professor of Economics at the University of Toronto Centre for Industrial Relations, Faculty of Management Studies, and Scarborough College. He obtained his B.A. in Economics from Queen's University in Kingston, Canada, and his M.A. in Industrial Relations and Ph.D. in Economics from the University of Wisconsin i Madison. In addition to his more recent work on the labour market behaviour of women, Professor Gunderson has published extensively in the area of manpower training and on the impact of institutional constraints on the labour market. He is also a member of the editorial board of the *International Journal of Manpower*.

Hicks, John
John Hicks graduated with a first-class B.Com. (Honours) from the University of Melbourne in 1972, and with a Diploma in Education in 1973. He is now a senior tutor in the Department of Economics, the University of Melbourne.

Nieuwenhuysen, John P.
John Nieuwenhuysen holds the degrees of M.A. (1961) from Natal, and Ph.D. (1963) from London. He is presently Reader in Economics at the University of Melbourne, and has previously been a research fellow at the University of Natal (1959-1961); a research officer at the International Labour Office in Geneva (1967); an economic adviser to the Department of Trade and Industry in London (1971); and a visiting associate professor of Economics at the University of Pittsburgh (1966 and 1970). He is the editor of *Australian Trade Practices: Readings* (Cheshire, 1970) and author (assisted by E. Oakley) of *Competition in Australian Bookselling* (Melbourne University Press, 1975). He is on the Council of the International Institute of Social Economics and the editorial board of the *International Journal of Social Economics*.

Pettman, Barrie O.
Barrie O. Pettman was educated at the City University, Graduate Business Centre, M.Sc. (1967), Ph.D. (1970). He has been a lecturer in the Department of Social Administration, the University of Hull since 1970. He has published widely on a number of topics including industrial training, equal pay and labour turnover. He has also undertaken consultancy work for the Office of Manpower Economics. He is presently Chairman of the International Institute of Social Economics, on the Council of the Institute of Scientific Business, a Vice-Chairman of the British Society of Commerce, and Editor of the *International Journal of Social Economics*, the *International Journal of Manpower*, and *Managerial Law*.

Sloane, Peter J.
After graduating in economics at the University of Sheffield in 1964 and undertaking research at the University of Strathclyde, Dr. Sloane has held appointments at the University of Aberdeen and the University of Nottingham where he has been a Lecturer in Industrial Economics since 1969. During 1973/4 he acted as Economic Adviser to the Department of Employment's Unit for Manpower Studies (on secondment) and he has also undertaken consultancy work for the Prices and Incomes Board, Commission on Industrial Relations, Office of Manpower Economics and OECD. He has published widely, mainly in the area of labour economics and industrial relations.

Thurley, Elizabeth F.
Elizabeth Fusae Thurley was born and educated in Tokyo, taking a B.A. degree in English literature in 1953, at Tsuda University, famous in Japan for its pioneering of higher education for women. She came to England in 1957 after marriage and has three children at school. She works at the B.B.C.

Thurley, Keith E.
Keith Ernest Thurley was educated at LSE, taking a B.Sc.(Econ.) specialising in Sociology in 1952. He served in the Commonwealth Division in Japan and afterwards worked as an Assistant Labour Officer in a textile company in Britain, returning to LSE in 1959. He has been lecturing in Personnel Management, Industrial Relations, Industrial Sociology and, more recently, on Social Structure in Japan. Publications include "Supervision; a Reappraisal" (with Hans Wirdenius) and articles on Japanese management and industrial development.

EQUAL PAY FOR WOMEN

Introduction

by Barrie O. Pettman and J. Fyfe

The seven countries covered in this volume have pursued the concept of equal pay for women but via varying methods. In none of the countries studied could it be said that the concept is fully accepted and implemented. However, the studies do emphasise the quite considerable movement in the direction of equal pay for equal work particularly during the last decade.

Unfortunately, the progress has been uneven within and between countries. There are, however, several significant similarities in the seven countries both with respect to the progress of the concept and problems encountered in its implementation. These similarities and problems are now discussed under the headings of:
—the role of women in the labour force
—industrial and occupational crowding
—education, guidance and training
—Government intervention
—female/male earnings differentials
—other factors hindering further progress.

The role of women in the labour force
The role of women in the labour force in the countries examined shows in many respects interesting similarities. For example, the overall activity rate of women since the second World War generally shows an increase, although with a stagnation over the period 1960-1971 in Germany. A variation on this theme is shown by the case of Australia where the activity of female migrants had a demonstration effect on the activity rates of Australian born women. The exception to this general trend is Japan but this is due to the rapid decline in the previously prevalent sector of unpaid family labour.

A large proportion of the increase in each country, including Japan, is attributable to the increase in the activity of married women with the biggest increase in the older age brackets [1]. In addition, a growing proportion of economically active women are working part-time and obviously the working patterns of both full-time and part-time women workers are closely related to family commitments.

Industrial and occupational crowding
Women are crowding into certain industries, especially in the services sector, as well as crowding into certain occupations, particularly white-collar ones. Many of these industries and occupations are precisely those not generally covered by collective

agreements[2] and where trade union organisation is often weak. This rigidity of industrial and occupational distribution based on traditional concepts of "women's work" and "men's work" is of the greatest importance not only as regards equal remuneration for work of equal value but also vis-à-vis the general level of women's wages as compared with that of men's. Women tend to be confined to a limited range of traditionally low-paying occupations or those ranked low in prestige, instead of penetrating a wide range of occupations at all levels[3]. Where they are concentrated in "women's occupations" the tendency is to undervalue the work performed rather than to evaluate it objectively on the basis of the multiple factors involved in its performance[4].

On the other hand, specifically here in the cases of the United Kingdom and Germany, it is emphasised that of the two major forms of discrimination, namely pre-entry (employment) discrimination and post-entry (wage) discrimination it is the latter which is more prevalent, that is the redistribution of females both occupationally and industrially would have less effect on average earnings in comparison with granting women the male earnings levels in their existing occupations or industries. Consequently, it is possible that, while they will need to go hand-in-hand, equal pay legislation is more significant than equal opportunity legislation. In fact, since the original commissioning of these chapters John Addison has widened this analysis to include other European countries without altering this conclusion[5].

Education, guidance and training

Generally there is a strong positive relationship between educational attainment and female activity in the labour force but coupled with a lower proportion of women with qualifications, at whichever level of qualification chosen. The same conclusions are true at the next stages, namely guidance and training. Often women are settling for jobs that do not fully utilise their talents. Insufficient attention to the basic and continued education and training of girls, combined with outmoded vocational guidance which ignores changes in employment opportunities evolving with technological change tend to exacerbate the situation in which the attitudes and backgrounds of many women are inimical to the application of the equal pay principle and to the improvement of the wage position of women.

Government intervention

Increasingly since the end of the second World War, Governments have in many cases seen the need for action on the concept of equal pay. However, this has been undertaken by differing means in different countries.

In the United Kingdom the pattern followed was the usual one of voluntary collective bargaining, TUC resolutions, Royal Commission and the activity of pressure groups which gradually achieved the acceptance of the equal pay principle in certain areas of the public sector, particularly in white-collar occupations. However, to reach manual occupations and the bulk of the private sector necessitated legislation which was finally passed as the Equal Pay Act of 1970 phased over a 5½ year period until the end of December, 1975.

Germany, on the other hand, approached the equal pay concept via the constitutional method of Article 3 of the Basic Law of 1949, strengthened by the law on the organisation of companies in 1952, 1955 and 1972, and reinforced by the decisions of the Federal Labour Tribunals.

At the other extreme, for many reasons relating to the differing cultural norms, Government involvement in Japan has only recently commenced with the Vocational Training Law of 1969 and the more important Working Women's Welfare Law of 1972. Thus legislative effects on the price of female labour have not as yet been felt but "is surely going to be seen in the near future".

The remaining four countries of Australia, America, Canada and to a lesser extent New Zealand are linked via the problem of central versus provincial legislation. Thus under the Canadian constitution legislation pertaining to labour and civil rights are under provincial jurisdiction. Ontario, however, passed equal pay legislation in 1951, but the Federal Government did not follow suit until 1956 and subsequently all other provinces, except Quebec, have adopted equal pay legislation.

America also has a federal/state problem. Montana and Michigan had enacted equal pay laws as far back as 1919 and by 1945 three other states had joined them. However, it was not until 1963 before Congress passed the Federal Equal Pay Act subsequently, although inadvertently, strengthened by Title VII of the Civil Rights Act of 1964 and explicitly by Executive Order No. 11375 of 1965.

Similarly, in Australia the Federal Government has left equal pay to the central Arbitration Commission, with its important 1969, 1972 and 1974 Cases, and the legislation of individual states. The complex set of procedures of Conciliation and Arbitration at Commonwealth and State levels has compounded the difficulties of introducing equal pay. Fortunately, New Zealand has learnt a lesson from Australia and introduced the Equal Pay Act of 1972 at the national level and has also possibly learnt from the United Kingdom's experience by introducing this legislation over a phased five year period.

The cases of America, Canada and Australia do highlight the aspect of differing interpretations that can emerge through different cases being heard in different States under slightly different legislation. Even in the United Kingdom where this federal/provincial split is not apparent this point is important in that there are numerous possible permutations in the future through the use of the country's tribunal system which will be used in the implementation of the Equal Pay Act.

Given the amount of time that equal pay legislation has been available in certain parts of several of the countries, in particular Canada, and despite recent changes it must be admitted that nevertheless such changes in legislation have had very little effect on the narrowing of pay differentials.

Male/female earnings differentials

In the countries studied the overall average weekly earnings of women workers remained a fairly stable proportion of those of men, both in manual and non-manual occupations, in the 1940s, 1950s and early 1960s. However, in recent years the wage rates of women in most of the seven countries have increased faster than those of men. However, for supply and demand reasons this movement has only been marginally reflected on the earnings front. Even in the more comprehensive studies of male/female earnings differentials, that is after corrections for differing skills and a variety of individual characteristics, although the differential decreases there is still a residual earning disparity due to discrimination.

Another relevant point in addition to the impact upon women's pay structures themselves is the wider impact upon pay differentials. For example there are the issues of the effect of narrowing pay differentials between groups of women as well as between women and men, and also as between different groups of men. There is still a noticeable gap in this area with respect to how these differentials work their way through, especially at plant and within plant level. For example, in the United Kingdom there is an indication that the equal pay legislation may in some cases have an unfavourable effect upon the position of low paid men. Thus it was found that by adopting a definition of "low pay" that included the lowest decile of all manual men's earnings, by agreement then in a high proportion of such agreements where progress towards equal pay had either been achieved or nearly achieved the earnings differentials between the highest and the lowest paid manual men in these cases had either stayed the same or widened. In a substantial part of these latter cases the lowest decile of earnings for men fell below that for all industries and services and would thereby be "low paid" by such a criterion[6].

Consequently, there are thus many factors which are hindering further progress in addition to those of industrial and occupational crowding and education, guidance and training problems already discussed.

Other factors hindering further progress

Thus, despite the Government involvement mentioned, problems still exist and interestingly these problems do not seem radically different between the seven countries although the relevant weight of these factors varies from one country to another.

A major obstacle to the achievement of equal pay for equal work is the technical difficulty of job grading and evaluation, that is the difficulty of finding a reliable and objective means of measuring job content and determining job comparability. Even where separate grades for men and women have been eliminated women often tend automatically to be placed in the lowest grade or in a special but also badly paid grade, for example the "light work" category in Germany.

Another and related problem has been the difficulty of interpreting the meaning of "work of equal value", especially in occupations in which women are exclusively or primarily employed. There has been a persistent subjective tendency to undervalue

vis-à-vis

the work done by women and the occupations and jobs in which they are employed have stood in the way of any objective appraisal of such occupations and jobs.

In addition, some employers still refuse to accept the principle of equal pay. Such attitudes are based on conceptions about the average output of women, their rates of absenteeism and labour turnover, their shorter time-span in employment such that women are less equal than men and this should therefore be reflected in their wages. However, while these characteristics may or may not be exhibited by younger women this is certainly not the case for older women returning to work with direct family responsibilities behind them and as we have seen already these are the majority of women workers[7].

Thus it is feasible that this "vicious circle" argument of employers could be reversed into a "virtuous circle" argument whereby equal wage payment would in the future lead to a reduction in the adverse characteristics listed such that equal expectations became a reality in the same way that present unequal expectations often become a reality. In fact there is little scientific support for these traditional views on the personal differences between the sexes, whether of physique, ability, personality, interest or values[8]; there is more basic similarity between them on all aspects. Although one sex may be significantly better than another on a certain type of ability, this group difference is small when set against the huge variation in ability found within each sex[9]. The largest differences between the sexes are to be found on those dimensions that are most closely interwoven with the differential sex-role that men and women are assigned by society.

The willingness to accept the equal pay principle is related also to the lack of adequate factual data about the sectors, industries within sectors, occupations and firms in which the principle of equal pay is not really being applied, the reasons why not, the economic and social effects of introducing equal pay by stages or immediately, the effects on women's employment opportunities and so on. Such ignorance breeds misconceptions which often reinforce comfortably held previous convictions. While it is hoped that this book itself will in a very minor way increase the information available much still needs to be undertaken in this field.

Another problem has been that while all the Governments in the countries studied have finally accepted the principle of equal pay in one form or another they have still encountered difficulties in applying the principle immediately and/or fully because of the problems involved in reconciling the consequences with the wider economic and social policies being pursued (or not) in that country, particularly vis-à-vis incomes policy. In addition, problems may be created by technological and employment market factors which may produce an economic climate not particularly conducive to the application of equal pay and may encourage discriminatory wage policies. This is more especially true where full employment does not exist and there is a fear of additional unemployment[10].

Other problems relate to the attitudes and behaviour of others in the employment situation other than Government and employers such as those of trade unionists, the public including consumers, and last but not least the attitude and behaviour of women workers themselves.

In most of the countries studied here the female unionisation rate, while still lower than the male rate, is on the increase. However, while trade unions generally endorse and support the equal pay principle they are not always willing or in a position in collective negotiations to give its complete application priority over other important competing claims. Often, there is a difference in attitude towards equal pay by national union leaders and the unwillingness on the part of the membership to accept such changes.

There is also a uniform pattern of public indifference whereby traditional attitudes towards the employment of women prolong the injustice of unequal pay by a slowing down of the rate of progress towards implementing the equal pay principle. Traditionally female employment is regarded as a temporary phenomenon and a marginal element in the labour force; generally women are viewed as having a short work life and are uninterested in participation in economic activity; and the public tends to ignore or depreciate the value of female work. Even a perusal of the following six chapters should explode these myths and Governments, aided by many other organisations, are attempting to reduce this public indifference.

Of course women form a large part of the public. However, women workers sometimes do not press their claims for equal pay either from fear of retaliatory discrimination or out of sheer neglect of their position or, in many cases, out of ignorance of their rights and the means of claiming them.

Conclusion

While the above obstacles do exist they are being overcome to varying degrees in the seven countries. However, despite the progress made so far it is necessary to emphasise that equal pay for equal work, although of utmost importance and the major theme of the next six chapters, is only one aspect of the broader question of women's wages and of the even wider question of female employment. The major characteristic of women's wages is their low level compared with those of men. While a failure to apply the equal pay principle fully and to evaluate the work of women fairly is an aspect of this situation, it is certainly not the only element nor is it the basic cause of the problem. Despite the considerable progress achieved so far on the discrimination front this clearly persists[11]. However, in addition to the removal of this discrimination what is required is a concerted and systematic effort to achieve more and better education, guidance and training for girls and women and to encourage them to make full use of such facilities in order to invest in the development of their skills and capacities partly for their own benefit and partly for the society to which they belong.

References

1. Department of Employment, *Women and Work: A Statistical Survey*, Manpower Paper No. 9, London: HMSO, 1974; and *Women at Work: Overseas Practice*, Manpower Paper No. 12, London: HMSO, 1975.

2. For examples of these areas in the E.E.C. see Sullerot, E., "Equality of Remuneration for Men and Women in the Member States of the EEC", *International Labour Review*, August-September 1975, 112(2-3), 87-108.

3. See for example in the United Kingdom, Pettman, B. O., and Fyfe, J., "Equal Pay and Low Pay", *International Journal of Social Economics*, 1974, 1(3), 268-279 and *Equal Pay and Low Pay*, Report and Survey No. 9, Bradford: Institute of Scientific Business, 1974.

4. Robinson, O., and Wallace, J., "Prospects for Equal Pay in Britain", *International Journal of Social Economics*, 1974, 1(3), 243-260; and "Equal Pay and Equality of Opportunity", *International Journal of Social Economics*, 1975, 2(2), 87-105.

5. Addison, J., "Sex Discrimination: Some Comparative Evidence", *British Journal of Industrial Relations*, July 1975, 13(2), 263-265.
   See also Sloane, P. J., and Chiplin, B., *Sex Discrimination in the Labour Force*, London: Macmillan, 1976.

6. Incomes Data Services, *Women's Pay and Employment*, IDS Study No. 100, London: IDS, June 1975.

7. Pettman, B. O. and Fyfe, J., *op cit*.

8. Department of Employment, *Women and Work: A Review*, Manpower Paper No. 11, London: HMSO, 1975.

9. Department of Employment, *Women and Work: Sex Differences and Society*, Manpower Paper No. 10, London: HMSO, 1974.

10. Sullerot, E., *op. cit.*, pp. 104-105.

11. Madden, J. F., *The Economics of Sex Discrimination*, London: D. C. Heath, 1973; Tsuchigane, R., and Dodge, N., *Economic Discrimination Against Women in the United States*, London: D. C. Heath, 1974; Sloane, P. J., and Chiplin, B., *op. cit*.

Equal Pay in Great Britain

by B. Chiplin and P. J. Sloane

Despite the relative importance of females in the British labour force and the lip service given to the concept of equal pay for men and women by employers, trade unions and the Government over almost a century, the issue has generally been pushed into the background by what have been considered to be more pressing policy objectives such as full employment, price stability and economic growth. In general few laws have been passed relating to the question of female employment. Exceptions include the Employment of Women and Young Persons Act 1936 and the Factories Act 1961. The latter which consolidated earlier legislation has the effect of limiting the hours and times of employment of women[1], protecting them from materials and processes which present particular health hazards for women, imposing restrictions on the lifting of weights and on working near moving machinery. The Mining and Quarries Act 1954, amongst other things, prohibits the employment of females below ground. Certain differences between the sexes are implicit in the fact that pensions have been payable to men at age 65 since 1925, whilst the age for women has been 60 since 1940. However, these are in general broad distinctions and until comparatively recently the "principle of voluntarism" has remained predominant in Britain, namely the belief that improvements are best effected by free collective bargaining between employer and employee representatives with minimum government involvement. The 1960's and after saw, however, an increasing government intervention in industrial relations, involving not only statutory wage control, but also eventually legislation on the broad field of industrial relations, training, redundancy and safety and health at work. The Equal Pay Act 1970 represents, therefore, not only an increasing aware-ness of the importance of paid female employment outside the household and a search for an equitable relationship between the work roles of the sexes but also part of a general move to effect change in the labour market by legislation rather than free collective bargaining.

The Role of Women in the British Labour Force

Over the century 1851 to 1951 the relative importance of women in the labour force was remarkably constant. Census of Population data show that women constituted about 30% of the occupied population throughout the period. Yet this constant percentage does mask a substantial increase in the number of women in the occupied population which rose from 2·8 million to 7 million. The only major fluctuations in this pattern occurred on account of the two World Wars.

During the First World War there was a rapid increase in female employment with the total number of occupied women being over 20% higher in 1918 as compared with 1914. The number of women employed in industry rose by some 800,000, largely at the expense of domestic service, and it was estimated that the number of females directly replacing males in all industries was some 704,000. In these cases the Atkin Committee[2] found, where the substitution occurred in heavy work, that output was lower, women were subjected to physical strain or an additional burden was placed on the remaining men; in skilled trades on the other hand no valid comparison could be made as there was insufficient opportunity for training and the development of experience; whilst in "repetition" processes and routine trades substitution was on the whole a success. Some employers made reference to the additional cost of female labour consequent upon higher proportionate overhead costs due to the lower output per head, the high cost of supervision, the cost of welfare, the cost of separate accommodation and the cost of special appliances or assistance to female employees. But the war did call into question the existing rigid divisions between "male" and "female" work.

The Second World War similarly transformed the position of women in industry. Between 1938 and 1944 the number of adult women (other than in non-industrial Central and Local Government) insured against unemployment increased from 25% to 37% of the total adult insured labour force (or by 0·8 million) and this despite a lowering of the age limit of insurability from 65 to 60 years in July 1940. Not only was there a net influx into industry, but also a switching to unfamiliar types of work, many of which were normally undertaken by males. In total, two and three-quarter million women were wholly or partly absorbed from the sphere of paid or unpaid domestic work. After the war the rate of withdrawal was rather slower than expected and, indeed, the female proportion of the occupied population was about one and a half percentage points higher in 1951 than it had been pre-war. There can be little doubt that the Second World War in particular has had a major influence on attitudes to female employment.

The growth in the relative importance of women in the labour force has in the main been a post Second World War phenomenon, with the percentage of women in the occupied population rising from 30·8 in 1951 to 36·6 in 1971. This represents an absolute increase of some 2·2 million women accounting for almost the whole of the growth in the labour force over the period. The latest projections[3] indicate that women will continue to increase in importance and that by 1991 they are likely to account for 38·8% of the labour force. Within this overall increase the most rapid growth has come from the employment of married women. They have increased from 38·2% of the female occupied population in 1951 to 63·1% in 1971 and by 1991 they are expected to be over 75%. Thus, rising activity rates amongst married women now constitute the major source of additional manpower in Britain. The main part of this growth has come from older married women re-entering employment as their families grow up. This has had an effect on the age of women at work; those in the age group 40 and over, where married women outnumber single women by 3 to 1, now form nearly half the female labour force. The growth in numbers does to some extent over-emphasise the importance of women since much of the increase in female employment in recent years has been due to the increase in numbers working part-time, with relatively little change in the numbers working full-time[4]. Census of Employment figures show that in June 1973, 36·3% of female employees worked on a part-time basis (see Table I). The majority of these are in service industries and form

Table I. Industrial Distribution of Female Employees, June 1973

INDUSTRY	Total Male	Full-time Female	Part-time Female	Total Female	Part-time as % of total Female	Total Male and Female	Total Females as % of total employed
Agriculture, forestry, fishing	306·2	66·6	48·0	114·6	41·9	420·8	27·2
Mining and quarrying	346·8	11·2	2·7	13·9	19·4	360·7	3·9
Food, drink and tobacco	433·5	192·9	101·7	294·6	34·5	728·1	40·5
Coal and petroleum products	36·0	3·7	0·7	4·4	15·9	40·4	10·9
Chemical and allied industries	301·5	97·0	26·0	123·0	21·1	424·5	29·0
Metal manufacture	459·3	46·5	11·8	58·3	20·2	517·6	11·3
Mechanical engineering	805·5	121·4	28·6	150·0	19·1	955·5	15·7
Instrument engineering	101·9	45·7	11·7	57·5	20·3	159·3	36·1
Electrical engineering	477·7	243·5	74·1	317·6	23·3	795·3	39·9
Shipbuilding and marine engineering	165·4	9·3	2·5	11·8	21·2	177·3	6·7
Vehicles	692·1	83·8	13·0	96·8	13·4	788·9	12·3
Metal goods not elsewhere specified	396·7	124·8	41·4	166·2	24·9	563·0	29·5
Textiles	298·9	208·8	47·3	256·1	18·5	555·0	46·1
Leather, leather goods and fur	24·9	14·8	4·3	19·1	22·5	44·0	43·4
Clothing and footwear	103·1	266·9	47·7	314·6	15·2	417·6	75·3
Bricks, pottery, glass, cement, etc.	234·4	53·3	11·4	64·7	17·6	299·1	21·6
Timber, furniture, etc.	231·2	43·2	12·1	55·3	21·9	286·5	19·3
Paper, printing, publishing	382·4	144·9	40·4	185·4	21·8	567·7	32·7
Other manufacturing industries	217·1	91·9	35·2	127·1	27·7	344·2	36·9
Construction	1244·0	63·3	30·6	93·9	32·6	1337·9	7·0
Gas, electricity and water	275·7	47·1	12·5	59·7	20·9	335·4	17·8
Transport and communication	1245·0	204·5	51·8	256·3	20·2	1501·3	17·1
Distributive trades	1204·1	813·9	672·5	1486·4	45·2	2690·5	55·2
Insurance, banking, finance and business services	503·4	398·4	141·6	540·0	26·2	1043·4	51·8
Professional & scientific services	1055·2	1166·8	948·6	2115·3	44·8	3170·5	66·7
Miscellaneous services	942·6	574·8	596·1	1171·0	50·9	2113·5	55·4
Public administration & defence	992·8	402·4	148·5	550·7	27·0	1543·5	35·7
Total, all manufacturing industries	5361·6	1792·5	510·0	2302·5	22·1	7664·0	30·0
Total, all industries and services	13478	5542	3163	8705	36·3	22182	39·2

(Source: Department of Employment Gazette).

a high proportion of the female labour force in these industries. About 60% work less than 21 hours a week and most are over 35, married, with small families. The growth in women employees is reflected in the fact that they now account for 26% of the membership of trade unions as compared with 8% at the beginning of the century and 15% in the inter-war period. This is still, of course, considerably lower than their share of total employment.

Full-time women tend to work fewer hours than men even though their normal weekly hours are broadly similar. The latter have fallen by about 4 hours for both men and women since 1951 and the normal basic week is now about 40 hours. In terms of actual hours worked these have fallen by about 2 hours a week for men and 4 hours a week for women over the same period. Consequently the percentage of female actual hours to male actual hours has fallen steadily over the post war period from 90% to 83%. The noteworthy feature is that whereas men's actual hours are about an eighth higher than normal hours, women actually work less than normal hours on average. Thus in terms of earnings, although the tendency of men to work more overtime is important, the fact that women tend to work less than normal hours should not be neglected.

The intensity of female employment differs considerably between industries as is shown in Table I, ranging from just under 4% of the work force in mining and quarrying to over 75% in clothing and footwear. The unequal distribution of women across industries suggests that the impact of equal pay is likely to have a disproportionate effect on certain industries and on particular firms. Just over a quarter of all females are employed in manufacturing and threequarters in services. Indeed over half of all women are employed in the three major services of distributive trades, professional and scientific services and miscellaneous services. There has been a substantial swing in favour of female employment which is most marked in services, where considerable substitution of female for male labour seems to have taken place.

Table II shows the occupational distribution as at April 1973 for both males and females as revealed by the New Earnings Survey. Female employment tends to be far more homogeneous than male with nearly 40% in clerical and related occupations, which are of course common to all industries and services. The concentration of women in non-manual occupations is clear and the distribution of males and females between manual and non-manual occupations is almost exactly reversed with 65% of women in non-manual occupations and 35% in manual compared with 35% and 65% respectively for males. Thus, women are heavily concentrated in certain industries and occupations, but to what extent are these industries and occupations those which on average pay low wages? To test this relationship Spearman's rank correlation co-efficients were calculated between male earnings and actual female employment as a proportion of total employment. In all cases the expected negative relationship was found but only for manual employees by industry was the co-efficient significant at the 5% level. It appears, therefore, that in general women are not so unfavourably distributed amongst occupations and industries as is frequently

Table II. Occupational Distribution of Employment of Full-time Adults, April 1973

Occupation	female as % of total employment	males as % total males	females as % of total females
Managerial (general management)	—	1·0	—
Professional and related supporting management and administration	—	5·1	—
Professional and related in education, welfare and health	61·4	3·9	15·1
Literary, artistic and sports	—	0·7	—
Professional and related in science, engineering, technology and similar fields	—	6·5	—
Managerial (excluding general management)	10·1	5·6	1·5
Clerical and related	63·9	9·1	39·0
Selling	38·5	4·1	6·2
Security and protective service	—	2·0	—
Catering, cleaning, hairdressing and other personal services	56·4	3·7	11·6
Farming, fishing and related	—	1·8	—
Materials processing (excluding metals)	25·4	3·8	3·1
Making and repairing (excluding metal and electrical)	33·4	5·5	6·7
Processing, making and repairing and related (metal and electrical)	6·2	20·4	3·3
Painting, repetitive assembling, product inspecting, packaging and related	41·3	5·0	8·5
Construction, mining and related not identified elsewhere	—	6·1	—
Transport operating, materials moving and storing and related	4·1	12·3	1·3
Miscellaneous	—	3·4	—
All manual occupations	18·5	64·7	35·5
All non-manual occupations	43·0	35·3	64·5
All full-time employees	29·2	100·0	100·0

*Results are generally given only for these occupations and main occupational groups represented by at least 100 persons in the sample and for which the estimates of average weekly earnings had a percentage standard error of not more than 2·0 per cent.
(Source: New Earnings Survey).

alleged[5]. But, given an unequal sex distribution one interesting aspect from a policy viewpoint is to examine the relative importance of unequal payment and unequal employment distribution. This can be crudely assessed, assuming constant employ·ment, by:

(1) Granting females the mean male earnings within each occupation (industry) but leaving the occupational (industrial) distribution unaltered;

(2) Re-distributing females in line with the "expected" occupational (industrial) distribution on the basis of the proportion of the sexes in the total labour force.

These exercises can be undertaken separately for manual and non-manual employees and a weighted average of female earnings calculated[6]. The results of the exercise suggest that the re-distribution of females both occupationally and industrially makes little difference to average earnings in comparison with granting females the male earnings levels in their existing occupations (industries). The results are based on the 1971 New Earning Survey and by way of illustration reveal, for example that for all occupational groups actual average female weekly earnings are £18·3; the average if they were paid the male earnings would be £29·4; if they were re-distributed and paid male earnings the average would be £32·9. Other results are of similar magnitude except that for non-manual women re-distribution by industry would reduce their average earnings. Of course, the data are only available in a fairly aggregated form but it is possible, for instance, from the 1973 NES to obtain information of 7 types of clerk. For these groups actual female weekly earnings are £22·32; payment of the male rate increases this to £32·97 and if they are then re-distributed this rises to £33·64. Even at this level of disaggregation therefore, earnings are more important than occupational distribution. The difference is not accounted for by hours of work since overtime is small and even for manual workers it does not account for the bulk of the difference. This important difference in occupational distribution seems to occur at a highly disaggregated level presumably related to age or seniority-based payment systems or other features favouring males. The results of the exercise nevertheless suggest that at the level of aggregation we have examined it is differences in payment rather than differences in occupation or industries which are most important in accounting for male/female earnings differences. This suggests that equal pay legislation is likely to be more significant than anti-discrimination legislation to the extent that they can both be made effective, although both may be required because of the inter-relationship between earnings and employment opportunities even within narrow occupational groups.

Reasons for the Difference in Male and Female Rates of Pay[7]

Before one can attempt to predict the likely effects of equal pay legislation it is necessary to understand the economic forces leading to differences in the rates of pay between men and women. For instance, it is necessary to know whether the major part of the difference can be explained by pre-entry or post-entry factors in terms of labour force participation, since *equal pay* legislation is only directly relevant to the second of these. Further, one must ascertain to what extent differences result from discrimination, practised either by employers or employees, jointly or separately. Also one must discover the extent to which differences result from supply and from demand side factors.

First of all examining the supply side two major influences are differences in labour force attachment between the sexes and difference in the extent and type of training. Thus on the former point Census of Population data show that the male activity rates for 1971 range from 86·6% in the age group 60-64 to 98·3% in the age-group 35-44. For single women the figure is over 80% between the ages of 20 and 54, whilst for married women the peak is 57·0% in the age groups 45-54 and falls to 38·4% in the age group 25-34. Indeed in every age group the activity rate for men is significantly higher than that of either married or single women, though there is a marked difference between the last two. On the question of training, of those young persons entering employment in 1973 49·3% of boys took up apprenticeships or employment leading to a recognised professional qualification whereas the corresponding figure for girls was 8·4%. No less than 58·2% of girls took up clerical appointments, indicative of the segmentation of the labour market. In the case of highly qualified manpower (i.e. those holding an academic or professional qualification recognised as being of at least first degree level) it was estimated that the total stock of highly qualified males stood at 1,060,000 in 1971 compared with 352,000 in the case of women[8]. The above points to the need to analyse male and female labour as a capital asset with a long run pay-off. The criterion for determining whether or not an investment in human capital should be undertaken is that it should earn a rate of return comparable with that in alternative uses. This applies not only to formal education but also to on-the-job training. The latter can in principle be categorized into completely general and completely specific. The rational firm would not pay any of the costs of general training, since the firm cannot create a property right in the worker, and there remains the danger that such a worker may be attracted away by other firms. Thus, we would expect the costs of general training to be borne entirely by the worker. For specific training the firm would be prepared to pay at least part of the costs since this training is by definition only useful to the firm in which it takes place. Therefore, both the worker and the firm have a vested interest in the worker remaining with the firm after completion of training.

The basic analysis is of relevance to the question of the investment in the training of women, whether it is the woman herself, or the firm which pays the cost. In the case of the worker, it is the early years following the completion of training which are given the greatest weight (since discounting techniques must be used in computing the return). Returns over later years are of only marginal significance. Yet, it is in this early period that married women are most likely to leave the labour force for family reasons. As we have seen the proportion of married women economically active is at a minimum in the 25-34 age group. Thus, from the female worker's viewpoint the investment in general training may not be an economic proposition. This is especially true in view of the fact that the majority of women fall into the secondary labour force with intermittent labour force participation over the economic cycle. Thus, there are sound economic reasons why women should not be willing to invest in themselves and out of choice are not found in the more skilled occupations requiring lengthy training.

From the point of view of the firm the key element in the decision to invest in the training of a worker is the probability of that worker leaving the firm. A high labour turnover will reduce the return on the investment to the firm and may even result in a capital loss. This is modified to the extent that the payback period on investment in human beings is relatively short and the available empirical evidence does, indeed, suggest that this is so (approximately two years in the case of manual apprentices). Empirically, at least as far as manufacturing is concerned, the turnover of women is higher than that of men by over 50% and absenteeism is also significantly higher. Thus firms may have a very good reason for not wishing to invest in the specific training of female workers. Consequently, the onus is put back on the worker to finance the costs. Thus, whilst firms may be willing to invest in male trainees, this may not be the case with females. One result of this would be to lower female relative wages, since the principal cost to the worker is foregone earnings[9].

Therefore, human capital theory may provide another explanation accounting for differences in pay between men and women, and also offer an explanation for the relative sparsity of women employed in highly skilled jobs. Certainly the removal of discrimination and the creation of equal opportunities for women may be important as an objective of social policy. But even if it is achieved it does not mean that women will be prepared to increase the investment in themselves and thus they may still continue to occupy lower paid jobs.

Together, the above differences suggest that a large number of women in the British labour force is likely to be grouped within a separate labour market from most male employees (i.e. men and women are non-competing groups in many cases). Not only does this follow from the fact that most males comprise the primary labour force, whilst most married women are members of the secondary labour force subject to alterations in their labour force status as the level of economic activity changes, but also from the fact that many females may be subject to the influence of a dual labour market. For in "male" occupations there exist high levels of skill and wages, employment mobility and promotion prospects, whilst in the "female" occupations in contrast there exist relatively low levels of skill and wages, few openings for promotion and high labour turnover. These differences are emphasised where there occur internal labour markets in which favourable treatment is given to existing over potential employees by means of job ladders internal to the organisation and recruitment only at lower skill levels[10]. In the case of certain non-manual grades it is possible that women do gain entry to the internal labour market but incremental seniority or age-related scales imply that they tend to be concentrated in the lower paid groups. Thus occupational differences tend to be narrowly rather than broadly defined. Some support for this is provided by age/earnings profiles of male and female employees, available from the NES, which show that females exhibit rising but flatter earnings profiles than males relative to age, suggestive of fewer opportunities of advancement to higher graded posts. Such differences are more marked in the case of non-manual employees.

Apart from these supply side factors, inequalities in earnings may result from demand side forces, reflecting differences in marginal productivity between the sexes (e.g. physical or legal limitations on female employment). As a rule of thumb the Atkin Committee suggested that a woman working without undue strain could produce four-fifths of a man's output. A majority of the Royal Commission felt that improvements in the general health of women and a closer matching of the job to the individual were likely to have reduced the margin. Given that some of these factors are important, economic theory would lead us to predict that, assuming no supply side differences and zero discrimination, market forces would operate to bring female wages to the point where inequality between men's and women's pay reflected only a difference in marginal net revenue product. If the discrepancy were greater than the difference in marginal productivity it would pay employers to recruit more females which would therefore have the effect of raising the women's rate relative to that of men. It is certainly the implicit assumption of the Equal Pay Act that inequality in wages exceeds any difference in productivity, and that part of this is discrimination. This can take the form either of employer or employee discrimination. The latter occurs when male employees dislike associating with females at work, particularly where the female is in a supervisory position, or entry of females into an occupation is opposed because the latter are seen as a threat to income and job security. It can be shown that the effect of employee discrimination is to diminish sexual wage differences in the long run and to ensure that the labour force is as far as possible segregated. In the case of employer discrimination on the other hand where it is the employer that has an aversion to employing women, sexual wage differences are likely to result and equal pay, as opposed to equal opportunity, legislation is appropriate.

The Historical Development towards Equal Pay Legislation
The TUC passed a resolution calling for equal pay as early as 1882[11] and the question was at issue in the matchgirls' strike of 1888 but the policy appears generally to have been subordinated to other union policy objectives, not surprisingly perhaps in view of the relative male/female sex ratio in terms of membership and the predominance of males in positions of authority within the union movement. Further, a large number of females are without the confines of union membership. Pinder[12] suggests that only when external pressures have demanded an active response have the unions extended the matter beyond mere annual or biennial resolutions and it is only comparatively recently that the TUC has abandoned the contention that equal pay is best brought about via collective bargaining rather than government legislation. In recent years apart from the pressure of the feminist lobby, incomes policy, low pay and race relations have served to focus attention on the issue and thus led unions to adopt a more forceful approach reflected in the fact that in a five year period prior to the passing of the Equal Pay Act individual unions had passed no less than 26 equal pay motions, and a number of women's conferences have subsequently devoted themselves to the question. However at local level the Office of Manpower Economics (OME)[13] found attitudes of union representatives to be equivocal and a certain degree of antagonism towards equal pay to be employed by part of the male membership.

As noted above, however, it is perhaps the contribution of females during the two world wars that has called into question prevailing attitudes. On 19 March 1915 the government made a pledge to all industrial workers contained in a memorandum on Acceleration of Output on Government Work, known as the Treasury Agreement. This suggested that all women who undertook work previously done by men should receive the full male wage. In 1918 a committee was set up to investigate and report upon the relationship between male and female wage rates, having regard to the interest of both as well as to the value of their work. The Committee recommended that women doing similar or the same work as men should receive equal pay for equal work "in the sense that pay should be in proportion to efficient output". In a minority report Beatrice Webb rejected the formula of "equal pay for equal work" because of its ambiguity suggesting that it might be variously interpreted as equal pay for equal efforts and sacrifices, equal pay for equal product or equal pay for equal value to the employer. "Hence any adoption of the formula would lead to endless misunderstandings between employers and employed and increased industrial frictions." In its place were proposed amongst other things the principle of the national minimum and the principle of the occupational rate together with the rejection of the principle of a male rate and a female rate. The clerical and administrative branches of the Civil Service were the subject of a Report of the Royal Commission in 1914 which recommended by a majority that where the character and conditions of work performed by women approximated in identity with the character and conditions of the work performed by men equal payment should be made to both sexes. This was accepted by the Atkin Committee which further recommended that the principle should be extended to the manipulative branches of the Civil Service.

In the inter-war years large scale unemployment appears to have pushed equal pay into the background although the London County Council applied the principle to its senior women officers in 1920. However, as discussed earlier, following the influx of women into industry during the Second World War the issue again came into prominence and the government eventually appointed a Royal Commission[15] to "examine the existing relationship between the remuneration of men and women in the public services, in industry and in other fields of employment; to consider the social, academic and financial implications of the claim of equal pay for equal work; and to report". The Commission found the explanation for unequal payment to be chiefly on the demand side. Three major demand side factors were legal restrictions on the employment of women, natural factors such as physical endowments, adaptability, absenteeism and welfare costs and conventional factors such as social attitudes towards feminine employment and pressure from male employees. It was found however, that there were important differences in the consequences of equal pay according to the sector of employment. In the Civil Service at that time female non-industrial employees (other than those engaged in a professional capacity) were entitled to the same pay as males only at the minimum of the scale on entry to any class. At the maximum of the scale the differential could not exceed 20% but an absolute limit kept the effective margin below this level. On the one hand there was the aggregation principle whereby men and women were employed on the same duties side by side and on the other hand the principle of segregation whereby they were employed in separate branches with separate lines of advancement, a particular form of internal labour market which amounted to the reservation of certain posts to men and others to women. There the Commission found that there was no reason to suppose that equal pay would effect a change in recruitment policy designed to restrict the employment of women, nor would such an alteration have a marked effect on recruitment. The effects would only be adverse if the common rate was set too low to keep this sector competitive with other sectors with respect to rates of pay. The results would be similar in the case of local government. Within teaching, however, there was recognition that there might be an adverse effect in terms of the male labour supply function. Among manual occupations the Commission found that few women received equal pay and where they did there tended to be either very few women employed or very few men (as in some textile and clothing occupational groups). There, the Commission found that there were difficulties which did not exist in the non-manual public sector. For instance, there were problems in defining comparable work, in determining how female efficiency compared with that of males and some opposition in union quarters. Furthermore, the Commission were inclined to accept the thesis put forward by Professor J. R. Hicks that there might be an inverse relationship between equal pay and equal opportunity such that "the probable consequence of a large scale application of equal time rates would be 'not merely that the process of penetration would be checked, but much (perhaps most) of the ground gained could not be held', since in general . . . at equal pay for men and women a man will always be preferred"[16]. The explanation of these differences, crudely between the public (predominantly non-manual) sector and the private (predominantly manual) sector, are to be found in the nature of competition and of training. The public sector is cushioned against competitive forces at least directly, whilst in the case of the private sector there is always the fear of undercutting if equal pay were to be granted. In the case of the professions and other skilled categories training is often provided free to firms with the educational system and thus there is no necessity to recoup a return on it.

Following pressure from various pressure groups the equal pay for non-manual civil servants was conceded by the government in 1955 to be granted in seven equal instalments, the last occurring on January 1st 1961. Women were taken to be performing equal work where there was a common recruitment of the sexes and common conditions of employment. Similar developments occurred in the nationalised industries, the health service, teaching and local government. Thus, "throughout this whole area of white-collar work in the public sector equal pay once accepted became the norm and can be seen to be applied without exception to those holding like posts irrespective of sex"[17]. Although in the manual field there were some examples of equal payment, sometimes as a carry-over from war-time experience, as when equal pay was granted to bus conductresses and differentials between male and female rates narrowed in some industries, equal pay was the exception[18]. When the Labour Party was returned to office in 1964 its election manifesto committed it to the principle of equal pay for equal work and the Equal Pay Act was passed in May 1970, the general principles, if not the details, being supported by all three major parties[19].

Subsequently attention has focussed on the question of occupational sex discrimination and the Conservative Government published a Green Paper, *Equal Opportunities for Men and Women*, in the autumn of 1973 which indicated the government's desire to introduce legislation to ensure equal access to potential benefits including equal opportunities for recruitment, training, promotion, overtime and shift-work and equal protection against acts to their detriment (e.g. in relation to questions of discipline and dismissal). Following the return of a Labour Government in 1974 a White Paper is in preparation at the time of writing which will include similar measures in relation to female employment and widen the scope of the legislation to cover education, housing, a wide range of commercial services and the supply of goods.

The Equal Pay Act 1970
A crucial feature of the 1970 Act is that its terms do not become effective until the 29 December 1975. This lag of $5\frac{1}{2}$ years was designed to allow firms and organisations sufficient time to plan and implement equal pay without major disruptive consequences and implicitly recognised the fact that females are employed in very diverse circumstances, such that some organisations would be virtually untouched by the legislation (at least directly) whilst to others it would represent a profound economic change. In addition the Act contained a clause which gave the Secretary of State for Employment the power to require that women's rates of pay should be at least 90% of men's rates as from 31 December 1973. In fact it was decided not to implement this particular provision, but rather to ensure orderly progress via special provision under incomes policy legislation (to which further reference is made below).

The Act is designed to prevent discrimination as regards terms and conditions of employment between men and women but does not seek to ensure equality of opportunity with respect to access to jobs. The main objective is to be achieved in two main ways:

(1) by requiring that employers grant equal treatment as regards terms and conditions of employment to men and women where they are employed on the same or broadly similar work, or where, with respect to different jobs, a woman's job has been rated as equivalent to that of a male employee by means of a job evaluation exercise;

(2) by providing for the Industrial Court (reformulated as the Industrial Arbitration Board under the Industrial Relations Act 1971) to remove discrimination in collective agreements, employers' pay structures and statutory wages orders which contain any provisions applying specifically to men only or women only and which have been referred to the Court.

In view of the complexity of implementing equal pay the Act is surprisingly short and in the event of a dispute with regard to interpretation leaves the problem to be resolved by the industrial tribunals (set up under Section 12 of the Industrial Training Act 1964([20].

It must be emphasised that the provisions of the Act imply equal treatment for men relative to women as well as the converse, so that it would seem to be unlawful where men and women were employed on the same or broadly similar work to provide for instance longer rest pauses for the women, which sometimes occurs in British industry[21]. In order for work to qualify as broadly similar there should be no work differences of practical importance, regard being paid to the frequency as well as the nature of such differences. The terms of the Act apply to male and female workers employed by the same employer or associated employer[22] at the same establishment or establishments in Great Britain at which common terms and conditions of employment are observed either generally or for employees of the relevant classes. The Department of Employment suggests that it is likely that a woman will need to point to a single agreement applying to those establishments and it is unlikely that all industry-wide agreement would normally be detailed or precise enough to be considered as fixing common terms and conditions[23].

It is also suggested by the Department that the Act covered all full or part-time employees although the Act itself makes no reference to the latter group. But it cannot be certain that there will always be a valid comparison between part-time females and full-time men (rather than part-time men)[24].

Another important aspect of the Act is that relating to collective agreements. Where a collective agreement made before or after the commencement of the Act contains a provision applying specifically to men only or to women only the agreement may be referred by any party to it or by the Secretary of State for Employment to the Industrial Arbitration Board for amendment with a view to removing the sex discrimination. Furthermore, this provision applies whether or not the men or women concerned are doing the same or broadly similar work or are covered by a job evaluation scheme. The Board may amend the agreement to extend to both men and women any provision applying to men only or to women only. Any resulting duplication must be eliminated, so as not to make the terms and conditions agreed for men, or those agreed for women, less favourable than they otherwise would have been. The Board cannot, however, extend the scope of a collective agreement to embrace men or women not already covered by the agreement. Where in such a case, for instance, a rate applying specifically to women only continues to be required the Board must amend the agreement such that the women's rate is raised to the level of the lowest men's rate within it. The effect of this, regardless of the work undertaken by the two sexes will be to distort relativities with men and may, indeed, imply a major reassessment of the wage structure.

A major problem facing any legislative provisions in this field is, of course, the precise definition of "equal pay" and "equal work". The British legislation falls between the Treaty of Rome and ILO definitions in terms of the extent of its coverage. According to Article 119 of the Treaty of Rome equal payment is to be made for equal work, although attempts to extend this definition have been made by the EEC Commission. The ILO Equal Pay Remuneration Convention (100) 1951 decrees on the other hand that there should be equal pay for work of equal value. The British example limits equal value to cases where this has been defined under a system of job evaluation, so that the extent of the coverage is a function of the incidence of job evaluation, which is rather a novel approach to the problem. It is not, however, clear under the British legislation what constitutes the same or broadly similar work or what constitutes a material difference, though this problem is to some extent avoided where job evaluation is utilised. It appears that equal payment is to include not only wage rates but also fringe benefits and any type of bonus rate. But differences may be justified if they are clearly related to difference in circumstances rather than sex, e.g. long service payments, shift-work allowances or overtime premium payments.

Progress and Problems in the Implementation of Equal Pay

The most obvious area for action prior to the implementation of the Act is to be found in differences in the levels of comparable male and female wage rates. This has been analysed by the Office of Manpower Economics (OME) and the Department of Employment amongst others. The former was invited by the Secretary of State for Employment on 3 May 1971, to carry out a study of equal pay as part of its general programme (in particular to study how employers were dealing with the problems involved in the introduction of equal pay) and also to assess the effects of the progressive introduction of equal pay on job opportunities for women and levels of pay generally[25]. The latter has since 1970 maintained a register recording broad movements towards equal pay in national agreements for manual workers and in wages council orders.

The Department of Employment[26] has classified collective agreements since 1970 as follows:

(1) Discrimination removed (V)—that is separate rates for women have been eliminated either by raising existing rates to the corresponding men's rates or by replacing women's rates by new occupational classifications;

(2) Phased plans (W)—whereby larger increases are granted to women as part of an agreed phased programme of movement towards equal pay by the end of 1975;

(3) Larger unphased increases (X)—that is women have been granted larger increases than men on a "one-off" basis without forward commitment;

(4) Equal unphased money increases (Y)—with the result that women retain a higher percentage increase than male employees;

(5) No progress (Z)—lower money increases to women widen the cash gap between men's and women's rates.

A summary of the position as at the end of March 1974 is given in Table III below. The main features appear to be that in most cases the parties to the agreement are making use of the time-period granted under the Act before full equality is obligatory and the actual approach of individual enterprises has been varied. If anything, wage councils have been slower to move than companies in areas where free collective bargaining generally prevails, but it is not known to what extent this represents inactivity rather than inherent problems resulting from the complexity of the arrangements or costs of the exercise.

A comparison with the OME investigation of the position under the latest agreements at the end of March 1972 reveals that in the latter case only 19% of agreements had moved substantially towards equal pay in contrast to over one-third in the table below. It should be noted that the statement that 10% or so of agreements had made no movement at the end of March 1974 hides the fact that a majority of them had made some moves towards equal pay at an earlier date. In fact only six agreements had made no movement at all towards equal pay either by March 1972 or by March 1974.

As noted earlier the Act empowers the Industrial Arbitration Board (IAB) to amend collective agreements and wages orders to raise any rate applicable to women only to the lowest rate for men. It is interesting, therefore, to examine the relationship between women's and men's minimum rates over the period since the Act was passed, which is shown in Table IV. This reveals a substantial movement towards full equality on the part of minimum female rates, only nine agreements paying female rates at less

Table III. Summary of Department of Employment's Register

Type of Agreement	Number of Agreements/ Orders at end of March 1974 which discrim- inated at January 1970	Movements in Agreement at end March 1974				
		Major Movement		Minor Movement		
		Discrimination removed (V)	Phased Plan to EP (W)	Larger Increases (X)	Equal Increases (Y)	No Movement (Z)
Collective Agreements	114	12	32	37	20	12
Wages Council and Boards Orders	44	4	5	15	15	5
All Agreements	157	16	37	52	35	17
Per cent of total %	100	10·2	23·6	33·1	22·3	10·8
No. of Women Covered* (000)	3372	391	988	1057	738	198
Per cent of total %	100	11·6	29·3	31·3	21·9	5·9

*OME estimates for 1972.
(Source: Department of Employment Gazette, August 1974).

Table IV. Lowest women's rate as a percentage of lowest men's rates in collective agreements and wages orders which were discriminatory in March 1970 (manual workers)

Percentage	Number of Agreements/Orders		
	March 1970	March 1972	March 1974
100	—	9	16
95—99	⎰ 9	3	20
90—94	⎱	12	61
85—89	⎰ 34	38	33
80—84	⎱	56	18
Less than 80	123	48	9
Total	166	166	157

(Source: Department of Employment Gazette, August 1974).

than 80% of the male rate in 1974 compared with 123 in 1970, and no less than 61·8% paying 90% or more of the male rate in 1974 compared with only 5·4% in 1970. This trend is confirmed by the index of hourly wage rates for all industries and services which reveals that over the period 1960-1970 male and female adult rates were moving very closely in line, but over the period 1970-73 women's rates increased by 153·1% and male rates by 145·2%. This relative improvement in female wage rates was not, however, altogether matched, by movements in relative earnings as is shown in Table IV.

New Earnings Survey data for April 1970-April 1973 (Table V) show that in the case of manual workers average weekly earnings of females tend to be about 50% of those of male workers and rather less in the case of non-manual workers in manufacturing. However, there is a clear tendency for males to work longer hours and allowing for this hourly earnings of manual women average approximately 60% of male earnings, the figure again being rather less in the case of non-manual women[27]. Over the 4 year period there has been a slight tendency for the earnings differential to diminish, presumably on account of the Equal Pay Act, (by between 1·0 and 2·6 percentage points in the case of weekly earnings and between 1·2 and 3·0 percentage points in the case of hourly earnings). However, clearer evidence on this is provided by the NES matched example which excludes the effects of labour turnover (Table VI) and shows again the relatively favourable movement in female earnings. It is also informative to note the make-up of payment in order to account for male/female earnings differences. Again data are available from the NES which are summarised in Table VII. These show a striking difference between non-manual and manual workers in terms of the importance of basic pay. For non-manual men, overtime premium, PBR and shift premia payments account for only 6·2% of gross earnings, whilst in the case of manual men these account for 28·5%. (For women the figures are 2·3% and 17·5% respectively.) Particularly noteworthy are the facts that 61·2% of manual men received overtime pay compared with 19·9% of women and that corresponding overtime pay accounted for a significantly higher proportion of male manual earnings

Table V. Earnings and Hours—Great Britain—Manual and Non-manual Full-time Adult Employees—(NES Estimates)

	Average Weekly Earnings including those whose pay was affected by absence			Average Weekly Earnings excluding those whose pay was affected by absence			Average Hours of those for whom earnings were calculated		Average Hourly Earnings including overtime pay and overtime hours			Average Hourly Earnings excluding overtime pay and overtime hours		
	Men	Women	Female as % of Male	Men	Women	Female as % of Male	Men	Women	Men	Women	Female as % of Male	Men	Women	Female as % of Male
MANUFACTURING INDUSTRIES	£	£		£	£				p	p		p	p	
Full-time Manual Workers														
April 1970	27·4	13·2	48·2	28·4	13·9	48·9	45·5	38·2	60·8	34·8	57·2	60·1	34·6	57·6
April 1971	30·2	15·0	49·7	31·1	15·7	50·5	44·4	38·0	68·2	39·5	57·9	66·5	39·3	59·0
April 1972	33·6	17·0	50·6	34·5	17·7	51·3	44·3	38·3	75·8	44·4	58·6	73·9	44·2	59·8
April 1973	38·6	19·6	50·8	39·9	20·5	51·4	46·4	40·0	86·0	51·2	59·5	83·7	50·7	60·6
Full-time Non-manual Workers														
April 1970	35·6	15·5	43·5	35·8	15·6	43·6	39·5	37·3	89·3	41·6	46·6	89·6	41·5	46·3
April 1971	39·5	17·5	44·3	39·7	17·6	44·3	38·9	37·2	100·3	47·0	46·8	100·5	46·9	46·7
April 1972	43·7	19·4	44·4	43·8	19·5	44·5	38·8	37·1	111·0	52·3	47·1	111·1	52·1	49·9
April 1973	48·4	21·8	45·0	48·7	21·8	44·8	39·2	37·3	122·4	58·5	47·8	122·4	58·3	47·6
ALL INDUSTRIES AND SERVICES														
Full-time Manual Workers														
April 1970	25·8	12·8	49·6	26·7	13·3	49·8	45·9	38·6	57·1	33·5	58·7	55·9	33·2	59·4
April 1971	28·8	14·7	51·0	29·4	15·3	52·0	45·0	38·4	64·0	38·3	59·8	62·2	38·1	61·3
April 1972	32·1	16·6	51·7	32·8	17·1	52·1	44·9	38·6	71·4	43·1	60·3	69·3	42·8	61·8
April 1973	37·0	19·1	51·6	38·1	19·7	51·7	46·7	39·9	81·7	49·6	60·7	79·2	49·1	62·0
Full-time Non-manual Workers														
April 1970	34·9	17·5	50·1	35·1	17·7	50·4	39·0	36·9	88·7	47·2	53·2	89·0	47·2	53·0
April 1971	38·9	19·7	50·6	39·1	19·8	50·6	38·7	36·9	99·2	53·0	53·4	99·5	52·9	53·2
April 1972	43·4	22·1	50·9	43·5	22·2	51·0	38·6	36·6	110·5	59·8	54·1	110·6	59·7	54·0
April 1973	47·8	24·5	51·3	48·1	24·7	51·7	38·8	36·8	121·6	66·2	54·4	121·7	66·1	54·3

Table VI. Percentage increases in average hourly earnings excluding overtime pay for full-time adult workers all industries and services, 1970-1973 (NES matched sample)

	April 1970— April 1971 %	April 1971— April 1972 %	April 1972— April 1973 %
Manual Men	11·6	12·2	15·2
„ Women	15·5	13·3	16·1
Non-Manual Men	13·0	14·0	13·1
„ „ Women	14·2	16·7	13·9
All Men	12·2	12·9	14·2
All Women	14·5	15·7	14·5

(Source: NES).

Table VII. Make-up of average gross weekly earnings of full-time adult workers April 1973 (All industries and services)

	MANUAL				NON-MANUAL				ALL			
	MEN		WOMEN		MEN		WOMEN		MEN		WOMEN	
	£	%	£	%	£	%	£	%	£	%	£	%
Make-up of gross weekly average earnings*	38·1	100·0	19·7	100·0	48·1	100·0	24·7	100·0	41·9	100·0	23·1	100·0
Overtime pay	6·2	16·3	0·8	3·8	1·4	3·0	0·3	1·2	4·4	10·6	0·4	1·9
PBR, etc. payments	3·6	9·6	2·4	12·3	1·3	2·8	0·2	0·6	2·8	6·6	0·9	3·9
Shift, etc. premium payments	1·0	2·6	0·3	1·4	0·2	0·4	0·1	0·6	0·7	1·7	0·2	0·8
All other pay†	27·3	71·5	16·3	82·5	45·2	93·8	24·1	97·7	34·0	81·2	21·6	93·5
% of employees who received overtime pay		61·2		19·9		18·9		10·4		45·3		13·5
PBR, etc. payments		39·3		32·8		7·9		3·3		27·5		12·9
Shift, etc. premium payments		18·4		8·3		3·9		6·3		13·0		6·9

*These results relate to all employees whose pay was not affected by absence whether or not they received payments of the kind specified.

†All other pay includes not only basic pay but any items other than overtime payments, PBR, etc. payments and shift, etc. premium payments[28].

(Source: NES).

than female. This highlights the importance of overtime hours which will not be directly affected by the legislation but nevertheless even in the case of manual workers these do not account for the bulk of the male/female earnings differential. Indeed, differences in basic rates can explain substantially more of the gross margin than overtime.

The differential effect between wage rates and earnings points to the need to examine what is happening to movements of male and female earnings and benefits at company level. The OME obtained information in 1971/2 on the progress being made towards equal pay from 142 companies, plus supplementary information from other concerns. Just under one-third of these had introduced equal pay and there was some evidence that progress was faster in the case of white collar as opposed to manual employees. 40% had made no move towards equal pay and were awaiting developments at national level before taking appropriate action, whilst others considered that there was little overlap between the jobs undertaken by males and females in their own concern.

NES data suggest that approximately a quarter of all female employees, mainly in service industries, are subject to individual rather than collective bargaining arrangements. The OME suggested that many of these were in white-collar occupations in small companies and consequently carried out a survey of 200 companies with less than 100 employees, where more than 10% were women, and where pay was not covered by collective agreements or wages council orders. Out of a total of 193 companies in which men and women were employed together, either on white-collar or manual work, 60% claimed that in no case was the work the same or broadly similar and only 13% had a formal pay structure, which would leave them subject to the collective agreement provisions of the Act. Furthermore, a quarter of the companies were unaware of the existence of the Act or its contents and the apparent lack of knowledge led to the launching of an equal pay campaign in June 1973. The Secretary of State for Employment sent a letter to 400,000 employers and industrial and commercial organisations. A booklet[29] was published which, amongst other things, urged firms not to assume that the Act did not affect them, that it applied only to men and women doing identical work, that they could wait until the union put in a claim, that they could introduce equal pay overnight or that the government's counter-inflation policy meant the issue could be postponed[30].

Progress in implementing equal pay in Britain has been effected in fact by the use of incomes policy. Under Stage II of the policy any remaining differential between men's and women's rates could be reduced by up to one-third by the end of 1973, outside the pay limit if necessary. But increases over the norm were only permissible where pay settlements within the limit did not have the effect of widening the existing relativity between men's and women's rates. It was presumably on account of this provision that the Government chose not to enforce the 90% maximum requirement regarding female wage rates relative to those of males at the end of 1973. Under Stage III of the incomes policy the equal pay provision was reinforced by allowing the parties to reduce any remaining differential by up to one half, again outside the pay limit if necessary. The Pay Board reported that of settlements under Stages II and III which included improvements outside the pay limits "the most striking improvements continued to be movements towards equal pay"[31]. In a later report the Board disclosed that up to the 31 May 1974 at least 2·9 million women or approximately one-third of the female labour force benefited from movements towards equal pay under 1,688 Stage II settlements made since the beginning of the policy on the 2 April 1973 and some 1·6 million from the 603 Stage III settlements made since 7 November 1973[32].

Indications from the Department of Employment Conciliation and Advisory Service were also that the main stimulus to progress towards equal pay over the period 1973/74 was derived from the provisions of the pay code. The investigations of the manpower advisers also give details of progress towards equal pay at company level by size of firm (Table VIII), which suggests that 70% of the concerns investigated had either achieved equal pay or had implemented phased plans for its introduction. For those with less than 100 employees this percentage falls to 50. 20% of all companies had still not made any progress towards equal pay.

British experience seems to support the need for a reasonable time period for adjustment in view of the complexity in many cases of collective bargaining arrange-ments and the lack of understanding of the legal provisions, particularly in the case of small firms. In the main the above information does not tell us precisely how women have been affected by the various changes that have been made. For instance, there is little advantage in full equality of rates if there are no women to enjoy them. Further-more, the obvious progress that has been made in terms of wage rates has only been reflected marginally in levels of earnings, partly because of the relative incidence of overtime between the sexes.

The OME Report found that a number of factors influenced the speed of introduc-tion of equal pay. These included in particular the complexity of collective agreements

Table VIII. **Progress towards equal pay and size of firm**

Size of Firm	Z(i)	Z(ii)	XY	W	V	
Less than 100	24	32	8	55	21	140
100—499	29	55	26	238	50	388
500—999	9	16	14	102	20	161
1,000—4,999	—	11	8	67	14	110
5,000+	—	2	2	13	3	20

Note: Z (i) = No progress and no intention to provide for it.
      Z(ii) = No progress but intention to make some provision
      XY = Some progress but unlikely to achieve equal pay by end of 1975
      W = Phased progress
      V = Equal pay achieved
      (Source: *Department of Employment Gazette*, August 1974).

and diversity of firms. In relation to the former where agreements were less complex progress tended to be quicker. The rate of progress at company level was to a large extent geared to what was happening at national level (i.e. whether the appropriate employers' association had taken any initiative on the question). Modifications were particularly facilitated where the collective bargaining arrangements were well established and effective. Many of the companies which had made little or no progress were small and without well formulated pay structures. On the other hand, some firms had failed to take action on the supposition that the Act did not affect them, whilst others had simply not given the matter any thought. Steps to implement equal pay had generally been taken earlier where job evaluation was utilised and companies frequently expressed the view that this greatly eased the introduction of equal pay. Few firms were found in practice to have adopted delaying tactics in order to take steps to avoid the effects of the Act by reclassifying jobs, etc.

Already a number of problems have been experienced by firms in implementing the requirements of the Act. Whilst the terms of the Act appear *a priori* to be relatively straightforward it seems that there are bound to be particular problems for the IAB and industrial tribunals. For instance most of those individual companies studied by the OME which were not using job evaluation had difficulties in determining what was broadly similar work, and many of them concentrated on introducing equal pay for identical work. A majority of firms investigated by the OME and 41 % of companies analysed by the Industrial Society utilised job evaluation schemes, the large majority of which were designed to match both male and female jobs. This is a much higher incidence than had been found to be the case by the NBPI in its investigation of job evaluation in 1968. This suggests that firms have not been deterred from introducing job evaluation by a fear that this would broaden the area of comparison between the two sexes and increase the costs of implementation of equal pay. Though there is no conclusive evidence on this it may be, however, that the result of the job evaluation exercise is to concentrate the large majority of females in the lower ranked grades, thereby minimising any consequential cost increase. Potentially there could be difficulties arising over the question of "associated establishments". For instance, depending upon the interpretation of common terms and conditions of employment it is possible that a multi-plant firm could be faced with the removal of regional wage differentials if females in a low wage area were able to gain comparability with males in a high wage area, and this could have a major impact upon its wage bill. Certain problems may also arise where there are differences in other terms and conditions of employment. For instance, an examination of collective agreements in *Time Rates of Wages and Hours of Work* shows that at April 1973 some 60 collective agreements and wage regulation orders specified different ages for men and women at which the adult rate becomes payable, most frequently but not exclusively expressing a higher age for men than for women. Under the terms of the Act these ages will have to be equalised either at one of the existing ages or at some intermediate level[33]. Other differences may arise with respect to hours of work, sick pay, holiday entitlement, service recognition and various fringe benefits. It should be noted, however, that the majority of problems may well arise after the end of 1975 when firms are required to eliminate the above sex differences and the problems will have been more clearly defined in the courts.

Effects of the Equal Pay Legislation

Any predictions on the eventual effects of the equal pay legislation must be dependent on particular circumstances, not least on the precise form of the proposed anti-discrimination legislation. Firstly, allowance must be made for the possibilities of evasion and avoidance, the former involving a failure on the part of organisations to fulfil the requirements of the legislation and the latter involving countervailing action to minimise its impact. Evasion may result through ignorance, as suggested by the OME survey of small firms, or through a fear that compliance would lead to severe economic problems or even bankruptcy. Avoidance could occur through organisations reducing the size of the overlap area within which comparison between male and female employees is valid under the terms of the Act. The OME found that "a very small number of firms were delaying the implementation of equal pay while they undertook a re-organisation of their labour force along the lines which would reduce the applicability of the Act; this mainly took the form of segregating men's and women's jobs in order to reduce the area of overlap". However, one must allow for the possibility that firms would not wish to publicise their moves in this direction and some cases may have escaped the notice of the OME. Indeed, some unions including the Association of Professional, Executive, Clerical and Computer Staff have suggested that a substantial number of companies have taken steps to avoid the consequences of the Act. Further, many of the firms which had made no progress towards equal pay may have been contemplating such a strategy. Most firms investigated by the OME, in fact, interpreted "the same or broadly similar work" to mean "the same work", which would tend to minimise the effective overlap area. As noted above, the Act does not seem to have deterred firms from introducing job evaluations, but the effect of the latter may merely be to rationalise the *status quo* by leaving women in the lower ranked (and consequently lower paid) jobs[34].

Given that evasion or avoidance does not occur the predictions of economic theory are not unambiguous. In a competitive labour market we would expect some female unemployment to result through consequential effects on price and the substitution of female by male labour (to the extent that the former are less efficient) and by further mechanisation[35]. However, where the labour market is imperfect it can be demonstrated[36] that equal pay could cause a rise in female employment as the monopolistic exploitation is removed. Thus, any prediction must be based on empirical evidence on the degree of competition in the female labour market. There are no available data on the distribution of females by size of firm in Britain which would cast at least some light on this question. But given general imperfections in both the product and labour markets the employment-creating effects of equal pay to women may be of some significance. As far as the production industries are concerned it does not appear that women are employed in more concentrated industries to any lesser degree than men. Analysis of three-firm concentration ratios based on 1958 Census of Production data does not suggest any close correspondence between the percentage of females in an industry and the degree of concentration[37]. It must be remembered, however, that the majority of women are not employed in manufacturing, but in the service sector which includes a substantial number of women employed in wages council sectors, where size of establishment tends to be small.

The above, however, assumes the absence of both employer and employee discrimination. As has been shown the former is likely to result in sexual wage differentials and to the extent that wage discrimination is practised the employment prospects of women are enhanced. The removal of the wage differential would have the effect of reducing female employment, assuming that reasons for discrimination remain constant[38]. The tendency towards unemployment will be strengthened in so far as more females make themselves available for employment at the new favourable wage rates via a substitution effect which outweighs any inclination on the part of the females to curtail their labour force participation (hours) via a negative income effect. It must be recognised also that many females may be prepared to accept employment at relatively unfavourable wage rates since their transfer earnings are low and they may be prevented from doing so by the legislation. On the other hand, where employee discrimination exists this is likely to result in forces operating towards equal payment and segregation; whilst equal pay legislation may be irrelevant in the long-run it may reinforce this tendency in the short-run. Here the predicted effect on employment is uncertain without knowledge of the relative sizes of the segregated labour forces in equilibrium. Thus one cannot be dogmatic about the effect of equal pay upon female employment, the total welfare of the female population or the total costs of its introduction.

The direct costs of equal pay to the enterprise are likely to be substantially different between particular industries and firms. In addition secondary effects may occur through the traditional rigidity of the British wage structure with the possibility that male employees may seek to maintain their customary differential over women by one means or another. In addition, female employees not affected by the clauses of the Act may seek to restore parity with those women so affected. This would not only add considerably to the inflationary impact of the legislation but also tend to generalise its effects. The OME found that less than half the companies investigated had made a systematic attempt to estimate costs and that secondary costs as outlined above were generally ignored. Whilst two-thirds expected the increase to be less than 5% of the total wage bill, one in six companies expected costs to increase by more than 10% and one or two in excess of 20%. Similarly, the Industrial Society found that anticipated increases in labour costs ranged from less than 1% to $33\frac{1}{3}$% whilst the larger group centered on between 1% and 3%.

Conclusions

The relative importance of females in the British labour force is likely to increase rather than diminish, for virtually the whole of the future growth of the labour force to the end of this century is likely to be derived from a further influx of married women into paid occupations. A major feature of the British wage structure has been the long-run stability of the male earnings differential over females and it remains to be seen whether this is susceptible to change via legislation. Analysis of the occupational and industrial distribution of females points to the importance of wage differences rather than occupational/industrial mal-distribution in explaining the gross earnings gap, suggesting scope for equal pay legislation, in so far as this is capable of removing differences within narrow occupational groups. Whilst the 1970 Act did not go so far as to seek equal pay for work of equal value, merely demanding equal pay for the same or broadly similar work, this definition has been widened by the novel approach, compared with other countries, of permitting comparison where the parties have implemented a job evaluation scheme, which appears to be increasingly the case in the British economy. A further distinctive feature was the inclusion of an adjustment period of over five years from the passing of the Act until its clauses were to be made fully effective. Whilst a substantial number of industry-wide and plant-level agreements appear to have made full use of this breathing space, in some cases it seems to have been treated as an excuse for inactivity. Whilst differences in wage rates have substantially narrowed this has only marginally been the case with respect to earnings. However, since the Act does not become fully operational until the end of 1975 it is not possible to ascertain the precise long term effects of the legislation. Much will depend upon its interpretation in the Courts, especially in view of the lack of detail in the wording of the Act. It is doubtful whether the Act by itself will reduce substantially the gross earnings differential between sexes, but this is implicit in the fact that anti-discrimination legislation in relation to sex is in preparation and considerable public debate is centred on these issues.

References

1. These in effect limit in general daily hours of women to 10 (or 10½) in any one day in some cases and to 9 hours a day or 48 hours in a week in others, and lay down that working hours are to be between 7 a.m. and 8 p.m. (7 a.m. and 1 p.m. on Saturday)—therefore limiting shift-work, that there is to be no Sunday work and that the maximum period without a break is to be 4½ hours. There are also fairly stringent restrictions on overtime hours, which may not exceed six hours in any week, 100 hours in any year, or be worked in more than 25 weeks in any year within any factory. However, the Secretary of State for Employment has powers of exemption where this is in the public interest and in practice exceptions are relatively freely given.
2. *Report of the War Cabinet Committee on Women in Industry* (Chairman, Sir James Atkin), Cmnd 135, 1919.
3. "Projections of the Labour Force", *Department of Employment Gazette*, April, 1974.
4. "Part-time Women Workers 1950-1972", *Department of Employment Gazette*, November 1973.
5. These calculations were made using 1971 NES data. It should be noted that using Department of Employment figures for total employees in employment produces a negative co-efficient significant at the 1% level. This series includes part-time workers and the implication is, therefore, that part-time females are relatively unfavourably distributed industrially in comparison with full-time females.

6. For more details and some discussion of the difficulties involved see Chiplin and Sloane, *op. cit*, 1974.

7. The substance of this section is more fully developed in the authors' "The Economic Consequences of the Equal Pay Act 1970", *Industrial Relations Journal*, December, 1970, and "Sexual Discrimination in the Labour Market", *British Journal of Industrial Relations*, November 1974.

8. Department of Employment, *Employment Prospects for the Highly Qualified*, Manpower Paper, No. 8, HMSO, 1974.

9. Morris and Ziderman, *Economic Trends*, 1971, estimated that the incremental rates of return to society of a first degree over an "A" level qualification were 10·4% in the case of men and 4·9% in the case of women, but these estimates are based on actual earnings adjusted for ability and differences in labour participation, and may reflect a degree of discrimination as well as other factors. It should be noted that it is the differential in earnings between levels of qualification both for men and women that is relevant to the decision to invest in training rather than the absolute levels of male and female earnings. Thus it does not necessarily follow that because female earnings of the highly qualified are below those of the highly qualified males that there is less incentive for females to invest in training for this reason.

10. For a development of this approach see N. Bosanquet and P. B. Doeringer, "Is there a dual labour market in Great Britian?", *Economic Journal*, June 1973.

11. A similar resolution was passed unanimously in 1887 to the effect that "In the opinion of the Congress it is desirable, in the interests of both men and women, that in a trade where women do the same work as men they should receive the same payment".

12. Pauline Pinder, *Women at Work*, P.E.P. Broadsheet 512, May 1969.

13. Office of Manpower Economics, *Equal Pay First Report on the Implementation of the Equal Pay Act*, 1970, HMSO, 1972.

14. Atkin Committee, *op. cit*.

15. Royal Commission on Equal Pay, 1944-46 (Chairman, Sir Cyril Asquith), *Report*, Cmnd 6937, October 1946. The Commission's findings are discussed by E. H. Phelps Brown, "Equal Pay for Equal Work", *Economic Journal*, Vol. LIX, September 1949.

16. In the case of piece-rates the Commission was of the view that common base-rates would not be detrimental to women since there would still be allowance for differential performances between the sexes.

17. Pinder, *op. cit*.

18. The OME suggest that by 1966 only 10% of women, predominantly professional, enjoyed equal pay.

19. A similar measure was passed by the Northern Ireland Parliament in December 1970.

20. In order to assist both employers and employees and their representatives the Department of Employment produced a document providing guidelines on the provisions contained in the Act. See Department of Employment, *Equal Pay: A Guide to the Equal Pay Act* 1970, HMSO, December 1970.

21. Questions relating to statutory controls on women's hours of work, childbirth, retirement and pension arrangements are, however, outside the scope of the Act.

22. Two employers are associated if one is a company of which the other (directly or indirectly) has control or both are companies of which a third person (directly or indirectly) has control.

23. *Equal Pay: What are You Doing About It?* Department of Employment, 1973.

24. The importance of this question has been referred to above (see 5) and has also been emphasised in a recent paper on low pay in retail distribution which suggested that there was a relationship between the incidence of part-time employment and low pay. See O. Robinson and J. Wallace, "Part-time Employment and Low Pay in Retail Distribution in Britain", *Industrial Relations Journal*, Vol. 5 No. I, Spring 1974.

25. *Op. cit*.

26. "Progress towards Equal Pay", *Department of Employment Gazette*, August 1974.

27. This difference is more marked in manufacturing than in all industries and services.

28. Whilst "other pay" includes items besides basic pay these are likely to be small. The 1970 NES distinguished basic pay as such which accounted for 91·3% of the weekly earnings of non-manual men and 96·5% in the case of non-manual women. For manual workers in all industries and services corresponding figures are 69·1% and 82·1% respectively.

29. Department of Employment, *Equal Pay; What are You Doing About It?* 1973.

30. Similar misconceptions were found to exist by the Industrial Society in its survey of 173 member companies. See *Implementation of the Equal Pay Act 1970*, Survey and Report Series, No. 174, September 1971.

31. Pay Board, *4th Quarterly Report*, HMSO, 1974.

32. Pay Board, *5th Quarterly Report*, HMSO, 1974.

33. In the case of Tobacco Manufacturer the National Joint Negotiating Council agreed to a phased timetable for the introduction of equal pay. As part of this the adult age for women was raised from 18 to 19 years in 1972 and to 20 years in 1973, whilst the adult male was lowered from 21 to 20 in 1974. Similarly in the Fibreboard Packing Case Industry the adult age for men was reduced in two stages from 20 to 18 in order to bring it into equality with the adult female age. Source: *Time Rates of Wages and Hours of Work*, April 1973, pp. 28 and 132.

34. Where payment by results is practised a similar result may be achieved by the method of using "tight" and "loosely" rated jobs in such a way as to favour men.

35. As regards the possibility of factor substitution the Reddaway Report (W. B. Reddaway and Associate, *The Effects of the Selective Employment Tax; Final Report*, University of Cambridge, Department of Applied Economics, Occasional Paper 32, Cambridge University Press, 1973) found that without the abnormal productivity gains after the imposition of the selective employment tax (SET) on non-manufacturing employees the distributive trades would have required more labour than they actually utilised. The difference in terms of full-time equivalents was estimated for 1968 at over 100,000 in retailing and 30,000 in wholesaling. Whilst the precise effect of SET is a matter of debate the above result is indicative of the scope for substantial labour productivity changes which could possibly arise as a result of changes in female wage rates.

36. See Sloane and Chiplin, *op. cit.*, 1970.

37. Chiplin and Sloane, *op. cit.*, 1974.

38. It may be possible that the legislation will influence attitudes towards the employment of women in so far as it forces employers to bear the full costs of their reasons for discrimination.

Equal Pay in America

by J. E. Buckley

Equal pay, in the context of men and women performing the same job under similar working conditions and having comparable occupational seniority with the same employer, is fast becoming a reality in America. Wage differences based on sex are destined for the same fate that overtook the 13-hour day and 6-day week. Those employers who still maintain an unjustifiable pay differential do so in violation of an equal pay law that is being enforced with growing vigour. However, since the concept of equal pay for equal work is cast in the framework of equality within individual companies or establishments, most American women who work for wages do not benefit from the law. In the American workplace there is still very little occupational integration of the sexes within establishments. There are "male" and "female" jobs and industries, with male predominance in the best of each. In recent years token employment of one sex in occupations that were considered the preserve of the opposite sex has occurred, but the larger society still views most occupations as having a male or female quality.

Historical Perspective
European immigrants who settled in America brought with them long-established perceptions of the roles men and women play in society. Although living on the edge of a wilderness often necessitated modification of these roles, tasks were largely "assigned" on the basis of one's sex. Men cleared and worked the land, hunted for meat, and built and maintained the physical settlement. Women mainly worked in and around the house caring for both family and livestock. In addition to cooking, cleaning, washing, and sewing, women were the family spinners, weavers, teachers, and nurses. Women later dominated in these areas when the tasks were performed in a larger industrial or institutional setting.

In the American colonial period—and for some considerable time after national independence was attained—the prerequisites for equal pay treatment were essentially absent. In the more advanced European countries the 100-year span from 1750 to 1850 roughly approximated the beginning and maturation of the industrial revolution; at the end of this period America was still a land being settled, and the increase in population from about 1·3 million to 23·2 million was mainly in the rural and agricultural segments. Robert Smuts wrote that "During most of the 19th century the United States was still predominantly rural and agricultural . . . Toward the end of the century, however, the United States was rapidly becoming a nation of cities, of commerce, and of industry"[1].

Although the occupational segregation of men and women was almost complete in the early industrial history of America, there were isolated instances in which both sexes performed similar, if not identical, work assignments. The scattered accounts of these instances nearly always placed women in an inferior earnings category, and women and children were sometimes considered as a single workforce to be treated apart from the male workforce. Also present in the early industrial period were signs of resentment toward women workers. An "Emigrant's Directory", published in London in 1820, warned tailors that their trade in New York had been "much injured by the employment of women and boys who work from twenty-five to fifty per cent cheaper than men"[2].

Pay Differences

Some strong indications of women's inferior position as wage earners, such as those found in the "Emigrant's Directory", survived the period prior to the mid-19th century—a period in which the gathering of wage data was in a primitive stage. An 1832 report to the United States House of Representatives, presented by Secretary of the Treasury, Louis McLane, showed numerous instances of women receiving considerably lower wages than men within the same establishment. For example, 100 tailoring shops in Boston paid 50 cents a day to their 1,300 women employees, while their male employees received two dollars a day[3]. (Men probably performed the more difficult tailoring tasks, as was the custom at that time, but the large wage differential could hardly be fully explained by differences in duties or skill.) Although the McLane Report lacked specific occupational data, the examples in Table I, taken

Table I.   Earnings of men and women in selected establishments and States, 1832

Area	Firm	Product	Men No.	Men Pay	Women No.	Women Pay
Maine	Bristol Satinet	Satinet	3	$500·00 (Y)	3	$150·00 (Y)
Maine	Cumberland Factory	Cotton goods	15	7·50 (W)	75	2·50 (W)
Massachusetts	Walley Co.	Cotton goods	6	1·25 (D)	15	·40 (D)
Massachusetts	J. G. Root	Satinet	6	·80 (D)	9	·33 (D)
New Hampshire	Exeter Co.	Cotton goods	40	1·12 (D)	212	·44 (D)
New Hampshire	Cocheco Co.	Cotton goods	219	1·50 (D)*	752	·465 (D)
Connecticut	Unknown	Hats	60	1·25 (D)	30	·50 (D)
Connecticut	Unknown	Bookbinding	16	1·25 (D)	16	·60 (D)
New York	Unknown	Woollen goods	15	6·00 (W)	23	2·00 (W)
New York	Unknown	Blankets	6	·90 (D)	8	·48 (D)

*Rate as reported on page 635, Vol. I. On page 581, Vol. 1, same firm reported 219 males at $1·15.

Note: Pay for men in the second and ninth entry above was converted from daily to weekly. A 6-day work-week was assumed. The "Y" after a pay rate refers to yearly; "W" refers to weekly; and "D" to daily.

Source: McLane, L., *Statistics of Manufactures in the United States*, (Washington 1833), Vol. I, pp. 6, 10, 127, 132, 581, 635, 1033; Vol. II, pp. 71, 84.

from individual firms reporting information for men and women, show that large pay differences existed in the 1830's.

Other evidence of pay discrimination in the early industrial period in America supports the pattern shown in Table I. In Cincinnati, the Workingmen's Shield reported in 1833 (12 January, 1833) that women earned about 25 cents for every dollar a man earned. During the same period, Mathew Carey, a crusader for better working conditions and pay for women, estimated that working women in Philadelphia ". . . do not receive as much wages for an entire week's work, 13 or 14 hours per day, as journeymen receive in same branches for a single day of 10 hours"[4].

By the middle of the 19th century it appears that some progress had been made in narrowing the earnings gap between the sexes, although available information still showed wide variations. In 1851, male doffers in the cotton goods industry in Massachusetts had average hourly earnings that exceeded the earnings of female doffers by about 70%; by 1860 the average earnings gap for doffers had temporarily disappeared in Massachusetts. During the 1850's, male and female speeder tenders in the same industry and State had average earnings that were almost equal. The narrowing of the earnings gap in the mid-century was not, however, universal. Women school teachers in New York in 1853 were reported to have received only one-tenth of the pay of men teachers[5]. (This huge earnings gap, if correctly recorded, represented an extreme departure from the earnings ratio found for this and other jobs before, during, and after the period.) In New York during the same decade, the average earnings of male spinners in the cotton goods industry exceeded those of female spinners by 60 to 131%[6]. Although there is no overall measure of the difference in the average earnings of men and women doing the same work during the 1850's, men's average earnings may be estimated at roughly double the average earnings of women.

In 1934, the Bureau of Labor Statistics published a report on the history of wages in the United States from colonial times to 1928 (with a supplement through 1933). The report, lamenting the fact that "Wages in and of themselves have been consistently overlooked by most writers of American history"[7], attempted to provide some insight into an area that had long been neglected. The report included occupational wage data for selected industries from 1840. Data on average earnings of male and female painters in the building trades in Pennsylvania appeared for the first time in 1853. These data, which were reported with some degree of regularity until 1891, represent one of the earliest series of reliable statistical information on earnings of men and women in the same occupation. Table II shows the earnings relationship of these painters for selected years.

The earnings relationship between men and women painters in Pennsylvania showed no discernible pattern over the 37-year period shown in Table II. In 1853, men's average earnings exceeded women's by 126%; in 1860 the difference was 80%. Ten years later the spread was 149%; in 1879 (not shown in Table II), average

Table II. Average daily earnings of building trades' painters in Pennsylvania by year and sex

Year	Men*	Women
1853	$1·58	$0·70
1860	1·35	·75
1865	1·66	·84
1870	2·42	·97
1875	2·01	1·15
1880	2·12	1·17
1885	1·83	1·04
1890	2·65	1·25

*Rates adjusted to eliminate differences in the average number of hours worked.

Source: *History of Wages in the United States from Colonial Times to* 1928, US, Department of Labor, Bureau of Labor Statistics, Bulletin No. 604 (Washington, 1934), pp. 195-198.

earnings differences between the sexes were the smallest over the entire period—50%. At the end of the period (1890) the average earnings of men painters in Pennsylvania exceeded those of women by 112%.

Beginning in 1890, and continuing through 1907, earnings information became available for male and female proof readers in the printing and publishing industries. This information, presented for broad geographical regions, showed a very definite narrowing of the earnings gap—at least when compared to jobs in other industries at other times. The information for proof readers also showed the lack of a reasonably stable earnings relationship from year to year or among regions. In the North Atlantic region, for example, men's average earnings exceeded women's by 21% in 1890; by 1894 the difference was reduced to 7%. A completely different picture emerged when earnings differences in the North Central region were compared for the same two years. In 1890, average earnings of male proof readers in the North Central region exceeded those of female proof readers by 43%; in 1894, men's earnings exceeded women's by 104%. The information for proof readers, shown in Table III, also indicates that the earnings gap between the sexes was narrower in 1890 than in 1907.

Earnings of male and female weavers in the cotton goods industry are available for selected years from 1907 to 1932. This information shows that the earnings gap was generally narrower for weavers during this period than the earnings gap for proof readers in the period from 1890 to 1970, or for painters in Pennsylvania from 1853 to 1890. Earnings of men painters exceeded those of women by 100% for the years shown in Table II (unweighted average difference); a similar computation for proof readers in the North Atlantic and North Central regions combined (Table III) shows a 34% spread. Data for weavers in Table IV indicate an unweighted average difference of 10%. (Data available for 1971 show a further narrowing of the earnings gap for

Table III.   Average hourly earnings of proof readers, by region and sex, 1890-1907

Year	North Atalantic Region Average hourly earnings		North Central Region Average hourly earnings	
	Men	Women	Men	Women
1890	$0·329	$0·271	$0·318	$0·222
1891	·332	·301	·318	·252
1892	·327	·289	·318	·230
1893	·327	·296	·326	·200
1894	·323	·303	·326	·160
1895	·333	·280	·329	·174
1896	·325	·265	·329	·210
1897	·331	·261	·323	·187
1898	·338	·265	·323	·197
1899	·306	·269	·348	·256
1900	·355	·286	·364	·303
1901	·357	·292	·389	·254
1902	·403	·320	·386	·281
1903	·392	·351	·372	·325
1904	·370	·302	·370	·326
1905	·381	·298	·368	·291
1906	·410	·293	·382	·274
1907	·420	·320	·402	·280

Source: *History of Wages in the United States from Colonial Times to* 1928, US, Department of Labor, Bureau of Labor Statistics, Bulletin No. 604 (Washington, 1934), pp. 346-347.

weavers in cotton and manmade fibre textile mills. Nationwide average hourly earnings of male weavers exceeded those of women by 4·5%[8].)

Although no broad inferences can be drawn from the limited data presented in Table IV, there is a slight hint of how the relationship of men's and women's earnings behave in a time of economic crisis. By 1930, the effects of the Great Depression had not yet been reflected in the earnings of weavers; by 1932, however, earnings of both sexes had dropped considerably, but in seven of the eight States for which data are shown, women's earnings fell less drastically than men's in five States and fell at the same rate in the two other States.

When the history of pay differences between men and women workers in America is examined, the pattern that emerges shows a slow narrowing of the earnings gap. (As seen in Tables II, III, and IV, the narrowing of the earnings gap quite often behaved convulsively—taking two steps forward and one back.) For the most part, this improved earnings picture occurred without the benefit of legislation. There was no national policy, until recent years, which stated that men and women should earn the same wages when doing the same work. Without such a policy, enforced by legislation, women workers were still subject to discriminatory pay practices. Strong Federal legislation was needed to rectify a long-standing imbalance.

Table IV. Weavers in cotton goods industry, by State and sex, 1907-28

Year	Alabama		Georgia		Maine		Massachusetts		New Hampshire		Rhode Island		North Carolina		South Carolina	
	Rate per hour		Rate per hour		Rate per hour		Rate per hour		Rate per hour		Rate per hour		Rate per hour		Rate per hour	
	Men	Women	Men	Women	Men	Women	Men	Women	Men	Women	Men	Women	Men	Women	Men	Women
1907	$0·124	$0·112	$0·116	$0·109	$0·192	$0·162	$0·179	$0·162	—	—	$0·192	$0·170	$0·124	$0·114	$0·132	$0·122
1908	·124	·119	·128	·141	·174	·149	·184	·163	—	—	·190	·169	·129	·121	·133	·122
1909	·128	·123	·127	·113	·171	·151	·161	·151	—	—	·187	·166	·128	·118	·134	·121
1910	·131	·122	·130	·120	·169	·149	·163	·150	$0·155	$0·145	·179	·195	·132	·121	·136	·122
1911	·135	·126	·128	·120	·178	·152	·164	·148	·167	·160	·182	·161	·139	·125	·138	·127
1912	·141	·125	·143	·131	·197	·163	·180	·167	·190	·180	·192	·171	·144	·131	·140	·127
1913	·144	·128	·145	·133	·199	·167	·182	·166	·191	·180	·195	·173	·146	·134	·143	·129
1914	·140	·132	·159	·140	·197	·166	·186	·168	·196	·188	·201	·181	·156	·139	·148	·130
1916	·163	·147	·161	·144	·235	·204	·225	·206	·235	·226	·245	·224	·167	·151	·153	·140
1918	·235	·190	·218	·187	·382	·341	·327	·303	·344	·319	·359	·333	·251	·221	·232	·200
1920	·439	·378	·476	·430	·658	·560	·598	·548	·626	·575	·607	·538	·582	·519	·532	·468
1922	·255	·231	·282	·274	·471	·419	·460	·415	·466	·428	·454	·405	·350	·313	·286	·260
1924	·298	·262	·314	·286	·539	·458	·543	·487	·532	·495	·542	·515	·401	·351	·328	·299
1926	·298	·278	·297	·284	·485	·449	·459	·420	·514	·488	·494	·455	·353	·316	·314	·276
1928	·311	·299	·309	·292	·424	·397	·431	·405	·501	·493	·498	·469	·370	·333	·313	·277
1930	·327	·300	·308	·303	·449	·408	·460	·415	·460	·493	·489	·463	·372	·337	·347	·312
1932	·275	·263	·280	·277	·353	·321	·366	·336	·371	·354	·313	·310	·298	·276	·272	·262

Source: *History of Wages in the United States from Colonial Times to 1928*, US Department of Labor, Bureau of Labor Statistics, Bulletin No. 604 (Washington, 1934), pp. 394, 395, 563, 564.

Activism and Response

Inequitable pay treatment has been part of the American scene from the time both sexes first shared the same workplace. Many men and women felt that men should get higher wages because of greater responsibilities in providing for their families. Others found this position unacceptable. In 1829, an "intelligent and respectable lady of New Jersey" wrote to Mathew Carey concerning the condition of women workers. She suggested that women also have families to support, and ". . . seeing that women labor equally with men . . . they are fully entitled to an equality of wages"[9]. Female activists of the 19th century endorsed the principle of equal pay for equal work. However, the plight of the relatively few women who worked for wages was not their main concern. The activists concentrated on gaining equality before the law on such matters as property rights, divorce, separation, child custody, and on the right to represent themselves at the polling place. Besides, many women wage earners regarded employment, even at low pay and in harsh working conditions, as preferable to unpaid labour and lack of independence in the home.

Unions

Labour unions were first among organised groups to call for equal pay legislation. In 1868, the National Labor Union passed a resolution which urged Congress to pass laws that would guarantee equal pay for equal work for Federal employees. The resolution also urged State legislatures to pass similar laws. This stand by organised labour followed a generation of internal conflict in the male dominated movement. Trade unions feared the consequences of women competing for jobs that were held by men. In 1835, the National Trades' Union saw as a two-fold problem that ". . . the extreme low prices given for female labor are scarcely sufficient to satisfy the necessary wants of life, and create a destructive competition with the male laborer". That same year the National Trades' Union passed a resolution to oppose ". . . by all honest means, the multiplying of all description of labor for females, inasmuch as the competition it creates with the males tends inevitably to impoverish both"[10].

In 1836 the National Trades' Union recognised that women had a necessary place in industry, but the advice given at that time was that women should organise and, if necessary, strike for better wages. (Women had, in fact, organised and struck for better working conditions some years before this advice was given. In 1828, 300 to 400 women in cotton mills struck in Dover, New Hampshire. In 1834, there was another strike in Dover over a proposed reduction in wages, and a similar strike involving 800 women mill workers in Lowell, Massachusetts. In 1836, the 2,500 members of the Lowell Factory Girls' Association went on strike to protest against an increase in the price of board that was tantamount to a 12·5% wage cut.) Even as the National Labor Union was passing an equal pay resolution in 1868, its national president was fearful that ". . . the effect of introducing female labor [into male dominated trades] is to undermine prices, [female] labor being usually employed, unjustly to the woman, at a lower rate than is paid for male labor in the same kind of work".

He went on to suggest that government should set ". . . the example of equal compensation for male and female labor"[11]. The resolution on equal pay that came out of the 1868 convention was limited to employees on public payrolls.

During the late 1800's there was also some conflict between the labour movement's leadership and membership on the question of equal pay for women. The leadership generally favoured equal pay for equal work, but there was a certain amount of unwillingness on the part of the membership to accept such changes. In the printing and publishing industries, where considerable numbers of women were employed, typographical unions were faced with the problem. One observer, writing during the period, said that "Typographical unions were much praised for their gallantry in forcing employers to agree to their terms of "Equal work, equal pay, equal terms of apprenticeship for both sexes". This chivalric aspect was somewhat dimmed by refusal afterwards of some union men to work in the same offices as with women. Employers were frequently given the option of choosing between having all men or all women at the cases, and the struggle usually ended in favor of the men"[12].

Government as Employer
Among major employers, the United States Federal Government took the lead in endorsing the principle of equal pay for equal work. The principle was first written into law in 1870, when department heads within Government agencies were permitted to pay equal salaries to women. (Interpretations of the 1870 law, however, gave appointing officials in Government agencies the option to specify the sex of an employee to fill a particular position. In 1962 the President of the United States removed this option when he directed Federal agencies to make appointments without regard to sex, while still allowing the Civil Service Commission to make exceptions on the basis of objective, non-discriminatory standards. In 1965, Congress repealed the 1870 law.) The Civil Service Act of 1883 was far more important than the 1870 law in that it set up a merit system under which women could compete in Federal civil service examinations on the same basis as men. The Federal Government, under the Classification Act of 1923, became one of the first employers to initiate a pay system where the salary of each job was tied to the duties and responsibilities of that job, and the sex of an employee holding that job was not to be considered.

Government as Consumer
On numerous occasions the Federal Government has used its power as a consumer of goods and services to rectify a specific social problem. The Davis-Bacon Prevailing Wage Law of 1931, the Walsh-Healey Public Contracts Act of 1936, and the McNamara-O'Hara Service Contract Act of 1965 are examples of how the Government, as a party to a contract, requires that certain conditions be met in order to satisfy the terms of the contract. The McNamara-O'Hara Service Contract Act, for example, requires that contractors and subcontractors, holding Government contracts in excess of $2,500, use the prevailing rate within a given locality as the

minimum rate that can be paid to their employees engaged in service functions. ("Service employee", as defined in the Act, include guards; watchmen; skilled tradesmen; and unskilled, semi-skilled, and skilled manual labour.)

For many years before "equal pay for equal work" became a general law applicable to most workers, the Federal Government also used its contractual leverage on behalf of women workers. In 1918, the National War Labor Board directed firms holding government contracts to pay women the same wages as men when both performed the same work. During the Depression of the 1930's, industry codes promulgated by the National Recovery administration included equal pay provisions. The Walsh-Healey Act, which set basic labour standards for work done on Federal Government contracts exceeding $10,000 for materials, supplies, and equipment, also required that the minimum wage for men and women be the same.

Although Government as an employer and consumer had led the way and exerted pressure on behalf of women in the labour force, there was still a great need for action on a broader scope. To a large degree this need was met by the enactment of the Equal Pay Act of 1963 and the Civil Rights Act of 1964. These Acts, and Executive Order No. 11375, have become the chief legal tools used to help eliminate inequitable treatment of women workers. They each deserve some further attention here.

Equal Pay Act of 1963

In the 20th century, three national emergencies—the two world wars and the Great Depression of the 1930's—gave strong impetus to the equal pay movement and to the enactment of corrective legislation. The wartime emergencies saw millions of women entering the labour market to replace the men who had gone into military service. The Depression compelled many women to seek employment when their men were unable to find work. In April 1930, women represented 21·9% of all workers. In March 1940, toward the end of the Depression and before America entered World War II, 25·4% of all workers were women. By April 1945, the figure jumped to 36·1%. Women had served with distinction in "male" jobs, and serious demands for equal pay were emerging.

When the first comprehensive Equal Pay Bill was introduced in the US Congress in 1945, five states—Illinois, Michigan, Montana, New York, and Washington—had equal pay laws in operation. (Later in 1945, Massachusetts enacted similar legislation.) Two states, Michigan and Montana, had enacted equal pay laws in 1919, setting the example for the other State and Federal laws that were to follow. The 1945 Bill was defeated, but proponents of equal pay introduced similar bills each year thereafter until one became law.

Early in the Kennedy Administration a renewed interest in women in the workplace had surfaced. In December 1961, the President established a Commission on the Status of Women. The Commission, chaired by Eleanor Roosevelt, had responsibility for examining the role of women in the nation and recommending remedies where needed. The Commission's report, *American Women*, was presented to the President on 11 October 1963. Acting on the recommendations of the Commission, President Kennedy signed Executive Order 11126 on 1 November 1963, thereby creating the Interdepartmental Committee on the Status of Women and a Citizen's Advisory Council. Earlier in 1963, the US Congress passed and the President signed the Federal Equal Pay Act.

By passing the Equal Pay Act of 1963, it was the intention of Congress "To prohibit discrimination on account of sex in the payment of wages by employers engaged in commerce or in the production of goods for commerce". Congress found that wage differentials based on sex depress wages and living standards below those necessary to the health and efficiency of employees; prevent the maximum utilisation of available labour resources; tend to cause labour disputes which burden and obstruct commerce; and constitute an unfair method of competition. The Act, as an amendment to the Fair Labor Standards Act of 1938, was confined to workers covered by the 1938 law.

The language in the 1963 Act, paraphrased here, requires employers to pay both sexes equal compensation for work demanding equal skill, effort, and responsibility, and performed under similar working conditions. The Act specifically prohibits employers from reducing the wage rate of any worker in order to equalise the rate for both sexes. It also prohibits labour organisations from entering into agreements with employers that would result in discriminatory pay practices. The Act, however, does allow for wage differentials based on (1) a seniority system, (2) a merit system, (3) a system which measures earnings by quantity or quality of production, or (4) a differential based on any other factors unrelated to sex.

Since the application of the 1963 Act was limited to workers covered by the Fair Labor Standards Act of 1938, about 15 million "exempt" employees, such as executive, administrative, professional, and outside salespeople, were not subject to its protection. This was a serious deficiency in that some of the most subtle pay discrimination existed for employees in these categories. (For example, some employers scheduled training courses for evening hours when family responsibilities precluded many women from participation. Completion of these courses was sometimes a necessary condition for advancement, even though their practical need or value may have been questionable.) Public Law 92-318, referred to as the Education Amendments of 1972, removed this deficiency by giving equal pay protection to these exempt employees. (The 1972 Amendments, however, did not completely change the exempt status of these workers. They are still exempt from the minimum wage and overtime provisions of the Fair Labor Standards Act.) As with many laws, provisions of the Equal Pay Act were tested in several court cases. Judicial interpretations of the Act have had considerable impact on women in the workplace.

The US Department of Labor is charged with the enforcement of the Equal Pay Act of 1963. From 1964, when the Act took effect, until 1970, the Department had tried 15 equal pay cases and won only four. This poor record was partially due to court interpretations of the word "equal" as it applied to skill, effort, and responsibility.

The question arose as to how equal a job must be in order to meet the terms of the Act. Some rulings held that a job must be almost identical in order to meet the test. Employers had also maintained, and some courts agreed, that the flexibility of male workers in performing extra duties, such as lifting heavier loads, justified a differential.

The sixteenth case tried by the Department of Labor, Shultz v. Wheaton Glass Company[13], was the first under the Act to reach the United States Supreme Court. It involved male and female selectors and packagers who worked side by side at the Wheaton Glass Company facility in Millville, New Jersey. Although both sexes performed identical work for at least 80% of the time, men were paid 10% (21·5 cents) more per hour. The company also employed "snap-up boys", whose main function was handling of materials. Snap-up boys earned 2 cents an hour more than the female selector-packagers. The male selector-packagers at times performed the duties of the snap-up boys, and the company justified its wage differential for men on the basis that they were more flexible and versatile than the women.

The Third Circuit US Court of Appeals, in its landmark decision, refused to accept the company's argument for maintaining a differential. The Court ruled that jobs need only be "substantially equal" to meet the test of the 1963 Act, and that the extra menial tasks performed by the males did not make the jobs unequal. The Court also found that all males received the differential, even though all did not perform the additional "snap-up" duties. This blanket payment to males, based on their "flexibility" and "versatility", was not an acceptable differential under that part of the Act which allows for "a differential based on any other factor other than sex". The Supreme Court, by refusing to review the decision, let the lower Court's ruling stand.

Another important court decision has been handed down since the Wheaton ruling; this one, however, has been a setback to advocates of equal pay. In the case of Hodgson v. Robert Hall Clothes, Inc.[14], the employer successfully maintained that wages of salesmen selling men's clothing were justifiably higher than wages of saleswomen who sold less expensive and less profitable women's clothing in a separate department. The Court determined that the salespeople in each department were not interchangeable because of possible embarrassment to customers and because of potential reduction in sales volume. A comment in the University of Pennsylvania Law Review said the ruling implied ". . . that the costs created by business policies catering to the perceptions of community sexual mores should be borne by the female labor force, rather than the firm"[15].

Civil Rights Act of 1964
The Civil Rights Act of 1964 is, by an ironic turn of events, one of the most helpful pieces of legislation available to advocates of women's rights in the workplace. When the Bill was being considered in Congress, its proponents were primarily concerned with the constitutional right of black Americans to exercise their vote, to enjoy public accommodations without discrimination, to have equal access to public schools, and

to have equal employment opportunities. Those who favoured the Bill wanted its scope limited to cases of discrimination based on race, colour, religion, or natural origin. A coalition of Southern congressmen, having no particular commitment to equal employment opportunities for women, supported an amendment that would also prohibit discrimination on the basis of sex. This amendment was offered in the hope that support for the entire measure would be weakened or that the legislation might at least be delayed; many of the amendments strongest "supporters" were among those who vigorously opposed the Equal Pay Act a year earlier. The amendment carried over the objections of some who favoured the original Bill, and is now part of Title VII of the 1964 Act.

Title VII, dealing with equal employment opportunities, goes beyond the Equal Pay Act in several important respects. As amended, Title VII makes it an unlawful employment practice for an employer of 15 or more workers to discriminate against any individual in the areas of hiring, firing, or terms of employment, because of one's sex, race, colour, religion, or national origin. (These five criteria are applicable throughout this discussion of the 1964 Act. Hereafter, reference to "sex" will be understood to include race, colour, religion, or national origin.) It prohibits employers from limiting, segregating, or classifying employees (or applicants for employment) in any way which would deprive an individual of employment opportunities (or adversely affect the worker's status as an employee) on account of the worker's sex. On the same basis, it prohibits discrimination as it relates to wages, fringe benefits, assignments or promotions, use of facilities, or training or retraining. Employment agencies are similarly forbidden from classifying, referring, or failing to refer for employment any individual on the basis of the jobseeker's sex. Labour organisations are also forbidden to limit, segregate, or classify its membership (or applicants for membership) on the basis of sex, or to administer apprenticeship programmes on such a basis.

Title VII also created the Equal Employment Opportunity Commission (EEOC), and vested with it the authority to issue, amend, or rescind suitable procedural regulations to carry out the Title's provisions. Soon after its passage, questions had arisen as to how protective labour legislation within the individual states could be reconciled with Title VII of the Act. Some State laws, for example, prohibited women workers from lifting weights in excess of a specified limit. Employers were unsure whether they violated the Federal Act by adhering to the State law, or violated the State law by adopting the Federal Act. Those who favoured retention of the State legislation contended that Congress had no intention to strike down such protective laws, but only to abolish those which denied equal opportunity to women. Other groups, led by female activists, called for the abolition of the State laws on the grounds that they hinder women rather than help.

The EEOC settled the matter on 19 August 1969 when it issued the following revised *Guidelines on Discrimination Because of Sex:*

(1) Many States have enacted laws or promulgated administrative regulations with respect to the employment of females. Among these laws are those which prohibit or limit the employment of females, e.g., the employment of females in certain occupations, in jobs requiring the lifting or carrying of weights exceeding certain prescribed limits, during certain hours of the night, or for more than a specified number of hours per day or per week.

(2) The Commission believes that such State laws and regulations, although originally promulgated for the purpose of protecting females, have ceased to be relevant to our technology or to the expanding role of the female worker in our economy. The Commission has found that such laws and regulations do not take into account the capacities, preferences, and abilities of individual females, and tend to discriminate rather than protect. Accordingly, the Commission had concluded that such laws and regulations conflict with Title VII of the Civil Rights Act of 1964 and will not be considered a defence to an otherwise established unlawful practice or as a basis for the application of the bona fide occupational qualification exception.

The Civil Rights Act of 1964 also supplements the Equal Pay Act of 1963 in one other important aspect. The older Act, as mentioned above, is limited to workers covered under the Fair Labor Standards Act of 1938, as amended. The 1964 Act covers those workers excluded by the FLSA, provided they work for an employer of 15 or more workers.

Executive Orders
As chief executive officer, the President of the United States periodically issues executive orders to the executive branch of government. President Lyndon B. Johnson issued Executive Order No. 11246 on 24 September 1965, dealing with discrimination in employment because of race, colour, religion, or national origin. This action was aimed at government employment, employment by Federal contractors and subcontractors, and employment under federally assisted construction contracts. Two years later, on 13 October 1967, President Johnson amended the earlier Order by issuing Executive Order No. 11375. This amendment added the word "sex" to the four categories listed in the 1965 Order.

Both of these Orders include a phrase that has been widely circulated in recent years: affirmative action. Employers subject to the provisions of the Orders must initiate affirmative action programmes that ensure the employment of both sexes for all occupations, unless sex is a bona fide occupational qualification (as defined). The Office of Federal Contract Compliance of the US Department of Labor has responsibility for issuing guidelines and ensuring compliance. An affirmative action programme, as spelled out by the OFCC (Revised Order No. 4), is a ". . . set of specific and result-oriented procedures to which a contractor commits himself to apply every good faith effort". Guidelines issued include the active recruitment of women for jobs where they had been previously excluded. Suggested recruitment includes visits by employers to co-educational and women's colleges where desired skills are taught, and also making it clear in job advertisements that women will be considered equally with men for vacant positions. A contractor must examine all major job classifications within his organisation and provide an explanation if women are currently underutilised. "Underutilisation" is defined as having fewer women in a given job classification than would be reasonably expected by their availability. The contractor, in making his workforce analysis, must determine the following eight points:

(1) The size of the female unemployment force in the labour area surrounding the facility;

(2) The percentage of the female workforce as compared with the total workforce in the immediate labour area;

(3) The general availability of women having requisite skills in the immediate labour area;

(4) The availability of women having requisite skills in an area in which the contractor can reasonably recruit;

(5) The availability of women seeking employment in the labour or recruitment area of the contractor;

(6) The availability of promotable and transferable female employees within the contractor's organisation;

(7) The existence of training institutions capable of training persons in the requisite skills;

(8) The degree of training which the contractor is reasonably able to undertake as a means of making all job classes available to women.

Under an affirmative action programme, the employer, after examining his own employment practices and finding them wanting, is expected to establish goals and timetables for meeting those goals. According to the guidelines, goals should be significant, measurable, attainable, and specific for planned results. However, a certain amount of flexibility is allowed, providing the employer can demonstrate his good faith in carrying out the programme. If an employer fails to develop and implement an acceptable affirmative action programme within a specified time, the Director of the OFCC issues a notice of proposed cancellation or termination of existing contracts and debarment from future contracts. If the employer fails to request a hearing within 14 days, all current contracts would be terminated for default.

Current Earnings Situation

As alluded to earlier, the problem facing American working women is not primarily one of equal pay for equal work, but rather equal employment opportunities in a greater variety of jobs and industries. The proposition that greater employment opportunities are needed is accepted widely; the proposition that equal pay for equal work has, with qualifications, essentially been attained is still debated.

In 1970, the median earnings of American women employed on a full-time basis were approximately 60% of men's earnings. This figure, taken from the Current Population Reports of the US Department of Commerce, is circulated widely by individuals concerned with pay inequities in the labour market. Unfortunately, it is sometimes used without qualification, tending to cloud the problem of equal pay for equal work. Some writers fail to mention that the Commerce Department's figure relates to all workers in diverse occupations. The figure is useful in pointing out the earnings relationship of all full-time men and women workers, but it sheds little light on the earnings relationship of men and women doing the same work.

In its regular Area Wage Survey Program, the US Department of Labor's Bureau of Labor Statistics (BLS) conducts annual surveys of occupational wages and related benefits in 85 Standard Metropolitan Statistical Areas (SMSA's). Data are collected from a variety of manufacturing and non-manufacturing establishments in the 85 areas and are appropriately weighted to represent all 229 SMSA's of the United States and four broad geographical regions. Occupational earnings data are collected by sex, although the main goal of the survey is to measure the level, distribution, and movement of wages by occupational category rather than determine if wage discrimination exists. Published results, however, have consistently shown men's average earnings to exceed women's average earnings in the same job and area.

In an attempt to determine the causes of the observed wage differences, the Bureau, in 1971, examined 10 of the 37 office, clerical and plant occupations for which men's and women's earnings were studied in the 1969-70 round of surveys. (For 29 additional plant jobs, the Bureau collected earnings information for men only.) After examining the data in detail, the Bureau found little to suggest that individual employers pay men one rate and women another for the same job[16]. Among the chief values of the BLS study were the occupational refinement of the data and their uniformity and reliability. The Bureau's full-time professional field representatives applied standard job descriptions (which allowed for some interestablishment differences) in determining whether workers found within establishments actually matched the jobs surveyed. The chief limitation of the special study was that only 10 jobs with a total of 751,000 workers, or approximately 1·2% of the full-time civilian labour force in February 1970, were studied.

In the BLS study, eight office, clerical and two workshop or plant occupations with significant numbers of both sexes were selected for examination. Based on data for all establishments combined, the simple average wage differential by sex for the 10 occupations favoured men by 18% in 1970 (Table V). In each occupation, men had higher average earnings than women, with advantages ranging from 8% for office boys to 34% for order clerks. There was no consistent relationship between the earnings level of an occupation and the size of the spread in average earnings between the sexes. Despite substantial differences in earnings levels, male tabulating-machine operators, class A and B, had an identical pay advantage of 11% over women in both

Table V.   Average earnings¹ of men and women in 10 occupational classifications in all metropolitan areas combined, February 1970²

Occupation	All establishments			Establishments employing both men and women			Establishments employing only men or women		
	Average weekly or hourly earnings		Percent by which men's earnings exceeded women's	Average weekly or hourly earnings		Percent by which men's earnings exceeded women's	Average weekly or hourly earnings		Percent by which men's earnings exceeded women's
	Men	Women		Men	Women		Men	Women	
Office									
Clerks, accounting, class A	$145·00	$122·00	19	$145·50	$129·50	12	$145·00	$118·50	22
Clerks, accounting, class B	119·50	96·50	24	119·50	105·00	14	121·00	94·50	28
Clerks, order	133·00	99·00	34	137·00	109·50	25	131·00	97·50	34
Clerks, payroll	139·50	110·00	27	144·50	128·00	13	134·50	108·00	25
Office boys or girls	88·50	82·00	8	88·00	83·50	5	88·50	81·00	9
Tabulating-machine operators:									
Class A	149·00	134·50	11	148·00	140·00	6	149·50	129·00	16
Class B	124·50	112·50	11	123·00	117·50	5	125·50	110·50	14
Class C	106·50	95·00	12	108·00	104·00	4	106·00	93·50	13
Plant									
Janitors, porters, and cleaners	2·46	2·13	15	2·42	2·14	13	2·53	1·92	32
Packers, shipping	2·90	2·48	17	2·89	2·62	10	2·91	2·39	22
Unweighted average difference	—	—	18	—	—	11	—	—	22

(1) Earnings of office workers relate to regular straight-time salaries that are paid for standard workweeks. Earnings of plantworkers relate to hourly earnings, excluding premium pay for overtime and for work on weekends, holidays, and late shifts.

(2) Average month of reference. Data were collected during the period of July 1969 through June 1970.

Source:: US Department of Labor, Bureau of Labor Statistics, Washington, D.C. 20212

levels, whereas the advantage of male class A accounting clerks, 19%, was considerably lower than the pay advantage of men in the class B accounting job (24%).

An interesting pattern developed in the BLS data when all-establishment information, which produced an unweighted average earnings advantage of 18% for men in the 10 jobs, was reduced to examine (1) sex-wage relationships in those establishments employing both sexes in the same job, and (2) earnings of workers in establishments that employed only one sex in any of the 10 jobs. The 18% advantage of men at the all-establishment level dropped to 11% for establishments that employed both men and women in an occupation, and rose to 22% when data for firms employing only men were compared to data for establishments employing only women in a given job. Table V shows that the average earnings of men were generally similar in each group of establishments, while women averaged substantially less in establishments employing only one sex in the job than in establishments that employed both sexes. Thus, in terms of earnings, women appeared to fare better in establishments where male occupational counterparts were also employed.

A further analysis was made of information for establishments employing both men and women in a job. Data presented in Table VI compare men's and women's earnings within *individual* establishments. The values shown were obtained by (1) dividing average earnings of women in an occupation into the corresponding average for men, to arrive at a plus or minus percentage relationship for the occupation and establishment, and (2) arraying these percentages to observe medians and middle ranges.

For 6 of the 10 occupations, median establishment percentage differences in men's and women's earnings amounted to 2% or less, including two jobs (class B and C tabulating-machine operators) in which women held a slight advantage. The largest median percentage difference (favouring men by 9%) was recorded for order clerks. As indicated by the middle range of percentage differences, women frequently average more than men performing similar tasks in the same establishments.

The 1969-70 special study on men's and women's earnings in the same occupation was the third such study undertaken by BLS; the previous studies were based on data from area wage surveys conducted in 1958-59[17] and 1965-66[18]. The 1958-59 study—limited to 20 individual areas—does not afford direct comparison with the two more recent studies, which provided estimates for all metropolitan areas combined. Comparisons of data for 1965-66 and 1969-70 show that the average wage advantage for men in the 10 jobs combined remained the same (11%) in establishments employing both sexes in the jobs, and about the same (21 and 22%) in establishments employing *only* men or women. As indicated in Table VII, this pattern was not consistent for individual occupations. The earnings gap for payroll clerks, for example, was considerably greater in 1970 than in 1966 in establishments employing both sexes (13% compared to 8%). For that same occupation the earnings gap was slightly narrower in 1970 than in 1966 (25% compared to 26%) in establishments employing only one sex in the job.

Table VI. Median and middle ranges¹ of within-establishment percentage differences by which men's earnings exceeded women's in 10 occupations, all metropolitan areas, by region and industry division, February 1970²

Occupation	United States		Northeast		South		North Central		West	
	Median	Middle range	Median	Middle range	Median	Middle range	Median	Middle range	Median	Middle range
					(Percents)					
Clerks, accounting, class A	4	-2 to 13	3	-3 to 10	7	0 to 17	6	0 to 14	1	-3 to 7
Clerks, accounting, class B	4	-2 to 13	2	-2 to 9	6	-1 to 15	8	0 to 16	1	-3 to 8
Clerks, order	9	1 to 25	7	0 to 17	13	2 to 29	15	2 to 31	5	0 to 16
Clerks, payroll	2	-3 to 14	1	-5 to 11	1	-4 to 15	4	0 to 17	1	-1 to 11
Office boys	1	-2 to 8	0	-3 to 7	1	-3 to 6	2	-2 to 10	1	0 to 5
Tabulating-machine operators:										
Class A	0	-5 to 6	0	-5 to 5	—	—	1	-5 to 7	—	—
Class B	-1	-7 to 3	0	-3 to 5	-1	-7 to 4	-2	-7 to 3	-3	-7 to 0
Class C	-1	-7 to 4	-3	-6 to 1	—	—	1	-7 to 5	—	—
Janitors, porters, and cleaners	6	0 to 14	6	0 to 16	4	0 to 9	8	1 to 19	3	0 to 10
Packers, shipping	1	0 to 8	4	0 to 10	1	0 to 7	1	0 to 8	0	0 to 4

Occupation	Manufacturing		Public Utilities		Wholesale trade		Retail trade		Finance		Services	
	Median	Middle range	Median	Middle range	Median	Middle range	Median	Middle range	Median	Middle range	Median	Middle range
Clerks, accounting, class A	3	-1 to 11	2	-1 to 7	7	0 to 12	5	-3 to 16	5	-3 to 12	3	-4 to 12
Clerks, accounting, class B	4	-2 to 14	1	-2 to 5	9	0 to 16	6	0 to 17	4	0 to 10	4	-3 to 9
Clerks, order	9	0 to 26	—	—	13	3 to 27	—	—	—	—	—	—
Clerks, payroll	3	-3 to 15	—	—	—	—	—	—	—	—	—	—
Office boys	0	-4 to 5	2	-1 to 8	0	-2 to 5	5	-1 to 8	2	-2 to 8	0	-6 to 14
Tabulating-machine operators:												
Class A	0	-4 to 7	0	0 to 6	—	—	—	—	-2	-8 to 6	0	-5 to 7
Class B	-1	-5 to 2	—	—	—	—	—	—	-1	-6 to 6	—	—
Class C	0	-5 to 3	0	-7 to 0	—	—	—	—	0	-6 to 5	—	—
Janitors, porters, and cleaners	3	0 to 8	—	—	5	0 to 15	11	4 to 20	13	1 to 22	5	0 to 12
Packers, shipping	1	0 to 7	4	0 to 16	0	0 to 8	4	0 to 12	—	—	—	—

(1) The median designates position – half of the establishments recorded greater differentials than those shown: half recorded less than those shown. The middle range is defined by 2 values – a fourth of the establishments recorded smaller differentials than the lower value shown and a fourth recorded differentials larger than the higher value shown.

(2) Average month of reference. Data were collected during the period of July 1969 through June 1970.

Note: A minus sign indicates that men's average earnings were lower than women's in the establishments. Dashes indicate that data did not meet publication criteria.

Source: US Department of Labor, Bureau of Labor Statistics, Washington, D.C. 20212.

Table VII. Percent by which men's average earnings exceeded women's in selected establishment groups, all metropolitan areas, 1966 and 1970

Occupation	Establishments employing both men and women		Establishments employing only men or women	
	1966	1970	1966	1970
Clerks, accounting, class A	12	12	23	22
Clerks, accounting, class B	14	14	27	28
Clerks, order	26	25	38	34
Clerks, payroll	8	13	26	25
Office boys or girls	4	5	6	9
Tabulating-machine operators:				
Class A	6	6	10	16
Class B	4	5	13	14
Class C	4	4	8	13
Janitors, porters, and cleaners	18	13	37	32
Packers, shipping	18	10	25	22
Unweighted average difference	11	11	21	22

Source: US Department of Labor, Bureau of Labor Statistics, Washington, D.C. 20212.

In order to span 1964, when the Equal Pay Act went into effect, published BLS averages for men and women in the 10 jobs in 1960, 1965, and 1970 were compared. Relative to men's average earnings, there was little change in women's earnings over the period. In 1960, men's earnings exceeded women's by an average of 19% for the 10 occupations; this figure dropped to 18% in 1965 and remained at that level in 1970. A look at individual jobs during the 10-year period shows mixed patterns (Table VIII). Among the notable declines in men's advantage were those in the two plant jobs: the spread dropped from 20 to 15% for janitors and from 23 to 17% for shipping packers, with most of the declines occurring between 1965 and 1970. It is difficult to observe from these data any consistent effect resulting from the Equal Pay Act. Preliminary information available for 1973 indicated that the per cent by which men's average earnings exceeded women's average earnings in all establishments was holding steady at 18% (unweighted average difference for the 10 jobs). As in past years, the relationship among the individual jobs changed somewhat. The average earnings of male shipping packers, for example, were 22% higher than women's averages in 1973 compared to the 17% difference in 1970. On the other hand, the 12% advantage for male class C tabulating-machine operators in 1970 was eliminated in 1973 when both sexes had the same average earnings.

Published averages are influenced by the manner in which men and women are distributed among establishments with different pay levels. In the BLS 1969-70 study, for example, an examination of manufacturing establishments revealed that the lowest average earnings for the 10 occupations were found in such labour-intensive industries as apparel and leather products. In most cases women represented a higher

Table VIII.   Percent by which men's average earnings exceeded women's in all establishments, all metropolitan areas, 1960, 1965, and 1970

Occupation	1960	1965	1970
Clerks, accounting, class A	24	21	19
Clerks, accounting, class B	27	22	24
Clerks, order	37	37	34
Clerks, payroll	29	28	27
Office boys or girls	4	4	8
Tabulating-machine operators:			
Class A	11	6	11
Class B	11	9	11
Class C	8	9	12
Janitors, porters, and cleaners	20	18	15
Packers, shipping	23	23	17
Unweighted average difference	19	18	18

Source: US Department of Labor, Bureau of Labor Statistics, Washington, D.C. 20212.

proportion of the employment in the selected occupations in these industries than in the higher paying capital-intensive industries such as petroleum refining and transportation equipment.

The comparisons of men's and women's earnings within the same job and establishment do not eliminate all factors that contributed to sex-wage differentials. An important factor not taken into account in the BLS comparisons is length-of-service wage increases under pay systems that include range of rates for a given occupation. Such systems are more prevalent for office than plant occupations. A 1968-70 study by John Howell Cox showed that 69% of office workers and 37% of plant workers in metropolitan areas were paid under range-of-rates systems[19]. Because of longer job tenure, men usually have higher average earnings than women employed under the same rate-range system. (In January 1968, the median length of time men worked without interruption for the same employer, 4·8 years, was double that of women[20].) Also, job descriptions used in BLS wage surveys are usually more generalised than those used in individual establishments because some allowance must be made for differences in duties that occur among establishments. An establishment may, for example, pay men performing heavy janitorial work more than women with light cleaning duties, but both would be classified as janitors in the wage survey.

Occupational wage surveys conducted by the Bureau of Labor Statistics are not designed to determine whether wage discrimination between men and women occurs. Consequently, the discussion of men's and women's pay relationships, based on BLS data, neither denied nor affirmed the existence of wage discrimination. There is no doubt, however, that some employers do engage in wage discrimination, the Equal Pay Act notwithstanding. As discussed earlier, another arm of the US Department of

Labor, which administers the Act, has been actively involved in the question of sex-wage discrimination. According to the Department's Wage and Hour Division, over 171,000 employees, almost all of them women, were awarded nearly 84 million dollars as of the end of May 1974. However, in spite of court rulings and awards of back pay to female workers, the employer with a "male" and "female" rate for the same position is the exception rather than the rule. The BLS study showed that the sex-wage differential narrowed substantially, and in some instances disappeared, when data for individual establishments employing both sexes were examined. Even at this level—the level where any investigation of wage discrimination should begin—it is difficult to measure the exact effect of length-of-service wage adjustments and problems related to job descriptions used in wage surveys, but it is thought that such adjustments would further narrow the earnings gap. This appraisal, as will be seen later, does not acquit employers in regard to their responsibility for hiring and promoting capable women workers in a broader range of occupations.

Other Studies
Although the BLS study was not designed to determine the existence of wage discrimination, other studies of men's and women's earnings have dealt with the question without arriving at a consensus. Henry Sanborn, using 1950 US Bureau of the Census data and BLS data, discounted wage discrimination as a major factor in the observed earnings gap[21]. Sanborn concluded that if discrimination exists, it probably accounts for fewer than 10 of the 42 percentage points of the overall differential in men's and women's earnings. He suggests that consumer discrimination (in sales and waitress occupations, where consumers may prefer to be served by men) and co-workers' discrimination (in managerial and craft occupations, where men may object to having women employed in a particular capacity) are more important than employer discrimination.

Victor Fuchs, using 1959 and 1960 Census of Population and Housing data, found no evidence that employer discrimination is a major direct influence of men-women pay differentials. In his opinion, "roles" assigned to men and women would explain most of the observed differential: "Role differentiation, which begins in the cradle, affects the choice of occupation, labor force attachment, location of work, post-school investment, hours of work, and other variables that influence earnings"[22]. Fuchs arrived at the same conclusion as Sanborn that consumer discrimination may be more significant than employer discrimination.

Sanborn's and Fuch's references to consumer discrimination in the area of service occupations were buttressed by findings of Charles O'Connor in the July 1971 issue of the *Monthly Labor Review*[23]. In a study of wages and tips in restaurants and hotels, he found that waitresses usually averaged less than waiters in both wages and tips, but the spread was much greater for tips. Table waiters in full-course restaurants, for example, averaged 13 cents an hour more in wages than table waitresses, but the men had an average of 84 cents an hour more in tips. O'Connor pointed out that differences in customer attitudes about tipping waiters and waitresses and differences in the types of facilities in which they are employed contribute to larger tip averages for waiters. He said that better-class restaurant facilities with higher meal prices and tipping patterns probably accounted for a greater proportion of the waiters than the waitresses.

Mary Hamilton, investigating the possible causes of wage differences, concluded that discrimination has a sex dimension. Data used in her analysis were collected as part of a larger 1963 study of the Chicago-Northwestern Indiana Consolidated Area, directed by Albert Rees and George Schultz. After making adjustments for factors other than sex, she found there was a tendency for women to be more qualified than men within the same job. While this is not direct wage discrimination as such, the end result is the same. If Hamilton's analysis is valid, women are settling for jobs that do not fully utilise their talents (vis-à-vis men), and consequently earn lower wages. Hamilton concluded by stating that "... it should be emphasised that wage discrimination need not take the form of different wages for identical work. The employment of workers of different quality for the same wage seems more plausible—and certainly less visible. What evidence there is suggests that wage differentials attributable to sex do exist"[24].

The Women's Bureau of the US Department of Labor, in examining the earnings gap between men and women, noted that differences in earnings "... do not necessarily indicate that women are receiving unequal pay for equal work. For the most part, they reflect the fact that women are more likely to be employed in low-skilled, low-paying jobs"[25]. The Women's Bureau gave examples of how this works in the American labour market:

(1) In public elementary and secondary schools, women are less than 20% of the principals, superintendents, deputy, associate, and assistant superintendents, and other central office administrators in 1970-71;

(2) Women are concentrated in the lower paying levels of computer programmer positions, while men are more frequently employed in the higher paying levels. Similarly, women are usually in the lowest category of draughtsmen and engineering technicians;

(3) Among managers and proprietors, women frequently operate small retail establishments, while men may manage manufacturing plants or wholesale outlets;

(4) In the manufacturing of men's and boys' suits and coats, women are likely to be employed in lower paying jobs such as hand finishers, thread trimmers and basting pullers, and sewing machine operators, while men are likely to be employed in higher paying jobs such as finish pressers (hand or machine), underpressers, cutters, and markers;

(5) In the service occupations, women are likely to be cooks, nurses' aides, and waitresses, while men are likely to be employed in higher paying jobs as firemen, policemen, and detectives.

Figure 1. Women as Percent of Total Workers

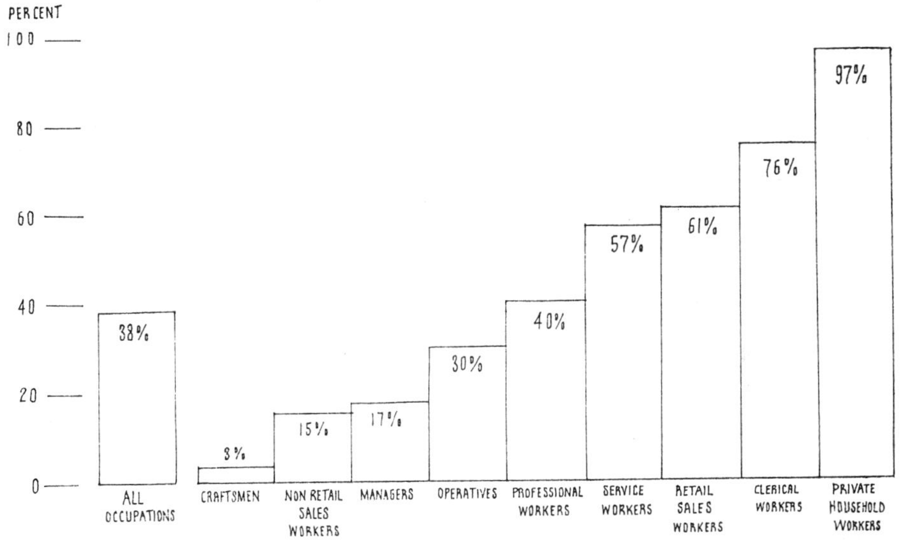

Source: Prepared by the Women's Bureau, Employment Standards Administration, from April 1972 data published by the Bureau of Labor Statistics, US Department of Labor.

As shown in Figure 1, women are heavily concentrated in such jobs as private household workers, clerical workers, and retail and service workers—historically areas in which low wages have been the rule. On the other hand, women have very little representation in the high-paying crafts and managerial occupations. Even the relatively large proportion of women in the high-paying professional workers' category, 40%, is somewhat misleading. Most of these women are at the lower-paying end of this category, in such jobs as elementary and high school teachers, nurses, and librarians.

Unresolved Problems

The problem of equal pay for equal work should be considered neither solved nor the major obstacle to the American working woman. There is little doubt or argument that the wide average earnings gap between all men and women workers is caused, in large part, by the concentration of women in low-paying occupations and industries. This finding, however, begs the question: Why are women concentrated in low-paying jobs and industries? There is no single explanation why women fare so poorly as wage earners, but rather a number of conditions acting to depress their earnings.

American women in the labour market today suffer financially and emotionally from the remnants of an earlier philosophy concerning women as wage earners. It was taken for granted that working women had fewer needs and family responsibilities than men and that a social benefit was being accrued when men, the "breadwinners", were given preferential treatment. A woman's place, especially if married and her husband present, was thought to be in the home and not in the labour market competing with men. Among some groups there was a certain stigma attached to women working for wages. Robert Smuts wrote that "In middle-class circles the employment of wives or daughters was taken as a sign of masculine failure. Conversely, one of the most acceptable ways for a man to display his success and bolster his prestige was to keep his wife and daughters in luxurious idleness"[26].

The restrictions placed on women workers by local laws and customs were reinforced by court rulings sympathetic to the male point of view. In 1872, for example, the United States Supreme Court upheld an Illinois State law that prohibited women from practising law. The Court stated in its opinion that ". . . the civil law, as well as nature herself, has always recognised a wide difference in the respective spheres and destinies of man and woman. Man is, or should be, woman's protector and defender. The natural and proper timidity and delicacy which belongs to the female sex evidently unfits it for many of the occupations of civil life." The Court went on to state that "The harmony . . . of interests and views which belong . . . to the family institution is repugnant to the idea of a woman adopting a distinct and independent career from that of her husband"[27]. (To its credit, the State Legislature of Illinois corrected the injustice by passing a law that same year (1872) which stated that "No person shall be precluded or debarred from any occupation, profession or employment (except military) on account of sex"[28].)

It is fair to assume that the decision handed down by the Supreme Court over 100 years ago reflected, and to some degree still reflects, the general attitude toward women. This attitude in no small way contributes to women's inferior position as wage earners. All segments of society, including working women themselves, share responsibility for the present condition.

Most working women participate in the labour market for economic reasons. Many married women (husband present) work outside the home to attain a higher standard of living for the family, to get more financial independence, or for some, to find greater personal fulfilment. (Single and other women may work for the same reasons, but the element of necessity is added.) However, the life cycle of the average woman runs counter to the accepted model for business success: Start at the bottom, work long hours, and slowly work toward the top. The typical young married woman starts at the bottom, but many of the extra hours she works are likely to be connected with family responsibilities in the home. It is estimated that the birth of a first child cuts the average years a married woman is in the labour force by 10 years, and each additional birth further reduces labour force participation by 2 to 3 years[29].

American working women, especially those whose attachment to the labour force is tenuous, have a greater tendency than men to sell their labour cheaply. This was recognised by Leonora Barry in the 1880's when the Knights of Labor hired her to organise women workers. After 5 years in that work she found among working women ". . . the habit of submission and acceptance without question of any terms offered them . . ."[30]. Mary Hamilton's study, cited above, also suggests that women settle for less than their talents demand. Women with family responsibilities are also more inclined to seek jobs in residential areas near home rather than commute to better paying jobs a greater distance from home[31]. Employers are aware of these tendencies, and some use them to justify less then equal treatment.

Perhaps the most important problem still facing the American working woman is the inability of men and women to neutralise years of "role" conditioning. Reinforcement of role playing by employers is suggested in tabulations published by the US Bureau of the Census in 1969. Of more than 250 distinct occupations listed by the Bureau, half of all women were employed in only 21 of them, whereas half of all men were in 65 occupations[32]. Employers must break away from the outdated concept that most jobs have a male or female quality. Gary Petersen and Linda Bryant writing in the August 1972 *Personnel Journal*, listed employers as a ". . . major target in the attack on discrimination . . .". They pointed out that "Management first must recognise areas of female underutilisation and take action accordingly. A top management policy must be initiated and enforced . . . Problem-solving will require focusing on the facts concerning female employment and dispelling the myths about women workers. Management must develop training that will assist in changing attitudes. They must help supervisors and managers recognise that subtle bias does exist and show ways in which it can be eliminated"[33]. In effect, Petersen and Bryant are calling on management in the private sector to set up programmes similar to the affirmative action programmes the Federal Government initiated under the executive orders discussed above.

The American educational system also must share responsibility for reinforcing sex roles found in the larger society. A typical charge levelled at the system is that schoolgirls are discouraged or forbidden from taking workshop courses and guided toward more traditional subjects such as commercial (clerical) courses. Boys are guided in the opposite direction. Career guidance counsellors form an important part of the educational system, and in recent years have been criticised for their lack of leadership in encouraging girls to train for jobs that are dominated by males. A simplification of the criticism is that a boy expressing interest in medicine will be advised to enter pre-medical school, whereas a girl with similar interests will be advised to enter nursing school. Whatever the reasons, America has one of the lowest ratios of female-male physicians among the industrialised nations. It was estimated in 1972 that only about 1 in every 14 physicians is a woman[34].

Some employment agencies also are targets of justifiable criticism for their actions in helping to perpetuate women's second-class status in the labour market. A recent study[35] by the Vermont Public Interest Research Group vividly displayed how role casting is immensely unjust to women entering the job market. Male and female researchers, posing as job hunters, contacted several employment agencies in Vermont to determine the type of jobs they might expect. Each researcher contacted the same agency within hours, giving identical sets of qualifications and attitudes. In nearly all instances the male was told he might expect employment in one of several high-paying fields, while the female was directed toward lower paying jobs. This discrimination, which is clearly in violation of Title VII, occurred nearly a decade after the passage of the 1964 Civil Rights Act.

As with all social problems, those adversely affected must work hardest to correct what is wrong. Women must start with themselves and reshape their own thinking if equal opportunity in the work place is their goal. A study by Peggy Hawley in the *Journal of Counseling Psychology* showed that "Women planning to enter male-dominated careers were more concerned with male support than those with traditional career goals. Only 10% said they would pursue present goals over the objections of significant men in their lives"[36].

Women must also give support to other women choosing non-traditional careers. Congresswoman Shirley Chisholm, the first Black woman elected to the US Congress, addressed this problem. She stated that prejudice against women ". . . is so widespread that, paradoxically, most persons do not yet realise it exists. Indeed, most women do not realise it. They even accept being paid less for doing the same work as a man. They are as quick as any male to condemn a woman who ventures outside the limits of the role men have assigned to females: That of toy and drudge"[37].

Elizabeth Duncan Koontz, the former Director of the Women's Bureau of the US Department of Labor, stated that the overriding goal of the Bureau has been to create ". . . a climate of acceptance for women as participants in every phase of American life, with equal rights and responsibilities". She went on to say that "This involves changing attitudes and dispelling myths about women's capabilities, motivations, and potentialities. For if our society is permitted to assume that the goal of every woman and the subsequent fate of every woman is marriage to a man earning enough to support her and educate their children, then much of what happens to the economic and social development of the country will be based on a false assumption"[38].

It may be stated then, in conclusion, that men and women in all walks of life must reassess their attitudes toward women as workers, and recognise the economic waste caused and injustices suffered to this point in time. More women must prepare themselves for jobs with greater responsibilities and rewards. Having done so, they must settle for nothing less than their talents demand. Likewise, employers must allow women to attain their full potential as workers and cease viewing them as a reservoir of cheap labour.

References

1. Smuts, R. W., *Women and Work in America*, New York, Columbia University Press, 1959, p. 2.
2. *View of the United States of America: A Complete Emigrant's Directory*, London, 1820, p. 371.
3. McLane, L., *Statistics of Manufactures in the United States*, Washington, 1833, Vol. 1, p. 465.
4. *Carey's Select Excerpta*, Vol. 13, p. 184. Quoted in United States Senate Document No. 645, 61st Congress, 2nd Session, Washington, 1910, Vol. IX, p. 27.

5. Sinclair, A., *The Better Half—The Emancipation of the American Woman*, New York: Harper and Row, 1965, p. 100.
6. *History of Wages in the United States from Colonial Time to* 1928, US Department of Labor, Bureau of Labor Statistics, Bulletin No. 604, Washington, 1934, pp. 363, 382, 386.
7. *Ibid*, p. 5.
8. US Department of Labor, Bureau of Labor Statistics, Bulletin 1801 (1974), p. 16.
9. "Free Enquirer", New York, May 6, 1829. Quoted in United States Senate Document No. 645, 61st Congress, 2nd Session, Washington, 1910, Vol. IX, pp. 25-26.
10. "National Trades Union", October 10, 1835. Reprinted in *Documentary History of American Industrial Society*, Vol. VI, p. 251.
11. "The Revolution", October 1, 1868. Quoted in United States Senate Document No. 645, 61st Congress, 2nd Session, Washington, 1910, Vol. IX, p. 30.
12. Mayer, A. N., ed., *Woman's Work in America*, New York: Henry Holt and Co., 1891, p. 302.
13. Shultz v. Wheaton Glass Company, 421 F. 2d 259 (1970), cert. denied, 398 US 905 (1970).
14. Hodgson v. Robert Hall Clothes, Inc., 326 F. Supp. 1264, (D. Del. 1971) rev'd 473 F. 2d 589 (3d cir.), cert. denied 414 US 866 (1973).
15. *University of Pennsylvania Law Review*, Vol. 122 No. 4, April 1974, p. 1034.
16. Buckley, J. E., "Pay Differences Between Men and Women in the Same Job", *Monthly Labor Review*, November 1971, Vol. 94 No. 11, pp. 36-39.
17. 20 *Labor Markets*, 1958-59 (BLS Bulletin No. 1240-22, 1959).
18. McNulty, J., "Differences in Pay Between Men and Women Workers " *Monthly Labor Review*, December, 1967, Vol. 90, No. 12, pp. 40-43.
19. Cox, H., "Time and Incentive Pay Practices in Urban Areas", *Monthly Labor Review*, December 1971, Vol. 94 No. 12, pp. 53-56.
20. O'Boyle, E. J., "Job Tenure: How it Relates to Race and Age", *Monthly Labor Review*, September 1909, Vol. 92 No. 9, pp. 16-23.
21. Sanborn, H., "Pay Differences Between Men and Women, *Industrial and Labor Relations Review*, July 1964, Vol. 17 No. 4, pp. 534-550.
22. Fuchs, V. R., "Differences in Hourly Earnings Between Men and Women", *Monthly Labor Review*, May 1971, Vol. 94 No. 5, pp. 9-15.
23. United States Department of Labor, Bureau of Labor Statistics, *Wages and Tips in Restaurants and Hotels*, Bulletin No. 1712, Washington: GPO 1970.
24. Hamilton, M. T., "Womenpower and Discrimination in the Labor Market", a paper presented to the North American Conference on Labor Statistics, Houston, Texas, June 1970.
25. United States Department of Labor, Women's Bureau, "Fact Sheet on the Earnings Gap", December 1971.
26. Smuts, *op. cit.*, p. 122.
27. Bradwell v. Illinois, 83 US (16 Wall) 130 (1872).
28. Mayer, *op. cit.*, p. 224.
29. Garfinkle, S., "Work Life Expectancy and Training Needs of Women", *Manpower Report* 12, United States Department of Labor, Manpower Administration, May 1967.
30. Sinclair, *op. cit.*, p. 306.
31. Fuchs, *op. cit.*, p. 10.
32. Hedges, J. N., "Women Workers and Manpower Demands in the 1970's", *Monthly Labor Review*, June 1970, Vol. 93 No. 6, pp. 19-29.
33. Petersen, G. G., and Bryant, L., "Eliminating Sex Discrimination—Who Must Act?", *Personnel Journal*, August 1972, pp. 587-591.
34. United States Department of Labor, Bureau of Labor Statistics, *Occupational Outlook Handbook* (1974-75), Bulletin 1785, Washington: GPO 1974.
35. "Washington Star-News", April 28, 1974.
36. Hawley, P., "Perceptions of Male Models of Femininity Related to Career Choice", *Journal of Counseling Psychology*, 1972, Vol. 19 No. 4, pp. 308-313.
37. Chisholm, S., *Unbought and Unbossed*, Boston, Houghton and Mifflin Co., 1970, p. xii.
38. Koontz, E. D., "The Women's Bureau Looks to the Future", *Monthly Labor Review*, June 1970, Vol. 93, No. 6, pp. 3-9.

Equal Pay for Women in Australia and New Zealand

by J. Nieuwenhuysen and J. Hicks

AUSTRALIA

Australia (the main focus of this chapter's attention) enjoys a reputation as a country in which the "three cornered suspension" afforded by conciliation and arbitration machinery has assisted both sense and sensibility in wage fixation. And in more than one newly independent nation in Asia, substantial elements of the Australian system have been incorporated in local institutions. Australians, for their part, may be excused if they on occasion feel that the arbitration system is not without honour save in its own country. This feeling is in a sense justified by the events outlined in this chapter. For, although the arbitration system now (at last) applies equal pay under all its awards, including the minimum wage, it is not clear that this is more than a Pyrrhic victory for female employment equality. This is because arbitrated awards are only part of the overall wage determining structure, and more particularly because unequal pay is of course only one aspect of discrimination against women. In brief, this chapter will argue that, in the Australian context, the establishment of equal pay in an only partially regulated wage system remains to be supplemented by a variety of other actions. Some of these actions depend on changes in social and psychological attitudes that cannot readily be legislated against or arbitrated upon.

Women in the Work Force

From 1901-1921 the proportion of women in the workforce remained quite stable at about 20%, and in the Censuses of 1933, 1947 and 1954 only small increases in this proportion were registered. But in the Censuses of 1961, 1966 and 1971 substantial increases—to 25·1% in 1961, to 29·5% in 1966 and to 31·7% in 1971—were recorded. More recent estimates[1]—in November 1973—show the percentage as 33·8. Table I, describing the changes in the size of the male and female labour forces in the post-war period, indicates the importance of these recent increases in female participation. Between June 1954 and November 1973, the total labour force grew by 57%. Women, who in 1973 represented about one-third of the total workforce, were responsible for over half of this increase. During 1954-1973, the female workforce increased by 130%, compared with the male sector growth of 35%. (But despite the growth of women entering the workforce, female participation rates in Australia—and, as later mentioned, in New Zealand—remain below those of some other industrialised countries[2].

Table I. Australia: Size of the Labour Force—by Sex 1954-1973

Year	Males	Percentage increase base 1954	Females	Percentage increase base 1954	Persons	Percentage increase base 1954	Females as a percentage of persons
	('000)	%	('000)	%	('000)	%	%
Census 1954	2,856·6		845·4		3,702·0		22·8
1961	3,165·9	10·8	1,059·2	25·2	4,225·1	14·1	25·1
1966	3,421·8	19·7	1,434·6	69·6	4,856·5	31·1	29·5
1971	3,639·6	27·4	1,690·8	100·0	5,330·5	43·9	31·7
Feb. 1973 (est.)	3,809·5*	33·3	1,901·5*	124·9	5,712·1*	54·2	33·2
Nov. 1973 (est.)†	3,862·2*	35·2	1,951·1*	130·7	5,813·7*	57·0	33·5

*Seasonally adjusted Figures
†Affected by industrial dispute
(Sources: CBCS, 1954, 1961, 1966 and 1971 Censuses
      ABS, The Labour Force, November 1973 (estimates), Ref. No. 6.20).

Married women have played a prominent part in the increased workforce participation of Australian women. Table II, setting out details of full-time married and other women workers by age, shows that in November 1973, the majority of full-time women workers (62·5%) were married. Table III gives the participation rate of married women in the workforce (that is, the number of married women in the workforce as a percentage of all married women). The Table shows that, of all married women, 17·3% in 1961, 32·8% in 1971 and an estimated 39% in 1973, were in the

Table II. Australia: Full-time Women Workers by Age and Marital Status November 1973†

Age Group Years	Married Women	All Females	Married Women as a percentage of All Females
	('000)	('000)	
15—19	22·3	319·3	6·9
20—24	170·5	340·6	50·0
25—34	133·5	416·4	32·0
35—44	331·0	381·5	86·7
45—54	277·0	343·2	80·7
55—59	64·6	96·7	66·8
60—64	25·7	48·1	53·4
65 and over	6·8	22·7	29·9
Total	1231·5	1968·5	62·5

(Source: ABS, The Labour Force, November 1973 (estimates), Ref. No. 6.20).
*Affected by industrial dispute.

Table III. Australia: Labour Force Participation Rate* of the Population 15 Years and Over, by Age 1961, 1966, 1971 and 1973

| | PARTICIPATION RATE (%) | | | | | | | | | | | |
| | MEN | | | | Married WOMEN† | | | | All WOMEN | | | |
Age Group	1961	1966	1971	1973 Est.	1961	1966	1971	1973 Est.	1961	1966	1971	1973 Est.
15–19 Years	69·6	66·2	55·7	59·6	19·9	29·4	36·4	43·8	64·5	62·2	52·1	55·9
20–24	94·9	93·8	89·1	90·9	24·5	37·0	44·1	50·4	50·8	58·9	58·6	62·2
25–34	98·4	97·5	94·8	97·4	17·3	26·4	33·0	40·3	25·5	33·3	38·9	44·8
35–44	98·3	97·3	94·9	97·6	21·2	32·5	41·3	49·9	27·5	37·0	44·4	52·1
45–54	96·7	95·5	93·0	94·9	19·1	29·2	36·1	44·2	27·2	34·9	40·0	46·6
55–59	92·7	91·2	88·4	88·7	12·6	20·0	23·2	26·7	22·3	27·2	28·3	30·4
60–64	79·7	79·5	75·6	76·6	6·5	11·1	12·0	14·2	13·3	16·5	16·0	17·3
65 plus	26·4	21·9	22·2	21·6	2·2	3·8	3·6	3·0	4·5	4·9	4·2	3·5
Total	85·9	83·9	80·3	82·1	17·3	26·6	32·8	29·0	28·9	35·2	37·1	41·3

(Sources: CBCS, 1961, 1966 and 1971 Censuses
ABS, The Labour Force, Nov. 1973).
*The labour force in each group as a percentage of the civilian population in the same group.
†Does not include widowed, divorced or permanently separated women.

workforce. The change is most noticeable in the age groups 20-24 years and 35-44 years. The first of these groups is composed of women who work in the period directly after marriage and before the birth of children. The tendency for more women to continue to work after marriage suggests a growing number of two income families. (As in many industrialised countries, this trend facilitates earlier marriage). The second age group corresponds to the period in which family responsibilities, notably child care, have declined sufficiently to permit a return to the workforce. Employment at this point in the family life cycle has become more feasible over the last two decades as tendencies toward younger marriages, smaller families, longer life expectancies and the reduction of the intervals between births, have enabled the completion of child-bearing while the woman is still comparatively young and has a number of active years ahead of her. In the early 1900s an Australian woman was likely to withdraw from the workforce at about 25 years of age and spend the rest of her life (about 30 years) outside it. Today the more likely pattern is earlier marriage with only temporary withdrawal from the workforce and a return at around 35 years of age to continue employment for 20 to 25 years[3].

Australia's post-war experience has been one of almost "brimful" employment, with only minor oscillations. Conditions very favourable for expanding female employment opportunities have been enhanced by industrial mechanisation and the growth of increasingly diverse services in the cities, where population and—as Table IV shows—employment are most heavilty concentrated. Although there are some exceptions, the proportion of women workers, married or unmarried, is in general far

Table IV. Australia: Labour Force Participation Rates, by Urban and Rural Location and Age Groups, June 1971

| | PARTICIPATION RATE* (%) | | | | | |
| Age groups | Men | | Married Woment | | Total Women | |
	Urban	Rural	Urban	Rural	Urban	Rural
	%	%	%	%	%	%
15–19 years	54·7	61·3	39·1	21·2	53·1	44·0
20–24	88·8	92·8	46·6	27·2	60·8	41·0
25–34	94·9	95·5	34·0	26·8	40·3	29·7
35–44	94·9	95·6	42·5	34·2	45·8	35·6
45–54	93·0	93·7	36·8	31·8	40·9	33·7
55–59	88·3	89·2	23·1	23·9	28·6	26·4
60–64	75·0	78·9	11·5	15·4	15·7	17·6
65 years and over	19·4	38·1	3·0	7·9	3·7	8·6
Total	79·9	83·4	33·7	27·4	38·0	31·1

(Source: CBCS, 1971 Census)

*The labour force participation rate is calculated by expressing the labour force in each age group as a percentage of the civilian population, aged 15 years and over, in the same age group.

†This category does not include widowed, divorced or permanently separated women.

lower in rural than in urban centres. Many of the jobs involved (e.g. machine operators in light manufacturing plants) have traditionally been a female preserve. New occupations considered suitable have emerged as a result of the expansion of service and manufacturing industries. An additional source of demand for female workers during the post-war years has its origin in the fall in the birth rate during the late 1920s and early 1930s[4]. The shortage of men entering the workforce in the late 1940s was coupled with rapid economic growth. Employers were encouraged to engage women for jobs previously performed by men.

At the same time, the Commonwealth Government was actively pursuing an immigration policy (by means of an assisted passage scheme) to alleviate the labour shortage. As Table V suggests, female (and male) migrants show a greater inclination to enter employment than do Australian born women (and men). Underlining this, Table VI shows that in June 1947, female migrants represented 8·7% of the female population and 7·3% of the female workforce, but by 1971 the figures were 23% and 26% respectively. However, the contribution of the female migrant to increased participation rates for Australian women is likely to be greater than these figures would suggest —a "demonstration effect" must certainly have helped to break down some of the inhibitions Australian women have suffered in considering employment outside the home. In addition, domestic labour saving devices have released the housewife from much drudgery and provided her with time in which to undertake work providing a

Table V. Australia: Labour Force Participation Rates of the Population Aged 15 Years and Over, by Place of Birth, June 1971 and November 1973

| | PARTICIPATION RATE | | | |
| | Men | | Women | |
Birthplace	1971	1973	1971	1973
Australia	79·6	*Est. 82·1*	*35·8*	*Est. 40·6*
United Kingdom	79·3	N.A.	38·3	N.A.
Italy	85·7	,,	37·9	,,
Greece	86·9	,,	48·8	,,
Yugoslavia	88·6	,,	51·7	,,
Germany	89·2	,,	48·8	,,
Netherlands	90·1	,,	39·2	,,
New Zealand	80·4	,,	44·3	,,
Poland	86·7	,,	48·6	,,
Malta	86·8	,,	38·3	,,
Rest of Europe	84·4	,,	45·5	,,
Other countries	75·3	,,	43·1	,,
Total born overseas	82·5	Est. 85·7	41·6	Est. 46·0

(Source: CBCS, 1971 Census.
   ABS, The Labour Force, November 1973 (estimates) Reference No. 6.20).

Table VI. Australia: Proportion of Female Migrants in the Population and Labour Force, 1947-1971

| | Labour force* | | Female migrants as a proportion of: | |
Census	Migrant female no.	Total female no.	Total female labour force %	Total female population %
June 1947	52,259	717,162	7·3	8·7
,, 1954	132,748	845,402	15·7	12·5
,, 1961	229,105	1,059,169	21·6	15·2
,, 1966	336,967	1,434,640	23·5	17·1
,, 1971	436,126	1,690,849	25·8	23·0

(Source: CBCS 1947, 1954, 1961, 1966 and 1971 Censuses).
*Includes both employed persons and unemployed persons who were either laid off without pay for the whole week, or who were actively looking for work.

monetary return. Somewhat circuitously, these labour saving devices (and other consumer durables) have meant increased claims on the family budget, and have induced wives to undertake outside employment in order to provide the additional income necessary for their purchase.

Table VII sets out wage and salary earners in civilian employment by industry group and sex. It will be noticed that for a select group of occupations women repre-

Table VII. Australia: Wage and Salary Earners in Civilian Employment by Industry Group and by Sex—May 1972
(Excluding employees in rural industry and private domestic service and defence forces)

Industry group and sub-group	MALES Number	As proportion of total males	FEMALES Number	As proportion of total females	As proportion of persons in industry group
	('000)	%	('000)	%	%
Forestry, fishing and trapping	14·3	0·5	0·7	*	4·7
Mining and quarrying	70·0	2·4	4·7	0·3	6·3
Manufacturing	1,022·0	34·3	350·3	22·8	25·5
Electricity, gas, water and sanitary services	108·0	3·6	8·5	0·6	7·3
Building and construction	368·0	12·4	18·1	1·2	4·7
Transport and storage—					
Road transport and storage	99·5	3·3	12·8	0·8	11·4
Shipping and stevedoring	37·0	1·2	3·0	0·2	7·5
Rail transport	58·0	1·9	6·1	0·4	9·5
Air transport	26·2	0·9	6·3	0·4	19·4
Total	220·7	7·4	28·3	1·8	11·4
Communication	93·9	3·2	27·9	1·8	22·9
Finance and property—					
Banking	55·6	1·9	36·3	2·4	39·5
Other	68·9	2·3	58·3	3·8	45·8
Total	124·5	4·2	94·6	6·2	43·2
Commerce—					
Wholesale trade	186·3	6·3	79·7	5·2	30·0
Primary produce dealing, etc.	24·1	0·8	6·8	0·4	22·0
Retail trade	220·7	7·4	246·6	16·1	52·8
Total	431·1	14·5	333·1	21·7	43·6
Public authority activities (n.e.i.)	142·3	4·8	67·1	4·4	32·0
Community and business services—					
Law, order and public safety	43·1	1·4	24·4	1·6	36·1
Religion and social welfare	20·5	0·7	22·6	1·5	52·4
Health, hospitals, etc.	49·7	1·7	204·7	13·3	80·5
Education†	102·0	3·4	139·2	9·1	57·7
Other services	46·7	1·6	42·5	2·8	47·6
Total†	262·1	8·8	433·4	28·2	62·3
Amusement, hotels, cafes, personal service, etc.—					
Amusement, sport and recreation	37·1	1·2	22·7	1·5	38·0
Hotels, personal service, etc.	82·3	2·8	145·6	9·5	63·9
Total	119·4	4·0	168·3	11·0	58·5
Grand Total†	2,976·2	100·0	1,535·0	100·0	34·0

*Less than 0·1
†Excludes trainee teachers, some of whom were classified as wage and salary earners prior to July 1971.
(Source: Commonwealth Bureau of Census and Statistics—"Employment and Unemployment, May 1972", quoted from *Equal Pay*, Department of Labour and National Service, 1972, p. 45).

sent the majority of workers. For example, in May 1972 women accounted for 80·5% of the workforce in "health, hospitals, etc.", 63·9% in "hotels, personal service, etc.", 57·7% in "education", 52·8% in the retail trade, and 52·4% in "religion and social welfare"—all of which fall under the general heading of service industries and follow closely the patterns of employment established in many other countries.

It is clear that education and vocational training play an important part in the nature of work Australian women are able to perform. Table VIII presents labour force participation rates for men and women by level of education attained. There appears in this table a strong positive relationship between educational attainment and activity in the workforce, i.e., those women who have progressed beyond secondary education are more likely to be part of the active workforce than those who have had no formal schooling or did not attend school beyond the primary stage. Table IX (which shows the percentage distribution of the population aged 15 years and over, by level of education attained as at 1966) emphasises this point. It suggests further that Australian women are "required" to have higher educational qualifications than men if they are to enter the workforce at a given level. Of all men in the labour force in 1966, 59% had ten years or less of schooling while only 52% of women in the work-force fell into the same category. Of greater importance is the feature that over 70% of women *not* in the workforce had less than the stated ten years of schooling. This suggests that a basic lack of educational training would severely restrict the employ-

Table VIII. Australia: Labour Force Participation Rates for Men and Women, by Level of Education Attained

LEVEL OF EDUCATION ATTAINED	Participation Rate (%) Men	Women
	%	%
Tertiary level		
University	94·0	62·4
Other Tertiary	94·1	63·2
Secondary school		
Leaving (approx. 12 years schooling)	82·2	47·6
Intermediate (approx. 11 years schooling)	88·9	44·6
Attended Secondary school (approx. 7-10 years)	85·6	33·8
Primary school Attended Primary school (less than 7 years approx.)	79·8	25·0
No formal schooling	60·1	18·8
Not stated	61·5	20·7
All Persons	83·9	35·2

(Source: CBCS, 1966 Census (unpublished data)).

Table IX. Australia: Percentage Distribution of the Population Aged 15 Years and over, by Level of Education Attained, 1966

Level of Education Attained	In the labour force		Not in the labour force	
	Males	Females	Males	Females
Tertiary level	%	%	%	%
University	2·5	1·3	0·8	0·4
Other Tertiary	3·5	3·9	1·1	1·2
Secondary school				
Leaving (approx. 12 years schooling)	10·6	11·7	12·0	7·0
Intermediate (approx 11 years schooling)	24·6	31·2	16·1	21·0
Attended Secondary school (approx. 7-10 years schooling)	29·1	27·0	25·5	28·7
Primary school				
Attended Primary school (less than 7 years approx.)	27·3	22·8	36·0	37·1
No formal schooling	0·6	0·4	2·0	1·0
Not stated	2·0	1·7	6·5	3·5
Total	100·00	100·0	100·0	10·00

(Source: CBCS, 1966 Census).

Comment: Labour force participation is related to educational attainment. Women in the labour force in 1966 were more likely to have had 11 and 12 years of schooling, and to have reached the "other tertiary" level. However, males were more likely to have reached "university" and to have had 10 or fewer years schooling than females. This latter difference may reflect the different age structures of the two groups.

ment opportunities available to these women should they wish to find jobs in the future. A study of vocational training (Table X) complicates this picture as relatively more females than males had not obtained any qualifications. One explanation of this is that men have open to them a greater number of job opportunities in which learned skills are more important than general educational achievements. They therefore tend to make the most of qualifications that can be gained after their formal education has finished. Women, on the other hand, can be expected to drift into areas of employment not requiring such expertise. The details in Table XI lend support to this argument, and show the large proportion (44·7%) of women compared with the relatively small proportion of men (14·7%) engaged in clerical and retail employment.

The expanding role of women in the Australian workforce, as described above, disguises an unemployment problem arising out of an uneven distribution of available jobs. Figure 1 depicts the trend in seasonally adjusted unemployment rates in Australia between 1964 and 1973. For the whole of the period, unemployment among females has been greater than for males and has exhibited considerably more variation. However, job opportunities taken in the aggregate have been more plentiful for female

Table X.   Australia: Distribution of Employed Population 15 Years and Over by Highest Level of Qualification Obtained, June 1971

Level of Qualification Obtained	EMPLOYED POPULATION					
	Males		Females		Persons	
	No.	%	No.	%	No.	%
No qualification	2,422,548	67·6	1,334,757	80·7	3,757,305	71·7
Trade	727,165	20·3	31,833	1·9	758,998	14·5
Technician	141,837	4·0	84,423	5·1	226,260	4·3
Other tertiary	135,824	3·8	85,289	5·2	221,113	4·2
First degree	100,462	2·8	27,749	1·7	128,211	2·5
Higher degree	16,865	0·5	2,681	0·2	19,546	0·4
Not classifiable	41,815	1·2	87,166	5·3	128,981	2·5
Total	3,586,516	100·0	1,653,898	100·0	5,240,414	100·0

(Source: CBCS, 1971 Census).

Comment: Almost three-quarters of employed persons have no vocational qualifications beyond formal schooling. Relatively more employed females than employed males have not obtained any qualifications.

An overwhelmingly higher proportion of employed males than females have obtained trade level qualifications. The most common qualifications obtained by females are at technician or "other tertiary" level. Completion of short specialised courses ("not classifiable" group) are also common qualifications obtained by women.

Table XI.   Australia: All Females and Males in the Labour Force, by Occupation— November 1971   ('000)

	Professional and Technical		Administrative Executive and Managerial		Clerical		Sales		Farmers, fishermen, timbergetters, etc.	
		%*		%*		%*		%*		%*
All Females	243·6	13·5	39·3	2·1	569·4	31·7	234·5	13·0	62·1	3·4
Males	360·8	9·7	316·3	8·5	320·3	8·6	228·9	6·1	397·6	10·6

	Transport and Communication		Craftsmen, production-process workers		Service, Sport and Recreation		No previous work experience		Total	
		%*		%*		%*		%*		%*
All Females	50·3	2·7	278·5	15·4	306·0	17·0	11·5	0·6	1795·2	100·0
Males	286·4	7·6	1649·0	44·1	163·5	4·4	11·8	0·3	3734·6	100·0

*Rounded percentages of total males and females in the labour force respectively.
(Source: The Labour Force 1971, CBCS, References 6.22).

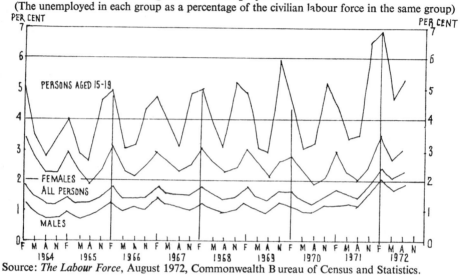

Figure 1. Unemployment Rates

(The unemployed in each group as a percentage of the civilian labour force in the same group)

Source: *The Labour Force*, August 1972, Commonwealth Bureau of Census and Statistics.

than males. A study by the Department of Labour and National Service[5] pointed out, for example, that in 1969 female unemployment increased by 5·9% and there were on average 11·5 unfilled vacancies registered with the Commonwealth Employment Service for every 1,000 females in the labour force; in contrast, male employment increased by 3·0% and there were on average 7·4 unfilled vacancies for every 1,000 males in the labour force. Job vacancies and job applicants were not as well matched for females as for males because of the imbalance in the geographical distribution of labour and the occupational imbalance between job seekers and jobs available. It was noted (in the Department of Labour study) that the geographical imbalance affected females more than males because of the former's concentration in jobs (such as white collar and light manual occupations) which are relatively scarce outside capital cities [6]. The occupational imbalance for females is illustrated by the figures for 1969 when over one-third of the registered unfilled vacancies were for nurses and clothing, textile and footwear operatives and 26% were in sales and clerical positions. In contrast, less than 3% of registered unemployed females were seeking jobs as textile and footwear operatives and more than 54% were looking for sales and clerical jobs.

Suggested corrections to the imbalance in the geographical distribution of labour include improved transportation systems to aid commuting between areas of insufficient and excess labour, and enlargement of the job range in different areas. If attempts currently being made to establish regional growth centres are successful, this problem may to some limited extent be attenuated. Occupational imbalance is, however, even more difficult to overcome, since this involves vocational training schemes which are only now beginning to come into government sponsored vogue in Australia.

Table XII. Australia: Employed Married Women, Full-time and Part-Time, by Industry, February 1973

Industry Group	Part-time workers ('000)	%	Full-time workers ('000)	%	Total ('000)	%
Agriculture	33·0	7·7	28·7	4·0	61·7	5·4
Manufacturing	46·6	10·9	191·1	26·8	237·7	20·8
Commerce	108·0	25·2	182·7	25·6	290·7	25·4
Community and business services	103·6	24·2	140·3	19·7	243·8	21·3
Amusement, hotels, personal services	74·1	17·3	60·1	8·4	134·2	11·7
Other industries	63·6	14·8	110·7	15·5	174·3	15·3
Total	428·8	100·0	713·7	100·0	1,142·5	100·0

(Source: CBCS, The Labour Force, February 1973 (unpublished estimates)).
Comment: Married women in part-time employment work mainly in the "commerce", "community and business services" and "amusement, personal services" industries, whilst married women working full-time are employed in "manufacturing", "commerce", and "community and business services" industries, in that order.

Certain structural aspects of the married female labour force are summarised in Table XII. Over one-third of married women workers have taken jobs on a part-time basis only[7]. But it is from this group that the major contributions to female employment have been made. Figure 2 depicts labour turnover rates for male and female manual workers from 1949 to 1972. For most years the turnover rate of female workers

Figure 2. Labour Turnover Rates for Male and Female Manual Workers. March 1949-1972

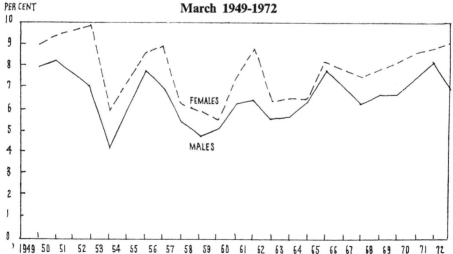

Source: *The Role of Women in the Economy*, Woman and Work No. 12, Women's Bureau Department of Labour, Fig. 1.

Table XIII.   Australia: Average Incomes for Men and Women ($), by Income Source 1968-69*

Average Incomes:	Wages and Salaries		Earned Income		All Sources	
	Median	Mean	Median	Mean	Median	Mean
	$	$	$	$	$	$
Men	3,090	3,290	3,120	3,490	3,050	3,390
Women	1,500	1,530	1,540	1,670	740	1,180
All persons	2,480	2,670	2,540	2,860	1,910	2,320

*Non-institutional population aged 15 years and over.
(Source: CBCS, Income Distribution, 1968-69, Part 1, Ref. no. 17.6).

exceeded that of males and in recent years there appears to have been a rapid widening of the gap. These features of relatively high labour turnover and part-time employment suggest that Australian women view their participation in the workforce rather differently compared with men. Many women seem still to be preoccupied with home and family duties. Work (either on a full-time or part-time basis) is in many instances only the means by which women secure additional income to meet family commitments, or a "stop-gap" between leaving school and getting married. The increase in the proportion of working married women mentioned above involves a redefinition of "the women's place". The role of the working mother has no doubt been inhibited by the strength of Australian social resistance to this change. The slowness of community recognition of the equal pay issue is perhaps a reflection of this conservatism. As Table XIII shows, female incomes are well below those of men. While the reasons for this pattern of income distribution are complex, one aspect must certainly be the continued retention in many occupations of (over-award) wage differentials based on sex. Until different attitudes are adopted, the likelihood of increasing the training of women for occupations in which labour is in short supply must remain rather slim. Australia will no doubt continue to have relatively high rates of unemployment among females, especially in the younger age groups where a large number of girls leave school with little consideration given to a future vocation.

Australian Wage Settlement Procedures
The fixing of women's wages in Australia has of course to be seen in the context of the overall system of wage settlement, which is chiefly characterised by the variety of tribunals operating under Federal and State law. Although generally referred to as "the compulsory arbitration system"—an indication of the ultimate powers of the tribunals—voluntary conciliation and arbitration are also employed. Industrial awards by State and Federal tribunals cover nearly 90% of all employees. Only about 40% of the workforce is covered by Federal awards. But the Federal tribunal, the Commonwealth Conciliation and Arbitration Commission, has a special status

derived partly from being the most important single authority. The Commission's position ensures that its decisions in major cases are usually followed by State tribunals. But this has not prevented State authorities from departing in important respects from standards recognised in Commonwealth awards (thereby creating pressures for alterations in Federal awards of which the Arbitration Commission has had to take note). As later described, award wages for women have been an example of Federal-State dispartities between the tribunals, with the Federal tribunal acting for sometime as the cart rather than the horse.

The diversity of sources of awards is not the only complicating factor in describing the equal pay issue in Australia, however. To the award wage determination system must be added the collective bargaining opportunities which have been encouraged rather than precluded by the arbitration system. Collective bargaining agreements are of two kinds. First, there is the certified and registered industrial agreement. This is an agreement in writing signed by both sides and presented to the Arbitration Commission for certification. Once certified, the agreement is deemed to be an award of the Commission. The second type of agreement could be described as autonomous collective bargaining, which has operated in some situations for many years. Unions have thus been able to exploit both the various avenues of award wage determination and the means available for collective bargaining. The growth of over-award payments has presented a difficult problem for the Arbitration Commission. It acknowledged in the 1969 national wage judgement that "an award increase or substantial portion thereof is likely to be added to amounts actually being paid, whether they be actual award figures or whether they include over-award amounts". However,

Table XIV. Australia: Average Weekly Earnings and Minimum Weekly Award Wage Rates

| | Average weekly earnings per employed male unit | | Minimum weekly award wage rates | |
	$	% increase on same period of previous year	$	% increase on same period of previous year
1961–62	47·60	2·6	36·54	3·0
1962–63	48·90	2·7	36·72	0·5
1963-64	51·50	5·3	37·61	2·4
1964–65	55·30	7·4	39·66	5·5
1965–66	57·90	4·7	40·74	2·7
1966–67	61·70	6·6	43·24	6·1
1967–68	65·30	5·8	45·40	5·0
1968–69	70·20	7·5	48·50	6·8
1969–70	76·10	8·4	51·09	5·3
1970–71	84·70	11·3	55·49	8·6
1971–72	93·20	10·0	61·26	10·4

(Source: Commonwealth Bureau of Census and Statistics, Wage Rates and Earnings, Average Weekly Earnings).

although as indicated by Table XIV over-award payments have been important down the years, it is at the level of award wages that the equal pay issue has mostly been debated in Australia. The discussion which follows is therefore confined to award wages.

In discussing award wages it may be useful to briefly mention a few of the major concepts employed, since the equal pay issue has been part of these. An important and long established division of Commonwealth award wages had been made into (1) the basic wage, which was roughly uniform across all Commonwealth awards and (2) margins, which were rates for particular jobs. Margins were intended to reflect an evaluation of different levels of skill, while the basic wage was a foundation element in award wages and was in effect the award wage paid to unskilled workers. There have been a variety of changes over the decades in the practices and principles of determining the components of award wages. Most important for our purpose was that in 1965 the Commission for the first time held a joint enquiry into the basic wage and margins, and in 1966 announced its intention to abolish, as from 1967, the basic wage and margins and to prescribe instead a "total wage". Also, in 1966, the Commission introduced a minimum wage designed to protect low-paid workers. This differs from the basic wage in that it is not a foundation element in award wages— instead it overrules any lesser wage which may otherwise have been prescribed.

The Equal Pay Issue

The practice, up to 1967, of adding to the basic wage a margin for skill, responsibility, or risk, necessary training, and so on was exercised irrespective of whether the job was for men or women or both. Down the years, however, it became the tendency to distinguish occupations which had been primarily for males from those regarded as open for both sexes. Though (as always with different tribunals at State and Federal levels operating over long periods of time) the record is patchy. In some cases different margins were awarded for men and women even though the titles of classification were the same; in others, the margins awarded were similar. Of course, similar classifications of titles in awards did not mean that precisely similar work was being performed by men and women; nor did it necessarily reflect an arbitrator's assessment of a wage so much as an agreement or compromise between the parties[8].

Until the Basic Wage Enquiry of 1949-50, the basic wage for females under Commonwealth awards was fixed at 54% of the male basic wage. In the 1949-50 Enquiry this percentage was increased to 75. Fixing the female basic wage as a proportion of that for men originated in the Clothing Trades Award of 1919, handed down by Mr. Justice Higgins. The first case in which female rates were discussed by the Commonwealth Court (as it was then called) was the Fruit Packers' case in 1912, and this was also presided over by Higgins. In the Fruit Packers' case he said that in fixing the minimum wage for a man he had been forced to act on "considerations other than those of mere earning power". He had based it on "the normal needs of the average employee regarded as a human being living in a civilised community . . . one of his normal needs being those of domestic life. If he has a wife and children, he is under an obligation—even a legal obligation—to maintain them. How is such a minimum applicable to the case of a woman picker? She is not, unless perhaps in very exceptional circumstance, under any such obligation. The minimum cannot be based on exceptional cases . . . The State cannot ask that an employer shall, in addition to all his other ancieties, make himself familiar with the domestic necessities of every employee . . ." He added that "there is much more danger incident to the forcing of men out of an industry to which they are suited than to the forcing out of women, even if they are equally suited"[9].

The principle of wage and employment precedence of men over women because of their assumed family responsibility enunciated by Higgins was still alive and well in the 1949 Basic Wafe Enquiry when the majority judgement said that "it was socially preferable to provide a high wage for the male because of his social obligations to fiancee, wife and family". The judgement went on: "while single females were said to be anxious to receive the higher wage their interest changed on their marriage . . . as married women they became concerned that their husbands should bring home the largest possible pay envelope"; and "the productivity, efficiency and the needs and the responsibilities, etc. of females were substantially less than that of males . . ."[10]. The Court therefore rejected the claim for an equal basic wage for female employees, but, as mentioned, increased the basic wage for adult females from 54 to75% of the male basic wage.

The Commonwealth Equal Pay Cases, 1969 and 1972
In June 1969 the Arbitration Commission gave judgement in the Equal Pay Cases brought before it in the form of two applications from the Meat Industry Employers' Union and eight applications relating to various areas of the Commonwealth Public Service. In its judgement the Commission stated that it assepted the concept of equal pay for equal work and proposed to introduce the principles of State Acts concerning equal pay to the extent of the claims before it. The Commission suggested that nine principles which it expounded should be applied in determining future applications for equal pay. The principles were:
  (1) the male and female employees concerned who must be adults, should be working under the terms of the same determination or award;
  (2) it should be established that certain work covered by the determination or award is performed by both males and females;
  (3) the work performed by both the males and the females under such determination or award should be of the same or a like nature and of equal value, but mere similarity in name of male and female classifications may not be enough to establish that males and females do work of a like nature;
  (4) for the purpose of determining whether the female employees are performing work of the same or a like nature and of equal value as the male employees the Arbitrator or the Commissioner, as the case may be, should . . . take into

consideration whether the female employees are performing the same work or work of a like nature as male employees and doing the same range and volume of work as male employees and under the same conditions;

(5) consideration should be restricted to work performed under the determination or award concerned;

(6) in cases where males and females are doing work of the same or a like nature and of equal value, there may be no appropriate classifications for that work. In such a case appropriate classifications should be established for the work which is performed by both males and females and rates of pay established for that work. The classifications should not be of a generic nature covering a wide variety of work;

(7) in considering whether males and females are performing work of the same or like nature and of equal value, consideration should not be restricted to the situation in one establishment but should extend to the general situation under the determination or award concerned, unless the award or determination applies to only one establishment;

(8) The expression of "equal value" should not be construed as meaning "of equal value to the employer" but as of equal value or at least of equal value from the point of view of wage or salary assessment;

(9) notwithstanding the above, equal pay should not be provided by application of the above principles where the work in question is essentially or usually performed by females but is work upon which male employees may also be employed.

The Commission in its decision in 1969 also established stages up to January 1, 1972 at which increases in female rates should occur, starting on October 1, 1969 at 85% of the male rate and finishing on January 1, 1972 at 100% of the male rate. Up to the end of August 1972 equal pay had been prescribed for a large number of classifications indicated in various Commonwealth awards. In the States between 1969 and 1972 a number of developments occurred relevant to the equal pay issue, but the main changes were concerned with the application of the 1969 Equal Pay case principles in award classifications satisfying the necessary requirements[11].

In 1972 another Equal Pay Case was heard by the Arbitration Commission. By this time (late 1972) some parties before the Commission estimated that about 18% of females in the workforce had received equal pay as a result of the 1969 decision. In its judgement, delivered on 15 December, 1972, the Commission stated that it had considered simply amending the principles of its 1969 judgement but had decided instead to "state positively a new principle. In our view", (the Commission said) "the concept of 'equal pay for equal work' is too narrow in today's world and we think the time has come to enlarge the concept to 'equal pay for work of equal value'. This means that award rates for all work should be considered without regard to the sex of the employee". The Commission decided that the new principle should be phased in over a maximum period of $2\frac{1}{2}$ years. The new principle was defined as follows:

"(1) The principle of 'equal pay for work of equal value' will be applied to all awards of the Commission. By 'equal pay for work of equal value' we mean the fixation of award wage rates by a consideration of the work performed irrespective of the sex of the worker. The principle will apply to both adults and juniors. Because the male minimum wage takes account of family considerations it will not apply to females.

(2) Adoption of the new principle requires that female rates be determined by work value comparisons without regard to the sex of the employees concerned. Differentiations between male rates in awards of the Commission have traditionally been founded on work value investigations of various occupational groups or classifications. The gap between the level of male and female rates in awards generally is greater than the gap, if any, in the comparative value of work performed by the two sexes because rates for female classifications in the same award have generally been fixed without a comparative evaluation of the work performed by males and females.

(3) The new principle may be applied by agreement or arbitration . . . [and]

(4) Implementation of the new principle by arbitration will call for the exercise of the broad judgement which has characterised work value inquiries"[12].

The Role of Government

In both the 1969 and 1972 judgements, the Commission pointed out that it had been influenced by the changing social and industrial climate affecting equal pay. In the 1969 judgement the Commission noted that it had always in appropriate cases "when dealing with broad social issues paid regard to views of States either expressed by submissions or implied by State legislation. . . the conjunction of views of the Federal Government and four State Governments . . . is a matter to which we must pay serious regard when considering a social problem of this magnitude"[13]. The four states referred to by the Commission were New South Wales, South Australia, Western Australia and Tasmania, which had passed virtually identical legislation on equal pay, beginning with the New South Wales Industrial Arbitration (Female Rates) Amendment Act, 1958[14]. The four State Acts were of especial importance in view of the relatively larger number of females covered by State than by Federal awards. The Commission felt that the legislation implied a social acceptance of the concept of equal pay and considerable support for the adoption of the concept by the Commission. In its 1972 judgement the Commission again noted further liberalisation of attitudes whether by legislation or submission by State Government. Also, a second submission by the Commonwealth Government (following the Labour Party victory in the November 1972 election [15]) had positively supported equal pay, though different views as to the method of implementation had been expressed.

Unlike some of the States, the Federal Government had (at least until November 1972) declined to take the initiative in the equal pay field. It had viewed the Arbitration Commission as the proper body to make an examination and determination on the issue. For example, in 1962, the then Minister of Labour and National Service, Mr. W. McMahon, had stated: "While the government does not oppose the principle of equal remuneration for work of equal value it does not consider that it would be acting responsibly if it were, by its own decision, to apply the principle to its own employees in advance of a definitive determination by the Arbitration Commission[16]".

Similar reasoning, i.e. that the Commission and not the Federal Government has jurisdiction over wage-fixing, has been used to defend the (former) Federal Liberal Government's failure to ratify conventions 100 and 111 of the International Labour Organisation. And in both the 1969 and 1972 Equal Pay Cases the Commission did not give great weight to the Conventions, although in 1969 it said that ILO documents "must be taken to represent international thinking on the question of equal pay for equal work". It does seem difficult to explain why, up to the end of 1972, Australia had not ratified the relevant ILO conventions, which had been adopted by a wide diversity of countries. In particular, the wording of the crucial articles 1 and 2 of Convention 111 would seem to be likely to be unexceptionable to any Australian government. (These articles cover undertakings by ratifying members of the ILO to eliminate discrimination "on the basis of race, colour, sex, religion, political opinion, national extraction or social origin"). The only plausible explanation is that the Liberal government felt that by taking the initiative on equal pay it would be unwisely fanning the flames of wage increase pressures. The succeeding Labour administration took an opposite view, and in 1973 ILO Convention 111 referred to above was ratified by Australia.

There are two issues here which will determine which is the more appropriate approach in the light of different objectives. First, will males as a result of the 1972 decision be able to restore their pre-existing wage relativities? The answer to this question is open to conjecture. In the 1972 case, no evidence was adduced that this had happened after the 1969 decision. The second issue is what the economic consequences of the 1972 judgement were. Did it add an unduly heavy burden to existing wage pressures? The employers estimated during the hearing that the cost of granting the claims would be some $645 million a year and the Commonwealth in its first submission said that "the ultimate costs could be very considerable". The Commission felt that the employers might have overstated the situation by not making allowances for part-time female workers. However, the Commission recognised that the increase in the total wages bill as a result of the decision would be "substantial but its effect will be minimised by the method of implementation . . . In our view", (the Commission went on), "the community is prepared to accept the concept of equal pay for females and should therefore be prepared to accept the economic consequences of this decision".

An important part of the Commission's 1972 decision concerned its rejection of the union claim that adult females be paid the same minimum wage as adult males. Echoing Mr. Justice Higgins, quoted above, the Commission stated that the minimum wage had since its inception in 1967 been considered as including a family component.

Indeed the unions have regularly presented the minimum wage in this light. The Commission remarked that "the material used by the unions in their various claims over the years for special increases to the minimum wage has principally been directed to family problems and the oral evidence, both expert and of employees themselves, has been similarly directed. However, the unions now argue as a simple matter of equity that females should receive the same minimum wage as males. We reject that argument because the male minimum wage in our awards takes account of the family considerations we have mentioned". The Labour Government made it clear that it wished to see this portion of the judgement reversed. The Commission, while on the one hand acknowledging the influence of governmental and social attitudes, has also repeatedly declared its independence. In the 1972 judgement for example, the Commission said that "it reaches its decision on the substance of the submissions put to it, rather than upon the nature of the party . . . putting these submissions". But in the 1974 National Wage judgement it was apparently the influence of governmental and social attitudes which weighed most heavily with the Commission. In an important reversal, the Commission in 1974 accepted what it had so firmly rejected in 1972—the application of the minimum wage to adult male and female workers alike.

In the 1974 National Wage case, the claim for equal minimum wages was argued by all the unions, the Australian Government, the Union of Australian Women and the National Council of Women in Australia. The Commission stated that the submissions made to it had demonstrated "not only widespread and deep social support but also the economic viability of the concept". It was able to point out that the application of the principles propounded in the 1972 Equal Case, and the increase in award rates generally, had lifted the pay of female workers substantially. The average Commonwealth award rate for adult females had risen from \$50·29 in December 1972 to \$62·17 in December 1973, an increase of 23·6%. The increase for adult males in the same period was 13·3%. In December 1973, female Commonwealth award rates averaged 82% of male rates compared with 75% a year earlier. On our estimate, it seems that some employers will have been faced with wage increases of 100% for female employees in the $2\frac{1}{2}$ years up to June, 1975. Since in May, 1974 the lowest rates applicable to adult females in most awards were close to the minimum wage, the Commission felt that the extension of the minimum wage to adult females was economically feasible. Nonetheless, it did so with a phasing-in period—adult females would be entitled to 85% of the new male minimum wage from the date of its operation (June 1974); 90% from September, and 100% by June 1975.

In logic, the Commission could only accede to the request for an equal minimum wage by discarding the "family component" from the concept of this wage. It pointed out that it had insufficient information to justify continuing to take account of the widely varying family obligations of workers on the minimum wage, that it was "an industrial arbitration tribunal, not a social welfare agency", and that "the care of family needs is principally a task for governments"[17].

Over-award Payments and Equal Opportunity

So far, only award wages and the role of the Commission and State and Federal Governments in affecting equal (award) pay have been mentioned. But it is important to remember that (as Table XIV shows) award wages in Australia represent only a share of the individual's pay packet. The impact of the equal pay decisions in levelling out male/female wages in the aggregate may therefore be circumscribed to the extent that unions in male dominated industries are able to win large over-award settlements.

It is also important that arbitration awards are, of course, only part of the broader issue of female equality in the labour market. Dr. Riach has rightly said that Australian women "stand to gain less in the long run from a direct equal pay award, which merely removed the symptoms of restricted employment opportunities, than they do if equal pay for work of equal value is achieved indirectly by the elimination of sexual discrimination in the labour market . . . (equal pay) will be a very limited victory if social prejudices continue to prevent women from occupying anything but a small proportion of responsible and well-paying positions"[18].

Action to bolster the equal pay decisions must now be considered a serious possibility in Australia. This action could include some of the suggestions made by Dr. Riach. In the public sector the Government as employer could remove any discriminatory practices which still exist, while in the private sector economic or legal sanctions and moral suasion could be considered. Certainly there is now available a whole range of measures that could be derived from overseas experience of the subject, the judicious application of which could serve to improve the employment opportunities for women in Australia. The record of the arbitration system on the equal pay issue as described above substantiates the claim made that Australian wage fixing machinery "demonstrates the practicability of public agencies established by law providing the forum of discussion and the means of determining the pay of employees throughout most of the economy"[19]. However, further progress in improving the employment status of women in the workforce seems now to depend mainly on developments outside the arbitration system.

Social versus Economic Issues

In Australia, as in other countries, there has been discussion of the extent to which wage differentials between men and women are the result of social (or "conventional" or "prejudicial") forces rather than economic ones. An early (1963) study by Dr. Blandy concluded that "if Australian society were more rational sex differentials would not be as wide as they are at present". Blandy suggested that "to raise wage and maintain employment opportunities for women it is necessary . . . to increase the demand for women workers considerably and to bolster supply factors in their favour. Employers must be persuaded that female efficiency and "overall value" are greater than they believe at present . . . To achieve this end a fundamental change in our whole set of social beliefs regarding the status of women in our society will be required"[20]. Although not yet meriting the adjective "fundamental" it is clear from the discussion above that official attitudes in Australia are undergoing a change. This change follows the fashion in overseas countries and has of course been partly prompted by pressure from increasingly active women's organisations and the growth of general consciousness on the unfair treatment accorded to women in the workforce and elsewhere.

The traditional influence of the (award) wage fixing tribunals in Australia on the rate of growth of total earnings, differentials for skill and aggregate differentials for women and men is uncertain. Now that the Arbitration Commission, with active support from Commonwealth and State Governments, has set out on an equal pay policy, the likely impact remains cloudy. Will the growth of collective bargaining and the possible decline of the relative importance of award wages mean that the battle for equal pay will be shifted from the tribunals to the shop floor? Will equal award pay bias employment opportunities in favour of men? How far can institutional and social changes affect wage differentials which may prove to have a strong economic genesis? These questions can only be answered by the future. But while an aura of indeterminacy surrounds these issues, it is clear that there remain (1) restrictions on the employment of women, and (2) discrimination against their earning potential. The recent Department of Labour study *The Role of Women in the Economy* has documented some of these. It noted that despite Australia's "fundamental" aim of full employment, there are a number of restrictions on females imposed by the relevant awards and State factory legislation. Usually these restrictions are in the interests of safety and general welfare "but in some awards they are intended to protect male employees from competition in industries . . . traditionally regarded as male (preserves)"[21]. In addition, therefore, to the equal award pay now won for women, it will be necessary for Australian and State governments to act carefully but forcefully in eradicating existing restrictions on the employment of women (perhaps on the basis of the New Zealand legislation referred to later in this chapter).

The second issue—that of discrimination against the earning potential of Australian women—is, by nature of its rather vague dimensions, more difficult to attack. What is needed first is a concerted research programme to present a comprehensive picture of the situation. In this respect, it is encouraging that the Women's Bureau of the Department of Labour is strongly aware of the need for this kind of investigation[22]. Questions that research needs to enquire into include the role of occupational distribution in wage differences based on sex; relative male and female productivity as a feature explaining wage differences; education and pay differences; flexibility in working life and work participation; and the need for child care facilities. It may be difficult to obtain all the information necessary to formulate a programme to create more equal opportunity for women. But there is little doubt that the attempt needs to be made. Although equal award pay has now been established in Australia, this achievement gives no ground for complacency. The concept of equal pay is indeed regarded by some as outmoded—they argue that "a standard, set by a male rate, acknowledges an inherent difference in the value of women's work and seriously disadvantages the women working in traditionally female occupations where no male rate of pay is prescribed. They ask 'equal to what?' "[23].

NEW ZEALAND

The Role of Women in the New Zealand Workforce

In 1956, according to the New Zealand population census, 18% of the female population was in active employment. This figure rose slowly but steadily to 21% at the time of the 1966 Census, and 22·4% in 1972[23]. This increased participation meant that the female component of the workforce rose from 27·9% in 1957 to 29·2% in 1973. (Table XV). Neither the increases nor the absolute levels attained are exceptional. Many countries (Table XVI) experienced female participation rates far higher than New Zealand. The New Zealand Department of Labour attributed this discrepancy to the "higher incidence of marriage, the higher New Zealand birth rates, and the social attitudes in New Zealand which expect a mother to care for her own children"[24]. Nonetheless, the increase in participation rates seems to result largely from the movement of married women into the workforce. As Table XVII indicates, the figure for married women in the labour force, expressed as a percentage of the female labour force, has risen from 8·5% in 1936 to 41·5% in 1966. Married women in the age group 35 and over have, as is shown in Table XVIII, been responsible for much of this increase. It appears that any further expansion in the female labour force will depend mainly on the re-entry of married women after their children have reached school age.

Table XV. New Zealand: The Sex Composition of the Work Force

Year	Males	('000) Females	Total	Females as a per cent of total
April 1957	386·3	150·0	536·3	27·9
April 1962	435·7	173·7	609·4	28·5
April 1966	744·5	277·3	1021·8	27·1
April 1973	814·7	335·5	1150·2	29·2

(Source: Department of Statistics, *Monthly Abstract of Statistics*, various issues).

Table XVI. New Zealand: Female Labour Force Participation Rates. Certain Countries (15 to 64)

Country	Date	Participation Rate %
United Kingdom	1966	50·1
Denmark	1965	47·6
Sweden	1965	44·3
France	1968	43·5
United States	1969 (est.)	42·4
Australia	1966	40·1
Canada	1961	34·9
New Zealand	1966	35·4

(Source: ILO Year Book 1970).

Table XVII. New Zealand: Married Women in the Labour Force as a Percentage of the Female Labour Force

	1936	1945	1951	1956	1961	1966
Number	11,291	31,958	41,932	62,033	84,556	116,314
Per cent	8·5	17·7	24·4	32·0	37·6	41·5

(Source: New Zealand census volumes).

Table XVIII. New Zealand: Married Women in Labour Force as a Percentage of All Married Women in the Same Age Group

Age	1926	1936	1945	1951	1956	1961	1966
16–19	3·4	5·7	18·2	14·5	18·5	20·0	23·5
20–24	3·5	4·3	17·4	16·0	19·4	20·7	26·7
25–29	3·2	3·7	10·3	9·7	11·6	11·9	15·8
30–34	3·3	3·6	8·0	8·9	11·3	13·3	16·4
35–39	3·6	3·6	8·4	10·5	13·9	18·0	21·8
40–44	3·9	3·9	8·7	12·2	16·6	21·3	26·9
45–49	4·2	4·4	7·8	13·1	17·5	23·1	27·7
50–54	4·0	4·2	6·1	10·7	15·5	20·7	25·2
55–59	3·8	4·2	4·6	6·9	10·8	14·9	18·5
60–64	2·7	2·8	2·5	3·7	5·2	7·5	9·5
65+	1·7	1·6	1·0	1·4	1·6	1·7	2·1
Married women of all ages— 16+	3·5	3·7	7·7	9·7	12·9	16·0	19·9

(Source: New Zealand census volumes).

Female employment is concentrated in the urban centres and, according to M. Gilson[25] varies not only according to whether a place is urban in nature but also with the size of the urban centre. The larger the centre, the greater the number of industrial and social organisations that can provide job opportunities. Perhaps more important is the social climate of a large city, which is on the whole more favourable to the employment of women.

New Zealand women have traditionally undertaken work in a fairly limited range of occupations. In Table XIX the four occupational groups listed in Part A include over 70% of women workers but only 26% of the men. The position is reversed for the six groups in Part B. Moreover women occupy the less prestigious positions in employment. Although on the figures examined above a higher percentage of employed women than men are in professional jobs, statistics for 1970 show that 80% of professional women were in nursing or teaching and, while 54% of school teachers were women, 90% of school inspectors were men. High status professions, such as law and medicine, boast few female representatives. There were no women judges or magistrates. Among doctors, 8% were women, and among surgeons, females represented a mere 0·03% of the total[26].

Table XIX. New Zealand: Occupational Groups—Percentage of Population 1966

Occupational Group	Married Women				All Married Women		All Other Women (mostly single)		Actively Engaged Women		Actively Engaged Men	
	Under 35		35 & Over									
	%	Sub-total	%	Sub-total	%	Sub-total	%	Sub-total	%	Sub-total	%	Sub-total
A.												
Clerical workers	32·5		20·1		24·2		32·6		29·1		8·0	
Professional, technical and related workers	14·1		7·8		9·9		21·1		16·5		7·8	
Services, sport, and recreation workers	10·5		15·6		13·9		14·7		14·3		3·3	
Sales workers	10·4		17·1		14·8		9·8		11·9		6·9	
Sub-total A		67·5		60·6		62·8		78·2		71·8		26·0
B.												
Craftsmen, production process workers, and labourers, etc.	17·9		25·0		22·6		13·5		17·3		41·2	
Farmers, fishermen, hunters, loggers and related	8·3		7·1		7·5		3·1		4·9		16·2	
Transport and communications workers	3·4		1·6		2·2		2·8		2·5		7·2	
Administrative, executive and managerial workers	2·7		5·7		4·7		1·1		2·6		7·0	
Armed forces and others (not classifiable)	0·3		0·2		0·2		1·5		0·9		1·8	
Miners, quarrymen and related	..		..		..		..		..		0·6	
Sub-total B		32·6		39·6		37·2		22·0		28·2		74·0
Totals ⎰Percentage*	100	100	100	100	100	100	100	100	100	100	100	100
⎱Base	38,665		77,649		116,314		164,130		280,444		745,595	

*Some rounding off.

(Source: Department of Labour Submission, New Zealand Census 1966, Vol. 4, p. 9).

The possibilities of acceptance into the more prestigious occupations depend partly upon qualifications and experience. It is difficult to collect data on experience, but Tables XX and XXI give some indication of the educational attainment of men and women in the New Zealand workforce. The Tables show that greater numbers of girls are attaining high level (school) leaving qualifications. The continuation of this trend is important in so far as a lack of general education is a restriction on the entry of women into the workforce.

Table XX: (a) New Zealand: Males at Educational Institutions as Percent of Mean Population, by Age Groups

Age Group	1961	1962	1963	1964	1965	1966	1967	1968	1969
15	71·5	80·3	81·0	79·5	80·7	82·0	84·8	86·8	87·7
16	45·5	46·3	52·2	51·8	51·8	54·3	55·3	61·5	60·8
17	22·5	23·9	23·1	26·2	27·5	27·0	28·7	32·1	32·1
18	10·5	11·5	12·5	12·6	13·8	14·8	15·0	17·1	16·9
19	8·2	7·8	9·4	9·8	9·6	11·5	11·7	12·0	13·7
20	6·3	7·2	6·7	7·9	8·2	8·4	10·2	11·1	11·2

(b) Females at Educational Institutions as Percent of Mean Population, by Age Groups

Age Group	1961	1962	1963	1964	1965	1966	1967	1968	1969
15	65·5	74·9	73·1	74·0	76·4	76·2	79·8	82·1	84·1
16	39·1	83·3	44·1	43·8	45·3	47·5	48·8	55·0	55·0
17	12·3	12·3	12·8	15·3	15·4	15·9	17·4	20·0	21·5
18	4·4	4·6	4·5	5·0	5·6	5·7	6·1	7·2	7·7
19	3·4	3·3	3·4	3·8	4·1	4·7	4·6	5·3	5·7
20	2·4	2·6	2·7	2·8	3·0	3·2	4·1	4·0	4·4

(Source: *Equal Pay in New Zealand*. Report of the Commission of Inquiry, Wellington, September 1971).

Table XXI. New Zealand: Levels of Female Secondary School Attainment

Level of Attainment	1961 No.	%	1965 No.	%	1970 No.	%
Non School Certificate	13,261	70·6	13,999	62·0	13,612	54·1
School Certificate	2,439	13·0	3,225	14·3	3,186*	12·7
Endorsed School Certificate	979	5·2	2,022	9·0	2,758†	11·0
University Entrance	1,417	7·6	2,233	9·9	3,560	14·1
Higher School Certificate	665	3·5	1,062	4·7	936	3·7
University Bursary	—	—	—	—	1,090	4·3
University Scholarship	11	0·1	23	0·1	36	0·1
Total	18,772	100·0	22,564	100·0	25,178	100·0

*3 or more subjects.
†Lower 6th Certificate included.
(Source: Department of Education—Research Section).

In recent years attention has been drawn to the limited range of subjects generally studied by girls. One of the effects of a narrow education is the restriction it places on the number and range of job opportunities. Further, lack of an adequate education limits the degree of advancement within employment which can be expected. Table XXII shows the probable employment destination of the current crop of school children. Fortunately, the problem has been recognised and this has resulted in a trend towards more vocationally useful subjects, such as mathematics, being undertaken by girls[27].

Table XXII. New Zealand: Probable Destination of State and Private Secondary Pupils

Probable Destination	Boys	Girls	Total	Boys	Girls	Total
		number			per cent	
Full-time education at university	4,012	1,962	5,974	15·11	7·79	11·55
Further full-time education—						
Teachers college	382	1,727	2,109	1·44	6·86	4·08
Kindergarten T.C.	—	171	171	—	0·68	0·33
Technical training	399	282	681	1·50	1·12	1·31
Commercial training	107	1,192	1,299	0·40	4·73	2·51
Art	65	94	159	0·25	0·37	0·31
Technical traineeships—						
Draughting cadets	374	57	431	1·41	0·23	0·83
Technical trainees	980	321	1,301	3·69	1·28	2·52
Health services	90	2,894	2,984	0·34	11·49	5·77
Office—						
Government	693	1,269	1,962	2·61	5·04	3·79
Local authority	100	315	415	0·38	1·25	0·80
Private enterprise	1,572	5,249	6.821	5·92	20·85	13·19
Shop and warehouse assistant	1,498	2,571	4,069	5·64	10·21	7·87
Skilled trades—						
Government	896	128	1,024	3·37	0·51	1·98
Local authority	178	24	202	0·67	0·10	0·39
Private enterprise	5,584	1,015	6,599	21·03	4·03	12·75
Farming	2,906	227	3,133	10·95	0·90	6·06
Factory and clothing workers	1,099	1,628	2,727	4·14	6·47	5·27
Domestic work and home	112	1,271	1,383	0·42	5·05	2·67
Armed forces	587	64	651	2·21	0·25	1·26
Other	4,917	2,717	7,634	18·52	10·79	14·76
Totals	26,551	25,178	51,729	100·0	100·00	100·00

(Source: New Zealand Official Year Book 1973. Department of Statistics, Wellington, p. 214).

As regards job training, population statistics from the 1966 census (Table XXIII) shows that 2% of men received training in a trade, compared with only 0·18% of women. However, 72·6% of men in the workforce had no qualifications at all, while only 67·8% of women fell into the same category. This suggests that men find jobs that do not require particular skills fairly easy to obtain while women, if they wish to be employed, must have a certificate indicating that they are capable of performing a particular task satisfactorily. While it is difficult to discern how far this tendency is caused by prejudice or other factors, it seems clear that the training facilities for women are still unsatisfactory in New Zealand. Although women must be taught the skills required for occupations in which labour is in short supply, their training will necessarily occur at stages different from that of men. Women need to be encouraged to undergo training before entering employment, after leaving school, and provision

Table XXIII. New Zealand: Workforce Qualifications

Qualification	Males	Females	Total
University—			
Doctorate	897	69	966
Master's degree	4,014	848	4,862
Bachelor's degree	14,876	2,652	17,528
Diploma	3,388	683	4,071
Other	3,419	81	3,500
Teacher's Certificate	7,164	9,925	17,089
Secondary—			
Higher School Certificate or equivalent, University Entrance Scholarship Examination	5,538	2,028	7,566
University Entrance	25,259	9,968	35,227
School Certificate	33,879	22,538	56,417
Other	22,343	8,532	30,875
Professional and higher trade	16,895	9,135	26,030
Trade certificate*	8,136	7	8,143
Other trade certificate†	7,495	498	7,993
Business college	795	9,376	10,171
Other qualification‡	50,478	13,612	64,090
No qualification	541,019	190,492	731,511
Totals	745,595	280,444	1,026,039

*Includes electricians', plumbers', carpenters', joiners', radio and TV servicemen's, and motor mechanics'.

†Includes Intermediate grades of Technician Certification Authority examinations, Police, Fire Brigade and Armed Forces examinations, overseas trade examinations, etc.

‡Mainly the Proficiency Certicate or Junior Free Place (43,029 male—and 11,308 females) and other primary certificates including the Certificate of Competency (6,531 males and 1,370 females).

(Source: New Zealand Official Year Book).

needs to be made for retraining when they are ready to re-enter the workforce after raising a family. To this extent the training that women receive will differ from that of men. The major problem to be overcome is the traditional (and internationally widespread) attitude that education is not a life-long process. Training and retraining may need to be regarded as feasible and necessary at most stages in a person's working life.

Table XXIV indicates, however, that women are not likely to be very receptive to training programmes initiated for them. The proportion of women working on a part-time basis has doubled in the ten years from 1962-1972 and now stands at 28·1% (compared with the male figure of 5%). As can be seen from the Table, the labour turnover rate of women is considerably higher than that for men. Women, it would seem, tend partly to look upon employment as a means through which they may supplement the family income in periods of extra need or as a way of passing the time between leaving school and being married. To the extent that such attitudes obtain it is difficult to persuade women to undergo training which they may feel will never be fully utilised.

These attitudes are compounded by the action of employers, which seem to be influenced by misconceptions about female absenteeism, interruption of service and the consequent economic doubts of training women for skilled executive or super-

Table XXIV. New Zealand: Sex Distribution of the Part Time Workforce (including Rates of Labour Turnover)

Date of Survey	Full-time employees and working proprietors			Part-time workers			Half-yearly percentage rate of labour turnover*	
	Males	Females	Total	Males	Females	Total	Males	Females
April—							%	%
1962	478,036	185,630	663,666	16,443	26,193	42,636	20	34
1963	491,568	190,830	682,398	16,908	27,906	44,814	18	32
1964	507,174	200,596	707,770	18,481	30,800	49,281	20	32
1965	526,455	211,599	738,054	20,386	34,669	55,055	21	33
1966	542,943	223,955	766,898	23,813	39,814	63,627	23	36
1967	554,644	233,899	788,543	24,372	44,453	68,825	21	34
1968	547,000	227,045	774,045	23,449	43,512	66,961	16	28
1969	558,695	235,077	793,772	25,074	48,221	73,295	20	30
1970	572,052	247,353	819,405	27,643	57,455	85,098	23	35
1971	584,793	255,687	840,480	29,110	66,000	95,110	24	36
1972	589,740	257,792	847,532	28,545	68,322	96,867	21	33
October—								
1972	581,577	256,914	838,491	29,740	72,379	102,119	19	30

*The relationship between the number of terminations over the previous half-year and the average number of employees during the same period.
(Source: New Zealand Official Year Book).

visory roles. The recurring theme of the 1971 New Zealand Commission of Inquiry into Equal Pay was the need to replace current "myths" with information based on better knowledge. The features which have shaped the roles of men and women have already altered considerably. There is little doubt that equal pay will produce a deeper questioning of the form of these roles, and their future interactions.

Wage Setting Procedures

New Zealand is one of the few countries in which wage determination methods approximate to those found in Australia. (At least this has been so until very recently). For many years the basis of wage determination for the majority of employees was a system of conciliation and arbitration supplemented by general wage orders. The system, which (as in Australia) evolved in the late 1890s, entailed the voluntary registration of unions, the regulation of agreements made between these unions and associations of employers, the reference of disputes to a Council of Conciliation and, in the event of a failure by the parties to reach an agreement, the reference of the dispute to the Court of Arbitration. The Court, after hearing the evidence, could then make an award binding all parties.

About half of New Zealand's wage and salary earners have been subject to awards and industrial agreements made under the Industrial Conciliation and Arbitration Act of 1954. However, in about 90% of cases the parties reached full agreement in the conciliation proceedings. The system was primarily concerned with maintaining industrial harmony and setting minimum requirements for pay and conditions. This left considerable scope for bargains to be made outside the formal awards. The divergences that emerged between award and ruling rates were a primary reason for the declining influence of the award system. In 1971 a comprehensive review of industrial legislation was undertaken. This culminated in the limitation of the role of the Court of Arbitration to the ratification of conciliation settlements, and an increased emphasis on direct bargaining outside legislative control[28]. The special status the Arbitration Court once enjoyed in wage determination was thus largely eroded and its influence on pay and conditions weakened.

Under the State Services Remuneration and Conditions of Employment Act 1969, a number of tribunals have been established which administer pay and conditions in the State Services. Amongst these are the Government Railways Industrial Tribunal, a Post Office Staff Tribunal, and a Hospital Service Tribunal, all with a common chairman and all, despite a wide variation in functions and powers, playing an essential role in salary determinations in the public sector[29]. In the private sector, there are a number of lesser wage fixing tribunals. These have limited legislative powers and, although their jurisdictions vary, they are normally confined to a particular industry or section of an industry. Notable examples are the Waterfront Industry Tribunal established under the Waterfront Industry Act 1953 and the Aircrew Industrial tribunal, which is given the task of settling disputes, including those over remuneration, in the air transport industry[30].

New Zealand has thus been faced with problems similar to those encountered in the Australian context. The implementation of equal pay through the existing institutional arrangement would have required the co-operation of several autonomous bodies. Such co-operation is rare. And even if it could be achieved, the more difficult problems of bringing workers and employers who prefer to bargain outside the system into line on the equal pay issue, and ensuring equality of job opportunity for women, would remain.

The History of the Equal Pay Movement

Pay differentials for men and women in New Zealand have been shaped by custom and tradition. The colonists sought to transplant British ideas into a new environment. This tradition was legally sanctioned in 1903 when differential rates were officially prescribed in the Christchurch Tailoring Trades Award, the Court of Arbitration granting male piece workers a rate of 1/- an hour, and females 8d. The principle was extended to all female workers in 1934 with the introduction of the Industrial Conciliation and Arbitration Amendment Act. This Act provided that the Court should set a basic wage for both adult male and female workers on the "needs principle", i.e. that pay should be sufficient to maintain a wife and three children "in a fair and reasonable standard of comfort". Only one award was made under this Act (in November 1936), when the Court set the basic wage for adult male workers at £1 16s. 0d. per week. However, the maintenance of the differential was reinforced with the Minimum Wage Act of 1945, which made provision for an adult male rate of £5 5s. 0d. and a female rate of £3 3s. 0d.

Rather surprisingly, the existence of a differential based on sex went unquestioned in the discussions leading up to the pronouncements of the Court. It was not until 1947 that workers' organisations made any attempt to alter the *status quo*. Even then, however, they sought not equality, but a reduction in the differential by raising the female wage from 65% of the male rate to 90%. The claim was rejected by the Court, which observed that:

> "It appears to us, for example, that one result would be to increase substantially the spending power of an important section of the community without the prospect of a commensurate increase in the production of consumer goods and services. Further we are inclined to the view that the main issue is fraught with such grave social and economic consequences that it is more a matter for the direct consideration of the legislature"[31].

For the next nine years the Court resisted union demands for equal pay, although it did make small concessions in 1949 and 1951. Even action on the international front by the ILO in requesting ratification of its equal pay conventions did not sway the Arbitration Court from its conviction that the introduction of equal pay would be ". . . a drastic departure from past and present industrial practice in this Dominion" and that any action on the matter was the responsibility of the Government.

Equal Pay in the State Service

By the early 1950s both the Government Service Tribunal and the Public Service Commission were subject to increasing pressure to introduce equal pay for state employees. Both bodies recognised the justice of the claim, but were not prepared to set a precedent which they believed would have serious economic effects. However, the first major change occurred in March 1957, when the Prime Minister announced the proposed establishment of a committee to investigate the issue of equal pay for women. But the committee never materialised. In the general election of late 1957, the Labour Party gained office, and began to implement its undertaking to introduce equal pay for the government services. By October, 1959, the Labour Government had established its own Equal Pay Implementation Committee, and following a report in July 1960, legislation entitled the Government Service Equal Pay Act 1960 was introduced. By 1965, the principle of equal pay had been extended to all Government employees[32].

The government was not, however, prepared to extend equal pay beyond this. No attempt was made to establish equal pay in the private sector. The lead provided was considered sufficient. Yet no dramatic change in the private sector took place. A study of awards and industrial agreements in force in 1966 showed that 415 applied to industries or occupations customarily employing members of one sex only. Of the remaining 301, only 8 had specific provisions for equal pay, while a further 18 specified a rate for a job irrespective of sex. Another 58 awards and industrial agreements contained partial provision for equal pay in limited circumstances[33].

The Commission of Inquiry into Equal Pay

Throughout the 1960s interest in equal pay in New Zealand grew. Pressure groups continually raised the question, but neither the Government nor the Court of Arbitration was prepared to take the responsibility of initiating any further change. Both argued that they had already done as much as possible, and that further action was outside their jurisdiction. However in January 1971, the Advisory Council on the Employment of Women, with the support of the Industrial Advisory Council, finally succeeded in its attempt to have the Government establish a Commission of Inquiry into Equal Pay[34]. This Commission held its first sitting in January 1971, and tabled its report to Parliament in September 1971.

The terms of reference of the Commission were to enquire into and report on how best to give effect in New Zealand to the principle of equal pay for male and female employees and in particular to consider the following matters: (1) a suitable formula for this purpose, having regard, *inter alia*, to the provisions of the Equal Remuneration Convention, 1951 (No. 100), of the ILO; (2) the most desirable means of giving effect to the principle; (3) the extent to which existing provisions (statutory or other) inhibit its application, any justification for such provisions, and the means of removing unjustified provisions; (4) the timing of the introduction of equal pay, the machinery for introducing equal pay, and the economic implications of the timing and the machinery; (5) the economic and social implications for the nation and for specific groups of the introduction of equal pay; and (6) any associated matters that it considered relevant.

The New Zealand Employers' Federation and the New Zealand Manufacturers' Federation argued before the Commission that equal pay should be implemented according to the same principles as established in the 1969 Equal Pay Case in Australia. (This judgement provided that equal pay would not apply "where the work in question is essentially or usually performed by females, but is work upon which a male employee may also be employed"). The Commission, however, did not think that this group of workers could be "swept under the carpet" and left to have its position clarified and determined by market forces. It took the view that the task set was not to replace the existing basis of wage determination, but to ensure that whatever other considerations were relevant, the sex of the worker would not be taken into account in fixing rates of pay. Further, it suggested the following criteria for determining whether any element of discrimination based on sex entered into the fixing of remuneration: (1) the extent to which the work called for the same or broadly similar degrees of skill, effort and responsibility; (2) how far the conditions in which the work was performed was the same or broadly similar; and (3) the rate that was paid to a male employee for the work.

There was almost complete agreement among those making submissions that equal pay should be introduced by legislation, and not through the various wage determination authorities, so that the rights and obligations of all concerned could be clearly specified. Progress toward equal pay was felt to have been slow and uncertain in New Zealand, and it was argued that without legislative direction, this pattern would continue. This belief was reinforced by the failure to achieve a substantial flow-on effect in the private sector after the introduction of equal pay in the State Services.

The Commission reported that the introduction of equal pay in the form of an Act of Parliament would have important timing implications. Particularly important would be the avoidance of the possible dislocation in the labour market which could accompany the introduction of equal pay at different times in different industries. The Commission recognised that adequate time should be provided for a smooth transition from female to male rates of pay, and it suggested that equal pay be introduced in five equal annual steps, so that all industries would be able to adjust to the new levels of female wages without index difficulty.

In the Report, special attention was given to the machinery for introducing and enforcing equal pay. The question of establishing a new body or bodies was dismissed as the existing agencies were considered by most Commissioners suitable for implementing the legislation. A minority of members suggested that New Zealand should adopt the legislative and administrative patterns of some other countries, notably the UK, USA and Australia. However, in the Australian instance, for example, the Commission majority argued that the complex set of procedures of Conciliation and Arbitration at Commonwealth and State levels had compounded the difficulties of introducing equal pay. The New Zealand system is a national one and, the Commission majority suggested, would best act as a structural support for an effective method of introducing equal pay. In order to ensure consistent and co-ordinated decisions, the Commission suggested that the Court of Arbitration have final authority in matters concerned with equal pay, even though this would mean encroachment on the jurisdiction of other wage fixing tribunals.

The workforce in New Zealand, as in many countries, includes a large number of workers whose rates of pay are not determined by any statutory or formalised procedures. Department of Labour estimates indicate that such workers constitute an important proportion of the workforce, possibly as high as 25%. Orders under the Minimum Wage Act provide an effective minimum rate of pay for some of these workers, but since vocations covered range from domestic workers to executive, supervisory and professional staff, the remuneration of those occupying the higher-paid posts would not be covered. In order to meet this problem, the Commission recommended that the equal pay legislation should be binding on all parties involved in the fixing of wages and salaries whether by "formal or informal procedures, by treaty, by contract of service, or unilateral decision". This clearly was in accord with the Commission's intention that "on full implementation it will be true in New Zealand that no contract of service shall provide in wording, spirit, or effect for a rate of remuneration based on a distinction between employees solely in terms of sex"[35].

The Commission's report was favourably received by the Government as "a balanced and realistic assessment of the issues"[36]. In a press release on 25 November, 1971, the Minister of Labour announced that the Government would introduce an Equal Pay Bill in 1972 which would follow the broad recommendations of the Commission of Inquiry. The Bill was introduced into Parliament on 29 August, 1972, and, with some modification, adopted the recommendations of the Report. The definition of equal pay in the Act was the same as that suggested by the Commission, and the criteria to be applied were only slightly different from those proposed. The Court of Arbitration was given the authority to amend any wage determination made between parties that did not conform to the new legislation, and provision was made to ensure that every award or associated instrument in force on 1 April, 1978, must provide for equal pay[37].

Equal Opportunity

The New Zealand Act is designed to cover all workers whether on award wages or not, and thus avoids the Australian problem in which equal pay has been introduced through the conciliation and arbitration system and consequently confined to award wages. Other problems are, however, apparent. The differential between male and female average rates (Table XXV) reflects more than inequality of job rates. Equally important is the number of persons in each occupational category. Most women withdraw, if only temporarily, from the workforce. In doing so they miss opportunities for promotion, so that a greater proportion of women than of men are found in positions

**Table XXV. New Zealand: Average Weekly Award Wage Male and Female Compared
1930 to 1967(NZ$)***

Year	Female weekly award	Male weekly award	Female as % of male weekly award
1930	5·21	8·98	58·0
1940	5·87	9·99	58·7
1950	10·60	15·85	66·9
1960	17·49	25·97	67·3
1967	22·90	32·62	70·2

(Source: Report on Prices, Wages and Labour, 1967).
*Later figures not available.

carrying lower rates of pay. Similarly relative lack of education and differences in physique are thought likely to help suppress the average female wage.

The introduction of equal pay in the New Zealand Public Service resulted in a rise in the average rate of female pay (expressed as a percentage of the average male rate) from 67% in 1960 to 73½% in 1965. However, by 1970 the average female wage had fallen back to only 71%[38]. This suggests that, although the introduction of equal pay aids in the reduction of the differential between male and female earnings, it cannot eliminate it entirely. This is because the difference reflects something more than unequal pay for equal work. The Commission of Inquiry recognised this and suggested that the major difficulties in implementing equal pay would be associated with the problem of changing the attitudes, habits and customary procedures which had emerged under various social climates. Despite progress, however, it probably remains true that "No report of a commission, or change in legislation, or change in wage fixing procedures, can do more than marginally accelerate the change in settled public opinion and attitudes upon which effective social reform depends"[39].

References
*This chapter has grown out of an article entitled Equal Pay for Women in Australia, by J. P. Nieuwenhuysen, in the *International Journal of Social Economics*, Vol. 1 No. 1, 1974.
  1. ABS, *The Labour Force* Nov., 1973. (In 1973, what used to be known as the Commonwealth Bureau of Census and Statistics—CBCS as referred to elsewhere—became the Australian Bureau of Statistics—the ABS).
  2. This point is noted in the 1974 *Committee of Inquiry into Labour Market Training Report*, Government Printer, Canberra, 1974, p. 9. The Report (p. 9) also notes that Treasury projections indicate that the participation rates of women in the workforce are expected to rise in the next decade, while that of men will fall. Of another kind are the studies recently made of the short term behaviour of female labour force participation rates. One of these, by Gregory, R. G., and Sheehan, P. J. found that there seemed to be an important "discouraged worker" effect, i.e. that at times of high unemployment, many women were sufficiently discouraged to withdraw from the workforce. See "The Cyclical Sensitivity of Labour Force Participation Rates", *Australian Economic Review*, 2, 1973.
  3. See *Women in the Workforce: Changing Horizons* Bulletin No. 9, Australian Department of Labour and National Service, October 1970, p. 12, and also Martin, J. and Richmond, C., "Working Women in Australia" in *Anatomy of Australia*, Melbourne: Sun Books, 1968, pp. 196-200. But the most comprehensive document is *The Role of Women in the Economy*, Department of Labour, 1974.

4. CBCS, *Demography* 1969 and 1970, Bulletin No. 86, Table No. 251, *Crude Birth Rates: States and Territories*, 1901 to 1970, p. 263.
5. *Female Unemployment in Four Urban Centres*, Labour Market Studies, No. 3, Australian Department of Labour and National Service, 1970, pp. 1-2.
6. A later study, by Mr. P. B. Beaumont, pointed out that in August 1973, the total unemployment rates and unemployment rates for women, respectively, were 2·2 and 2·7% in metropolitan areas, and 2·2 and 3·5% in non-metropolitan areas. See Beaumont, P. B., "The Non-Metropolitan Unemployment Position of Women in Australia", *Journal of Industrial Relations*, June 1974, p. 139.
7. A recent study by the Department of Labour deals at length with the details of part-time work. See *Part-Time Employment*, Government Printer, 1974.
8. *Equal Pay: Some Aspects of Australian and Overseas Experience*, Australian Department of Labour and National Service, 3rd edition, 1968, p. 3.
9. *ibid*, p. 12.
10. *ibid*, p. 19.
11. The large number of relevant classifications are set out in *Equal Pay*, supplement, 1972, Australian Department of Labour and National Service, August 1972.
12. National Wage and Equal Pay Cases 1972, Judgement, Sydney, 15 December 1972.
13. Equal Pay Cases Judgement, 19 June 1969.
14. This legislation is described in *Equal Pay: Some Aspects of Australian and Overseas Experience*, *op. cit.*, p. 50.
15. After the Commission had reserved judgement in the case, there was a change of Government, and the Commission received an application (which it granted) to re-list the matters so as to hear counsel for the Commonwealth.
16. House of Representatives, October 18, 1962. Quoted from P. Riach, "Equal Pay and Equal Opportunity", *Journal of Industrial Relations*, July 1969, 11(2), pp. 99-110.
17. These issues are discussed in Nieuwenhuysen, J. P., "The National Wage Case, 1974", *Journal of Industrial Relations*, September 1974.
18. *Journal of Industrial Relations*, July 1969, *op. cit.*, p. 107.
19. Phelps Brown, E. H., "Industrial Relations and the Law", *Three Banks Review*, March 1971, No. 89, p. 26.
20. Blandy R., "Equal Pay in Australia?", *Journal of Industrial Relations*, April 1963, 5(1), pp. 13-28.
21. *The Role of Women in the Economy*, *op. cit.*, p. 173.
22. *ibid*, p. 174.
23. Department of Statistics, *Monthly Abstract of Statistics*, April 1974.
24. *Equal Pay in New Zealand*. Report of the Commission of Inquiry, Wellington, September 1971.
25. Gilson, M., "Women in Employment" in John Forster (ed.), *Social Process in New Zealand*, Longman, 1969, pp. 183-97.
26. Timms, E., "The Social Implications of Equal Pay" in *Proceedings of a Seminar on Equal Pay for Equal Work*, Industrial Relations Centre, Victoria University of Wellington, pp. 115-31.
27. Commission of Inquiry, *op. cit.*, p. 26.
28. Department of Statistics, *New Zealand Official Year Book*.
29. Szakats, A., "Recent Developments in New Zealand Industrial Relations", *Journal of Industrial Relations*, December 1972, p. 384.
30. The Aircrew Industrial Tribunal Act, 1971.
31. As quoted in Atkinson, L. A., "The History and Implementation of Equal Pay in the New Zealand State Services, pp. 1-17 of *Proceedings of a Seminar on Equal Pay for Equal Work*, *op. cit.* Industrial Relations Centre, Victoria, University of Wellington, October 12-14, 1970, p. 5.
32. *Ibid*, p. 15.
33. *Equal Pay: Some Aspects of Australian and Overseas Practice*, *op. cit.*, p. 68.
34. *Equal Pay in New Zealand*. Report of the Commission of Inquiry, *op. cit.*, Wellington, 1971.
35. *Ibid*, p. 21.
36. *Equal Pay*, Department of Labour and National Service, *op. cit.*, p. 69.
37. *Ibid*, p. 71.
38. Rose, W. D., "Economic Aspects of Equal Pay", in the *Seminar on Equal Pay*, *op. cit.*, pp. 73-4.
39. Atkinson, L. A., *op. cit.*, p. 17.

Gleichberechtigung—The German Experience

by J. T. Addison

This study attempts to document and to comment upon the progress made toward the achievement of equal pay for women within the German Federal Republic. Whilst a certain emphasis must be placed upon equal pay legislation and application together with the facts of male/female earnings disparity an examination of the rôle played by females within the work-force is absolutely central to the equal pay theme. Accordingly, the study is in three principal sections. The first section examines the nature of female employment in terms of its activity, social structure, industrial and occupational distribution, training and qualification profiles. The second section outlines the appropriate legal framework and jurisprudence and reviews the status of equal pay in practice within collective agreements. The final section presents an empirical over-view of the relative earnings of females, prefaced by a critical theoretical commentary.

I. THE NATURE OF FEMALE EMPLOYMENT

Social Composition

The German Mikrozensus of April 1969 revealed that females constituted 36·5% of all economically active persons; that is, of a total labour force of 26,382,000 some 9,631,000 were females[1]. The corresponding female share in April 1970 was 35·8%. Indeed, there has been a certain stagnation in female activity over the period 1960-71. This phenomenon is indicated in Table I. The observed stagnation corresponds to an actual decline in the absolute number of gainfully employed females over the period in question[2]. Despite this stagnation, there have, nevertheless, occurred pronounced changes in the social composition of the female labour force. Firstly, there has been a significant increase in the average age of gainfully employed females. This process is documented in Table II which presents female activity rates by age group over the period 1961-70. The material shown indicates the dramatic decline in the activity rates of the 15-19 age group; the declining activity of intermediate age groups; and a continuing growth in activity of the gainfully employed aged between 40-60 years[3]. The reduced activity of the former groups is to be explained by an increased demand for general and vocational schooling and that of the 60 + age group to be attributed to earlier retirement possibilities. Secondly, and corresponding to this changing age profile, there has been a dramatic change in the family status of gainfully employed

Table I.   Aspects of Female Activity, 1960-71. Yearly Average Estimates

Year	Female employment Total civilian employment (%)	Female labour force* Female population (%)	Female labour force Female population Aged 15—64 (%)
1960	37·8	33·6	49·3
1961	37·5	33·3	49·3
1962	37·5	33·0	49·4
1963	37·0	32·4	48·9
1964	37·0	32·2	49·0
1965	36·9	31·9	49·0
1966	36·8	31·5	48·6
1967	36·5	30·3	47·3
1968	36·3	30·0	47·1
1969	36·3	30·1	47·6
1970	36·2	30·6	48·6
1971	36·2	30·4	48·5

*Economically active females (employed plus unemployed).
Source: *Labour Force Statistics* 1960-71, Paris, OECD, 1973.

Table II.   Female Activity Rates* by Age Group, 1961-71 (%)

Age Group	1961	1963	1965	1966	1967	1970
15—19	73·7	67·1	68·0	65·6	61·6	53·6
20—24	75·9	72·9	70·4	69·8	68·7	69·8
25—29	52·8	52·3	51·4	50·1	49·4	51·1
30—34	44·1	44·3	43·4	43·2	41·9	45·4
35—39	45·1	44·8	45·4	44·0	43·3	46·2
40—44	45·2	46·6	48·3	48·8	47·3	48·4
45—49	41·5	44·6	46·3	47·4	46·7	48·9
50—54	38·1	40·4	41·1	42·6	42·3	44·8
55—59	33·3	34·3	36·3	36·3	36·4	37·2
60—64	21·4	23·2	23·3	24·1	23·6	22·5
65 and above	8·1	8·1	7·8	7·8	7·9	6·5
All Groups	41·1	40·2	39·8	39·3	38·3	38·0

*Share of gainfully employed females in the female resident population per age group.
Source: Bericht der Bundesregierung über die Massnahmen zur Verbesserung der Situation
der Frau: Printed Matter VI/3698, Bonn, 1972, p. 36.

females. Whereas the proportions of widowed, separated and married females in gainful employment have increased, the share of the single female has sharply declined. This movement is charted in Table III, for the period 1950-70.

Not only has the participation rate of married females risen in general since 1950

**Table III. Distribution of Gainfully Employed Females by
Marital Status, 1950-70**

Year	Single (%)	Married (%)	Marital Status Widowed/ Separated (%)
1950	53·0	36·2	9·8
1961	44·0	46·2	9·8
1968	34·0	53·2	12·0
1970	30·0	57·3	12·0

Sources: 1950–68—Frauenkonferenz der I.G. Metall 24th–25th September 1970,
Frauenerwerbsarbeit, Realitäten-Konsequenzen, Dortmund, 1971, p. 13.
1970—*Statistisches Jahrbuch der BRD,* 1971, p. 128.

but also by each marriage interval and age group[4]. Indeed, the Federal Statistical
Office predicts that the absolute number of married females within the labour force
will increase by 8·9% over the period 1975-85. The size of the female labour force is,
however, predicted to increase by only 311,000 units, or 3·3%, as a result of declining
numbers of economically active single females (— 3·5%) and separated/widowed
females (— 6·2%). Today, over 50% of married females aged under 25 are gainfully
employed. Thereafter, the participation rate of married females declines until the
35-45 age group at which point the downward trend is reversed only to be re-established
in the interval 50-plus years[5].

Thirdly, and corresponding to the pronounced upward shift in the employment
activity of married females, there has been an appreciable increase in the number of
gainfully employed females with dependent children. Whilst the participation rate of
mothers with children under the age of 3 years has remained more or less constant at
the 27% level, the number of working mothers with children under 14 years has
doubled since 1950. Although the participation rate of childless married females
aged 40 years and less (81%) is considerably higher than that of, say, married females
whose youngest child is aged between 3-6 years (33%)[6] it is nevertheless the case
that the absolute number of gainfully employed married women without children has
increased by only 21% over the period 1950-70 whilst the corresponding increase in
gainfully employed married females with children under the age of 14 years stands at
118%[7].

Finally, with the increase in the share of married females and working mothers in
the labour force, there has been a corresponding increase in part-time employment.
Between 1961 and 1970 the number of gainfully employed females with a working
week of between 1 and 24 hours increased by 83%[8]. This trend would appear to
have been maintained in both the secondary and tertiary sectors of the economy.
Today, 27% of gainfully employed females work less than a standard (40 hour) week
as opposed to only 4% of males[9].

Employment Structure

In 1971 the percentage distribution of economically active females within the primary, secondary and tertiary sectors was 12·1%, 33·1% and 44·8%, respectively[10]. Over the period 1964-71 the number of gainfully employed females within the three sectors has declined by — 0·3%. Whereas female employment within the tertiary sector rose by 6·0% over the period in question, employment falls of — 30·0% and — 3·1% were registered in the primary and secondary sectors, respectively[11].

The distribution of gainfully employed females by economic branch is recorded in Table IV, which uses 1969 Mikrozensus data. Clearly, the bulk of females (84·2%) find employment within manufacturing industry, services, trade and agriculture. Females are over-represented within 3 main sectors, namely agriculture, trade and services. Over the period 1961-71 female employment across all the branches shown in Table IV has modestly declined by 2·6%. The principal increases in employment have been centred on services (70·8%), community and social services (39·4%), finance and insurance (37·5%) and construction (37·5%). The principal downward movements have occurred within agriculture (— 38·1%) and activities not adequately defined (— 32·6%)[12]. A peculiarity of female employment within the Federal Republic is the significant proportion of gainfully employed females either self-employed or engaged as unpaid family workers. In 1971, of the 9,557,000 gainfully employed females some 1,942,000, or 20·3%, fell within these categories. Consequently,

Table IV. Total and Female Civilian Employment by Economic Sector, April 1969

Sector	Total employment (000)	Female employment Absolute (000)	%
Agriculture, forestry, hunting and fishing	2,577	1,370	53·2 (14·4)*
Energy, water supply and mining	571	40	7·0 (0·4)
Manufacturing industry (excluding construction)	10,029	2,905	29·0 (30·5)
Construction	2,077	116	5·6 (1·2)
Trade (wholesale and retail)	3,129	1,655	52·9 (17·4)
Transport and communication	1,435	235	16·4 (2·5)
Finance and insurance	621	275	44·2 (2·9)
Services (not elsewhere specified)	3,493	2,090	59·8 (21·9)
Activities not adequately defined and private households	444	311	70·0 (3·3)
Community and social services	1,727	512	29·6 (5·4)
Without information	64	26	40·3 (0·3)
	26,169	9,534	36·4 (100)

*Figures in parenthesis indicate female sectoral employment as a percentage of total female employment.
Source: Mikrozensus, April 1969. *Statistisches Jahrbuch der BRD*, 1970.

when we examine the distribution of *employees in employment* by economic branch then a rather different picture from that depicted in Table IV emerges. In 1967, for example, only 1·2% of such females were employed within the primary sector. The corresponding values within the secondary and tertiary sectors were 39·2% and 59·6%, respectively. 82% of female employees in employment were concentrated within 3 branches: manufacturing industry (37·6%), services (22·9%) and trade (22·0%). Females were over-represented in the latter two branches—63·9% and 54·0% of all employed workers in services and trade, respectively, were females[13]. Indeed, we find females concentrated in those very sectors which have recorded the greatest increase in recorded vacancies over the period 1962-70[14].

The breakdown of female civilian employment by broad occupational status is indicated in Table V, which again uses 1969 Mikrozensus data. It will be observed that females are heavily over-represented within the unpaid family worker classification and heavily under-represented within civil service occupations. Over the period 1960-71 the absolute numbers of self-employed females and unpaid female family workers have declined by — 26·2% and — 53·8%, respectively. Female civil servants and white collar, or salaried, employees have increased in number by 49·6% and 29·2%, respectively, whilst the female industrial or manual worker total has declined by — 11·4%[15]. The centre of gravity of female employment has evidently shifted to the white collar sector. In 1950, for example, only 19·0% of all female employees in employment were salaried staffs. By 1970 this figure had risen to 35·0%. The share of industrial workers on the other hand declined from 40·2% to 36·2% over the period in question[16].

The not uncharacteristic facet of female employment within the Federal Republic is the concentration of females within a limited number of economic sectors and functions. In manufacturing industry, where 3/5 of female industrial workers and 1/5 of female salaried staffs find employment, females are principally located in 3 industrial

Table V. Total and Female Civilian Employment by Professional Status, April 1969

		Female employment	
Status	Total employment (000)	Absolute (000)	%
Employers and self-employed	2,857	586	20·5 (6·1)*
Unpaid family workers	1,942	1,630	83·9 (17·1)
Civil Servants	1,427	215	15·1 (2·3)
Salaried employees	7,540	3,683	48·9 (38·6)
Wage earners	12,403	3,419	27·6 (35·9)
	26,169	9,533	36·4 (100)

*Figures in parenthesis indicate the percentage of total female civilian employment within each professional status category.
Source: Mikrozensus, April 1969. *Statistisches Jahrbuch der BRD*, 1970.

Table VI. Gainfully Employed Females within Manufacturing Industry, by Selected Industry Groups*

1. Manual/Industrial Workers

Industry Group	All manual workers		Skilled workers		Other workers		Apprentices	
	Males & Females	Females	Males & Females	Females	Males & Females	Females	Males & Females	Females
Clothing	319,135	280,169(88)†	153,305	131,972(86)	149,835	130,057(88)	15,995	15,140(94)
Tobacco	23,211	15,673(68)	4,997	2,392(47)	18,186	13,275(72)	28	6(21)
Textiles	401,223	233,521(58)	127,184	57,370(45)	269,766	174,455(64)	4,273	1,696(39)
Musical instruments	47,180	25,211(53)	14,834	3,369(22)	31,018	21,538(69)	1,328	304(22)
Sport, leisure & jewellery								
Paper & associated products	108,488	52,666(50)	22,523	3,194(14)	84,670	49,418(58)	1,295	54(4)
Ceramics	64,536	30,452(46)	13,742	2,301(16)	50,030	28,076(57)	764	75(9)
Precision engineering, optics & watch making	126,077	56,166(45)	38,311	2,377(6)	81,383	53,656(66)	6,383	133(2·5)
Electrical engineering	784,244	334,450(43)	209,336	4,683(2)	536,487	329,249(61)	38,421	518(1)
Plastics & synthetics	133,632	51,785(39)	29,852	2,302(0·9)	101,254	49,460(49)	2,526	23(0·9)

2. Salaried Workers

Industry Group	All salaried workers		Commercial and administration employees		Technical employees		Commercial apprentices	
	Males & Females	Females	Males & Females	Females	Males & Females	Females	Males & Females	Females
Clothing	14,558	5,136(42)†	8,156	4,356(51)	5,353	367(6)	749	413(55)
Tobacco	7,253	2,435(33)	5,325	2,121(39)	1,739	195(11)	189	119(12)
Textiles	95,707	37,039(39)	53,209	28,004(52)	35,971	4,987(13)	6,527	4,048(62)
Musical instruments, sport, leisure and jewellery	12,083	5,821(48)	7,220	4,386(60)	3,908	796(20)	955	639(66)
Paper and associated products	28,061	10,844(38)	18,821	9,334(49)	7,627	670(8)	1,613	840(52)
Ceramics	14,558	5,136(35)	8,456	4,356(51)	5,353	367(6)	749	413(55)
Precision engineering, optics and watches	44,116	16,233(36)	21,451	12,655(58)	20,383	2,263(11)	2,282	1,315(57)
Electrical engineering	325,303	103,362(31)	149,533	81,940(54)	163,902	15,586(9)	11,868	5,836(49)
Plastics and synthetics	37,712	14,158(30)	22,396	11,917(53)	12,975	1,025(7)	2,341	1,216(51)

*Only those industries with high female employment.
†Figures in parenthesis indicate the percentage employment share of females.
Source: *Arbeits-und Sozialstatistische Mitteilungen,* 5/1972, p. 30.

groups. These are the consumer goods sector, food and luxuries and the capital goods sector in which females constitute 50%, 36% and 24%, respectively, of the total number of employees[17]. Within these industry groups females chiefly find employ-

Table VII. The Distribution of Female Employees in Employment by Selected Occupational Groups*, 1971

Occupational Group	Employees in employment	
	Males	Females
Other ceramic workers	5,900	8,400(59%)†
Book-binders	15,900	23,900(60)
Box and carton makers	4,600	13,700(75)
Other paper product makers	12,500	16,000(56)
Printing assistants	11,800	23,400(66)
Spinners, preparatory workers	24,400	42,200(64)
Knitters, rope makers	13,300	24,500(65)
Tailors	40,900	108,900(73)
Shoe makers	26,100	45,700(64)
Cooks	32,500	44,300(58)
Other metal-fabrication workers	7,400	13,800(65)
Electrical machinery builders	21,200	24,200(53)
Other electrical machinery and apparatus builders	18,300	72,100(80)
Hairdressers	32,200	118,400(79)
Welfare and social workers	10,300	25,800(73)
Hospital sisters and nurses	15,700	162,800(91)
Masseurs, hospital therapists	2,400	6,500(73)
Other treatment therapists	6,100	22,200(78)
Technical, professional and work teachers	23,300	23,900(51)
Waiters and stewards	38,800	76,900(66)
Other hotel workers	7,100	18,800(73)
Room and domestic cleaners	6,500	367,000(98)
Laundry workers	13,200	96,600(88)
Wholesale and retail trade workers (marketing, purchasing and sales)	302,600	784,300(72)
Book sellers and publishing sales	7,100	7,900(53)
Telephonists	10,900	34,800(76)
Office professions (management, industrial and secretarial)	812,800	877,100(52)
Bookkeepers	176,700	206,900(55)
Punched card operators, machine servicing	9,000	24,400(73)
Checkers and sorters	58,300	74,700(56)
Packing and despatch workers	125,400	191,300(60)

*Occupational groups with a female employment share of 50% and more.
†Figures in parenthesis indicate the female employment share.
Source: *Materialien aus der Arbeitsmarkt—und Berufsforschung*, MAT AB, 13/1972.

ment either in industries with a traditionally high female labour force (such as textiles and clothing) or in industries with a high rate of economic growth and a rising employ-ment trend (such as electrical engineering, precision engineering and optics together with synthetics). Table VI indicates this concentration of female salaried and industrial workers within a limited range of manufacturing industry. In parenthesis, it should be observed that in overall terms females constitute 30·1% of all employees in employ-ment within manufacturing industry and 28·3% of all industrial or manual employees in employment[18].

Much the same tendency towards high female density in a narrow range of economic branches is to be found within the trade (wholesale and retail) and service sectors. In retail trade no less than 61% of all employees in employment are females. In the private service sector females are principally located in health services, hairdressing, hotels, laundry and cleansing services. In the above branches females constitute 71%, 71%, 58% and 74%, respectively, of all employees in employment[19].

The sex orientation of certain branches of industry, trade and service sectors observed earlier appears in sharper relief when one examines the distribution of females by broad occupational spheres or Berufsbereiche[20]. This is not altogether surprising since the Berufsbereiche are analogous to the eight principal sectors of economic activity. To illustrate the clustering of female employees within particular elements of these occupational spheres we have somewhat arbitrarily selected those occupations in which females constitute 50% or more of all employees in employment, Table VII indicates 31 such occupations[21]. The clear impression of sex-oriented professions is reinforced when one examines the league-table of occupations ordered by the absolute number of female employees.

The Qualification Structure
The performance group (Leistungsgruppen) classification system adopted by the Federal Statistical Office permits us to very crudely sketch the skill structure of female industrial and salaried employees[22].

Performance groups 1, 2 and 3, in the manual workers context, broadly correspond to skilled, semi-skilled and unskilled occupational groups. The distribution of male and female industrial workers by performance group, over the period 1951-66, is detailed in Table VIII. Not only is there a marked discrepancy between the skill profiles of males and females but there has been little or no improvement in the degree of female skill acquisition over the period in question. Moreover, the skill structure of female workers would appear to be inversely associated with age. Of those females aged under 30 years some 7·4% occupy performance group 1 and 53·4% performance group 2. The corresponding values for females aged 45 years and above are 5·3%—5·4% and 46·4%—41·5%, respectively[23]. This so-called "down-grading" process is considered subsequently.

Over the period 1966-71 there has, however, been a modest improvement in the proportion of skilled females within those branches of the consumer goods and

Table VIII. Distribution of Manual Workers in Industry by Wage Group and Sex

Year	Sex	% by Performance Group 1	2	3	Total (%)
1951*	Males	58	25	17	100
	Females	12	46	42	100
1957*	Males	56	29	15	100
	Females	5	47	48	100
1962	Males	56	32	12	100
	Females	5	50	45	100
1966	Males	57	32	11	100
	Females	6	49	45	100

*Excluding Saarland and West Berlin.
Source: Statistisches Bundesamt, *Wirtschaft und Statistik*, Vol. 3, 1969, p. 143.

capital goods sectors having a high female employment share, and an opposite move-ment of equally modest dimension in the food and luxuries sector[24]. A more significant operation is, however, the very high proportion of females populating semi-skilled and unskilled occupations within these sectors. The consumer goods sector is dominated by semi-skilled female groups—of all female workers employed within the textile and clothing industries 64·0% and 70·4%, respectively, are semi-skilled. Female employment within capital goods and food and luxuries sectors on the other hand is typically unskilled—59·2% and 74·4% of all females within the respective sectors are classified as unskilled[25].

In the case of female salaried employees it is again observed that females are concentrated within the lower performance grades, namely Leistungsgruppen IV and V of the five element salary structure. The position is identified in Table IX, which distinguishes between commercial and technical salaried staffs. It can be seen that at the end of 1966 some 77·0% of male commercial employees and 85·0% of male technical employees were classified as occupying skilled performance groups I-III ("experts" and higher). The corresponding female proportions were 35·0% and 40·0%, respectively. Despite the obvious disparities in skill acquisition it is clear that there has been a certain improvement in the proportion of skilled females in both categories. Against this has to be set the marked under-representation of females within the technical employee group as a whole—only 10% of such employees are female as compared to 50% of commercial employees[26]. Again, there is some evidence to suggest a "down-grading" process at work within the older age groups. Females appear principally to achieve higher performance grading between the ages of 30 and 45. Thereafter, an inverse association between age and skill level may be discerned. There is the suggestion that those females who have attained skilled positions accept re-employment, after a break in the continuity of employment, in lesser skilled occupations[27].

Table IX. The Qualification Structure of Salaried Employees, Selected Groups, 1951-66, by Sex

Performance Group	Commercial employees								Technical employees							
	Males (%)				Females (%)				Males (%)				Females (%)			
	1951	1957	1962	1966	1951	1957	1962	1966	1951	1957	1962	1966	1951	1957	1962	1966
I	3·7	4·6	4·7	6·0	0·2	0·2	0·2	1·0	6·0	4·9	4·9	5·0	0·6	0·5	0·4	1·0
II	15·6	19·6	20·5	22·0	2·6	2·8	2·9	4·0	25·1	28·7	31·6	29·0	9·3	5·3	4·6	5·0
III	37·4	45·0	46·9	49·0	18·2	22·1	23·6	30·0	39·2	47·6	46·5	51·0	23·8	26·9	28·6	34·0
I-III	56·7	69·2	72·1	77·0	21·0	25·1	26·7	35·0	70·3	81·2	83·0	85·0	33·7	32·7	33·6	40·0
IV	37·3	26·8	24·0	20·0	61·4	59·7	59·2	55·0	26·5	17·2	15·7	14·0	52·6	53·2	54·2	52·0
V	6·0	4·0	3·9	3·0	17·6	15·2	14·1	10·0	3·2	1·6	1·3	1·0	13·7	14·1	12·2	8·0
Total	100	100	100	100	100	100	100	100	100	100	100	100	100	100	100	100

Sources: (1951, 1957)—*Statistik der BRD*, Vol. 246, Book 2, p. 9 *et seq.*
(1962)—Statistisches Bundesamt, *Gehalts-und Lohnstrukturerhebung*, Technical Series II, Preise, Löhne, Wirtschaftsrechnungen, Series 17, p. 7.
(1966)—Statistisches Bundesamt, *Wirtschaft und Statistik*, Book 6, 1969, p. 309 *et seq.*

Training

Material from the 1964 Mikrozensus reveals that whereas only 29·9% of gainfully employed males were without a completed professional training no less than 54% of females were within this category. The training status of male and female employed persons is examined in Table X.

The proportions of males and females having received vocational training within the school system appears similar, yet when this particular training form is broken down by school-type marked differences emerge between the two sexes. Whilst the shares of boys and girls within the primary and continuation school sectors are more or less equal, females are significantly under-represented within grammar school and secondary school sectors. In 1969/70, for example, females constituted 44% of all secondary pupils and 39% of matriculated pupils (Abiturienten). This position has only modestly improved over the period 1961-70[28]. Females are heavily under-represented in the intake of technological and engineering schools, where they respectively account for only 10% and 20% of all students. Moreover, only 24% of all university students are female[29]. In this latter context, not only is the female share low but it is also highly subject-specific; that is, females dominate the teaching (to include languages) and pharmacy areas[30]. Correspondingly, we observe a considerable over-representation of females within teacher-training establishments where they constitute more than 60% of the total intake[31]. Females are again over-represented in continuation and vocational/trade schools where they opt for educational courses of limited time duration and hence of limited job scope.

Turning to the subject of business or industrial training, 31·5% of all employed females had, in 1964, received a professional training in industry via apprenticeship and trainee schemes (Table X). This share has more than doubled over the period 1950-66, although clearly there still remain marked differences between males and females. Over the period 1950-66 the number of female apprentices and trainees increased by 120·1% and 43·1% respectively. The corresponding male increases were

Table X.   Professional Training of Employees in Employment, by Sex, 1964

Training Status	Sex	
	Males (%)	Females (%)
Without professional training*	29·9	54·1
Business training†	55·9	31·5
School vocational training‡	14·2	14·4
	100	100

Notes: *Factory on-the-job training alone.
        †Apprenticeship and trainee schemes.
        ‡Vocational schools, technological schools, engineering schools, universities.
Source: *Gewerkschaftliche Monatshefts*, 11/72, p. 705.

18·8% and 63·9%, respectively. However, it is to be noted that females dominate the lower skill training areas: females constitute 92% of all trainees but only 35% of all apprentices[32]. Moreover, female apprentices and trainees are concentrated within a narrow range of professional spheres (Berufsbereiche): in 1969 almost 70% of females were occupied within distribution, administration and planning[33]. In less aggregated terms, we find that 88·7% of females were at this time concentrated within 14 of the 559 recognised trainee and apprenticeship professional groups[34]. Female apprentices appear to be principally engaged in domestic economy, health and nursing professions. Female trainees, on the other hand, dominate the textile, food and luxury, trade, cleansing, administration and office professional groups[35].

Finally, in the context of further professional training or occupational improvement it is again the case that females are under-represented. Of the 50,132 persons receiving such job-enrichment training at the end of 1969, only 20% were females[36]. This share has shown little improvement over recent years despite the new law on occupational improvement (Arbeitsförderungsgesetz) of June 1969 and to which the above figures relate. Females comprised 14·1% of those receiving intra-occupational improvement training, 22·0% of those undergoing re-training, and 37·5% of those receiving on-the-job training.

II. THE EQUAL PAY ISSUE

Equal Pay Legislation

The constitution of the Federal Republic establishes the equality of men and women. Specifically, Article 3 of the Basic Law (Grundgesetz) of 8th May 1949 states that "Men and women have equal rights" and that "Nobody may be placed either at an advantage or at a disadvantage because of his or her sex" (sections 2 and 3). Indeed, such rights had been established in the constitutions of several Länder even before 1949[37]. The principle of prohibiting discrimination again finds expression in the law on the organisation of companies of 11th October 1952, in the new law on the organisation of companies which came into effect on 19th January 1972, and in that of 5th August 1955 on staff representation. Doctrine and jurisprudence—in particular the decisions of the Federal Labour Tribunal (Bundesarbeitsgericht)[38]—indicate that Article 3 of the Basic Law is a positive legal standard directly applicable to equality in respect of pay and equally binding upon State authorities and the signatories of collective agreements[39]. This results in the complete invalidity of all discriminatory clauses in collective agreements which could, ultimately entail the invalidity of all agreements.

However, the Government does not have the power to cancel a discriminatory agreement and no administrative checks are provided for within the above legislation. In Germany the responsibility for taking a case of job and/or wage discrimination before the labour courts rests with the individual. These courts exist at Federal and district (Land) level.

In addition to this "internal" legislation, two Conventions and one Recommendation[40] of the International Labour Organisation (ILO) relate to equal pay. The first Convention, namely No. 100, establishes "the principle of equal remuneration of men and women for work of equal value". Convention No. 111 extends this principle of equality to other terms and conditions of employment. Conventions Nos. 100 and 111 were ratified by the Federal Republic in 1956 and 1961, respectively.

Apart from the ILO, the Council of Europe's European Social Charter calls upon, in Article III (3), the signatories to recognise "the right of men and women workers to equal pay for work of equal value". Article 119, of the Treaty of Rome, backed-up by the Resolution of the Conference of Member States of 30th December 1961, is, however, more specific and different in character. Article 119 is very explicit in respect of "equal pay" but the situation is quite different in the context of "equal work". There is no precise definition of "equal work" apart from stating that pay for *the same work* at piece-rates shall be calculated "on the basis of the same unit of measurement" and that pay for work at time rates "shall be the same for the same job".

Clearly there is an important difference between the ILO and Treaty of Rome definitions of equal pay. In legal terms, however, jurisprudence exists in Germany which implies that:
(1) When men and women are paid by the hour, it is not admissible to pay a reduced rate to women on the basis of the lower yield of their work, because remuneration by the hour is based not on the result obtained but on the period of time during which the company commands the services of the worker.
(2) The notion of "equal work" cannot depend on the economic equivalence of the work done: it ought to be defined by the use of objective criteria for the scientific evaluation of jobs.
(3) Equality is, therefore, determined exclusively by the job done, independently of the results obtained and the sex of the worker.

Furthermore, this jurisprudence stipulates that no weight may be attached to the fact that the cost of female labour is higher—owing to the laws on the social protection of women.

Equal Pay in Practice
In discussing the progress made toward the implementation of equal pay for women it is useful to follow the conventional distinction between *direct* and *indirect* discrimination. The former relates to the express stipulation of distinct male and female rates within collective agreements. The latter concerns the practice of reserving certain categories almost exclusively for women and the systematic under-rating of female labour within categories ostensibly "common" to both sexes.

Despite the provisions of the Basic Law, reinforced by the Equal Rights Law of 18th June 1957, which forbade separate women's wage groupings in collective agreements, direct or overt discrimination existed within the Federal Republic until comparatively recently. The most significant movement towards the elimination of distinct sex rates would seem to have followed a statement by the Minister of Labour calling upon employers and unions to carry out the obligations assumed at Community level. This statement itself followed the Resolution of the Conference of Member States of 30th December 1961. The appeal, then, generally resulted in positive effects when it came to the renewal of collective agreements. By 1964 direct discrimination was alone practised within the agricultural sector of one Land (Hessen) and within one branch of manufacturing industry (leather goods). Distinct wage scales for male and female agricultural workers in Hessen were replaced in March 1965 by a system of wage rates related to work performed. Progress was less immediate in the leather industry[41] but this area of anomaly has since been removed.

A single classification of the wage and salary structure was theoretically arrived at between 1955 and 1964. Despite the progress made during this period it has proved possible for employers to avoid the provisions of an "equal wage" via *vertical* and *horizontal* discrimination. The former method has consisted in establishing job categories ostensibly open to both males and females but paying a lower rate than that established for unskilled labourers. These categories have to a greater or lesser extent been defined in such a way as to reserve them almost exclusively for women. The second, and well documented[42], method has consisted of laying down, besides the lowest paid job categories, certain "light work" grades (Leichtlohngruppen), which are again defined in such a way as to become essentially female domains. Low wages of this type lie approximately 25% below the wage rate of a skilled worker (Ecklohn); that is, they represent approximately 92% of the unskilled male worker rate. "Light work" grades, typically wage grades I and II in German collective agreements, are defined almost solely in terms of limited physical effort input (low calorie consumption) and lack of specialised knowledge. They applied to approximately 1·5 million female workers in 1970 and were significant in the chemicals, paper and pulp and food sectors[43].

The existence of "light work" groups has occasioned a lively controversy. The Employers' Federation (Bundesvereinigung der Deutscher Arbeitgeberverbände) maintain that "light work" categories do not give rise to discrimination in that they are applicable to both sexes and since all workers are classified in terms of the same principles and in accordance with the description of jobs cited in the collective agreements. That is, they maintain that the differentiation between physically light and heavy work is based on objective criteria without regard to the sex of the worker[44].

The Federation of Trade Unions, on the other hand, (Deutscher Gewerkschaftsbund) maintains that the lowest wage categories shown in collective agreements are almost exclusively female domains. The DGB also consider that companies systematically interpret the "light work" categories as representing purely physically light work which as such is contrary to the spirit in which collective agreements were negotiated. The DGB interpret the over-emphasis on physical strength as causing a systematic under-rating of women, particularly in those sectors where females comprise a high proportion of the labour force. The latter allegation receives qualified support from a survey conducted by the union I.G. Metall which suggests that 80% of women working within the metal industry are in this very position. And whilst bonuses are paid to men and women under the same conditions they are themselves directly related to wage rates.

The Federal Government has confined its rôle to one of establishing a committee, comprising the Minister of Labour and Social Affairs together with representative organisations of employers and employees, to study the application of the principle of equal pay. The committee, originally convened in 1955, has as its remit an examination and analysis of the work performed by all wage groups with a view to establishing whether, in those cases where women do different work from men, wages accurately reflect the value of the work performed. The committee was thus to study the measures required to ensure the application of the principle of equal remuneration for men and women workers for work of equal value and to establish appropriate criteria for the evaluation of women's work; that is, to clarify and settle the equal pay question in the framework of a general study on job evaluation. The committee has had a not uncontroversial history and indeed lapsed after a number of meetings when it became clear that agreement could not be reached on an appropriate questionnaire. It was reconvened in 1969 and after initial difficulties seems to have at last agreed on the method to be followed in a study of job evaluation which forms the general framework of the discrimination remit. However, because of the difficulties encountered in the evaluation of different jobs it is unlikely that a general survey on these lines could be voluntarily carried out. Further progress may thus require the compulsion of law.

And yet progress has been made in the context of these "light work" categories. A series of joint agreements have been reached in several sectors in order to abolish either the categories as such or the lower wages which they entail. Job analysis systems have been established in certain branches of the *iron and steel industry* with a view to eliminating every form of discrimination and to increasing the remuneration presently received by women workers. In the *paper industry* the wages of the light-work groups have been brought into line with those of unskilled workers. In the *chemicals sector* an agreement reached in 1969 provides for the gradual reduction of lower wages with equality being planned for 1975, by which time "light work" categories will have been abolished. As regards certain branches of the food industry where "light work" groups exist, there are plans and instructions from the Food and Hotel Industries Union (NGG) on a modification or re-definition of the present wage groups. These plans and instructions provide for the introduction of new criteria and new qualifications in the various wage groups with a view to achieving equal pay for equal work not merely in theory but also in practice. The NGG model, which provides for an integrated method of calculating salaries and wages, takes account of all the characteristics of a job to include "skills and responsibility", "space and surrounding" and "the carrying out of the work". In the *metal manufacturing industry* a new agreement of July 1973, applicable to the Nordrhein-Westfalen region, amalgamated "light work" wage groups I and II and improved the value of the newly consolidated rate to 80% of the Ecklohn—hitherto wage groups I and II respectively represented 75% and 78% of the Ecklohn—pending a further re-appraisal of the wage or performance group structure.

Despite the above moves, "light work" categories are still widespread in the Federal Republic, and the union consensus would appear to be that, with the possible exception of the *food sector* agreement, the relative position of men and women has been little changed by the various agreements.

Approximately 4 million salary earners in offices and businesses are graded into performance groups. It is alleged that discrimination, analogous to that discussed above, applies equally within this white collar sector. For these workers and for the 0·5 million to 1·0 million females not covered by collective agreements it is difficult even to make a tentative evaluation of how far such overt discrimination extends.

III. WAGE DISCRIMINATION BY SEX

Some Preliminary Observations

The degree of sex discrimination is particularly difficult to identify empirically. The fundamental problem, as we have seen in Section I, is that female labour force attachment differs substantially from that of males. The labour force participation of females should properly be regarded as a family decision in which female entry and exit from the labour force may reflect changes which do not relate directly to the female herself[45]. Most married females will thus form part of the secondary labour force liable to enter and leave employment as economic conditions change. Consequently, the supply conditions of married women to the labour market are less favourable to a high wage than those of single women. The important point here is that male and female supply curves (and transfer earnings) can at least partly explain wage differences. Female wages which are low do not then necessarily indicate an underutilisation of female labour and this substantially complicates the discrimination issue.

An examination of the gainfully employed by age group reveals differences in participation between the sexes. Table XI indicates that females constitute a disproportionate share of the total labour force in the 15-19 age group, reflecting the fact that relatively more males than females postpone entry into the labour market in order to acquire qualifications. The female/male employment ratio is, thereafter, markedly lower. This leads on to a second fundamental distinction between the sexes, namely the question of training (see Section I). On-the-job training can be classified according to whether that training is either completely *general* or completely *specific* in nature[46]. In the case of general training the costs, which under perfectly competitive conditions will be borne entirely by the worker, comprise foregone earnings and the returns comprise higher than average wages in the future after completion of that training[47]. In the case of specific training the costs are at least

Table XI. Number of Employees by Age and Sex

Age	Number of Males (000's)	Number of Females (000's)	Female as a percentage of Males (%)
15	8	10	125·0
15—19	1,239	1,127	91·0
20—29	3,230	2,253	69·8
30—39	4,367	1,844	42·2
40—49	3,495	2,043	58·5
50—59	2,487	1,461	58·7
60—64	1,228	510	41·5
65 and over	696	383	55·0
Total	16,751	9,631	57·5

Source: *Statistisches Jahrbuch der BRD*, 1970.

partly paid by the employer with the expectation of higher than average productivity and profits in the future. In both cases the investment decision is a function of the expected length of employment, since the latter determines the rate of return on the investment. In the case of the workers it is the early years following the completion of training which will be given the greatest weight because of discounting technique computations. Yet it is precisely in this early period that married females separate from the labour force. We have seen earlier, in Table II, that there is a very significant drop in the activity rates of female workers between the ages of 25-29[48], which suggests that female workers may very well consider the investment in general skills to be uneconomic. From the point of view of the firm the crucial determinant of the investment decision is the rate of labour turnover. Lower male turnover will induce a preference for male recruitment for jobs in which an investment in training is required. Lower wages for female workers may thus be seen as a method of raising the rate of return on investment in training. Hence, differences in the rate of pay of male and female workers engaged on similar work or operating within similar occupations do not necessarily imply discrimination.

The implication of the above is that a substantial section of the female labour force may not directly compete with male workers in the market; that is, male and female workers may be imperfect substitutes because of their different supply characteristics. Indeed, female workers may form the lower tier of the so-called dual labour market[49]. To the extent that females are largely confined to this secondary market—characterised by low skill levels and wages, limited promotion potential and high labour turnover—differences between the male and female wage and skill structure may be perpetuated. A study of the structure and distribution of manual worker wages in 1966 conducted by the Statistical Office of the European Communities sheds some light on the dual nature of the labour market in the Federal Republic[50]. The age/earnings profile of female manual workers is a less steeply sloped function than that of males[51] which perhaps suggests their having fewer opportunities of advancement to higher graded posts. The female age/earnings profile attains its maximum value between the ages of 25 and 30 and thence declines. The male profile is more clearly parabolic in form, climbs steadily to its maximum value in the 30-40 age group and hence declines. Again, male earnings in the younger age groups represent a smaller proportion of male mean earnings than is the case with the corresponding female groups. Specifically, the average earnings of males aged under 18, between 18 and 20 and between 21 and 24 represent 57%, 84% and 98%, respectively, of the male mean earnings value. The corresponding female values are 70%, 94% and 104%, respectively[52]. This result would seem to reflect the greater incidence of training within the male worker group and also to indicate support for the view that women are disproportionately confined to secondary employment. In part, this will reflect the fact that female labour turnover is significantly higher than that of men. According to the above study, whereas 26% of male manual employees had been employed by their current employer for less than 24 months this was the case for 35% of females[53].

Labour market segmentation may then reflect economic forces but may also reflect discrimination where there exist unequal opportunities for entry into the primary labour market between equally qualified males and females. Pre-entry discrimination may of course lead to post-entry forms of discrimination.

There exist two forms of discrimination, namely wage discrimination (or post-entry discrimination) and segregation by occupation and industry (pre-entry discrimination). Part of wage discrimination may reflect productivity differences. Segregation or exclusion will in part reflect differing natural endowments and skill acquisition. If sex does affect the price of human capital this will of course in turn affect the human capital decisions of the sexes. Each form of discrimination may reflect pure discrimination but there are often other economic explanations of inequalities between the sexes. On the supply side differences in personal characteristics (family circumstances, age and education) will give rise to unequal earnings opportunities between the sexes. This implies the existence of different supply functions which in turn may indicate that females are prepared to work at jobs similar to males at lower wages. Similarly, much of what at first sight appears to be discrimination may be exploitation[54] which although applicable to both men and women may be reduced by the unions in the case of the former.

In conclusion, then, sex wage differentials within occupations or the unequal distribution of the sexes among industries and occupations do not necessarily indicate evidence of pure discrimination. As intimated earlier, the non-homogeneity of male and female labour must be allowed for. Indeed, where there is an unwillingness on the part of both females and employers to invest in human capital formation, the optimal allocation of labour may require substantial differences in the male and female occupational structure and lead to the considerable over-representation of females in relatively low paid occupations. Alternatively, the optimal allocation of labour may imply substantial wage differences between the sexes in similar jobs.

Some Empirical Observations

As at October 1972 the average gross hourly earnings of female industrial workers within manufacturing industry stood at Dm 5·60; that is 70·6% of the corresponding male earnings value of Dm 7·93. Female earnings as a percentage of male earnings ranged from 61·8% in printing and publishing to 84·9% in the manufacture of motor vehicle, parts and accessories[55].

It is, however, perhaps more useful to examine sex earnings differences by broad occupational groups[56]. Accordingly, Tables XII and XIII chart the gross monthly earnings of male and female industrial and salaried employees over the period 1951-70. In the case of manual workers it can be seen that not only do females earn even less than males because they are concentrated within the lower performance groups but also there they earn less than their male counterparts within each performance group classification. The relative wage position of females has only modestly improved over the period in question and, moreover, female relative earnings would appear to be inversely associated with skill. Despite the elimination of the purely female wage grades in German collective agreements the improvement in female semi-skilled and unskilled relative wages appears minimal. In the case of salaried workers, sharp differences between the sexes are again observed. In all performance groups the gross monthly earnings of female salaried staffs stand at approximately 75% of the corresponding male values; that is, a less pronounced discrepancy than is to be observed within the manual worker sector. Nevertheless, females are again concentrated within the low performance grades and, moreover, the improvement in

Table XII.   Gross Monthly Earnings of Full Time Manual Workers in Industry by Wage Group and Sex

Year	Sex	Absolute Values (DM) Performance Group			Female values as a percentage of male values Performance Group		
		1	2	3	1	2	3
1951	Males	389	354	309			
	Females	215	221	207	55·1	62·2	66·3
1957	Males	516	477	407			
	Females	298	289	269	57·4	60·3	66·4
1962	Males	737	681	597			
	Females	471	453	421	63·7	66·4	70·3
1966	Males	997	901	797			
	Females	654	607	572	65·6	67·3	71·6
1970	Males	1,348	1,208	1,079			
	Females	867	806	771	64·4	66·9	71·5

Sources: *Statistik der Bundesrepublik Deutschland*, Vol. 90. Die Verdienste der Arbeiter in der gewerblichen Wirtschaft im November 1951, p. 84.
Statistisches Bundesamt: *Preise, Löhne, Wirtschaftsrechnungen*, Series 15, I, II. Years 1957, 1962 and 1970.

Table XIII.   Gross Monthly Earnings of Full Time Salaried Employees in Industry, by Wage Group and Sex

Year	Sex	Absolute Values (DM) Performance Group				Female Values As a percentage of male values Performance Group			
		II	III	IV	V	II	III	IV	V
1951	Males	631	441	369	303				
	Females	482	370	268	207	76·2	83·4	72·2	69·0
1957	Males	879	652	481	372				
	Females	703	516	375	277	79·9	79·9	77·5	74·2
1962	Males	1,203	891	664	528				
	Females	979	710	521	419	81·5	79·6	78·3	79·2
1966	Males	1,532	1,153	878	706				
	Females	1,238	912	686	544	80·8	79·0	78·1	77·0
1970	Males	2,009	1,523	1,170	960				
	Females	1,581	1,202	894	714	78·6	78·2	76·4	79·3

Sources: *Statistik der Bundesrepublik Deutschland*, Vol. 91; Die Verdienste der Angestellten in der gewerblichen Wirtschaft im November 1951, p. 106 *et seq.*
Statistisches Bundesamt: *Preise, Löhne, Wirtschaftsrechnungen.* Series 15, I, II. Years 1957, 1962, 1966 and 1970.

female relative earnings is less pronounced than in the manual sector with the exception of performance group V (namely, commercial and technical employees engaged in simple or mechanical job tasks and having no professional training).

A less highly aggregated view of female relative earnings is presented in Tables XIV and XV. Table XIV documents the relative earnings position of female manual workers within industry overall and for 7 branches of manufacturing industry. The use of hourly earnings data yields a slightly improved relative wage position over Table XII since there is a clear tendency for males to work longer hours. Again, a weakening in the relative wage position of females is observed with increasing skill level. The relative wage position of females appears particularly weak in the foodstuffs and luxuries sector and particularly strong in footwear and to a lesser extent in precision engineering, optics and watch-making. Table XV presents a parallel examination of female relative earnings within selected areas of the white collar sector. Again, as with manual workers, the examination of salary levels by performance group serves to reduce the crude earnings disparity of females observed when using average earnings values cutting across occupational lines. In the case of salaried employees, however, there is little evidence to suggest a weakening in female relative wages with increasing skill levels. On balance the statistical wage discrimination to be found within the white collar sector appears marginally less than that occurring in the manual worker context.

For the reasons advanced earlier it is extremely difficult to quantify the extent of pure wage discrimination operating against female workers. The study conducted by

Table XIV. **Wage Structure and Gross Hourly Earnings of Industrial Manual Workers, by Sex, October 1971**

Sector	Performance Group*	Females Distribution (%)	Females Absolute hourly earnings value (DM)	Males Distribution (%)	Males Absolute hourly earnings value (DM)	Female hourly earnings as a percentage of male hourly earnings (%)
Industry (excluding construction)	1	6·0	5·63	50·9	7·82	72·0
	2	46·5	5·24	36·3	7·00	74·9
	3	47·5	5·01	12·8	6·23	80·4
Overall average			5·15		7·32	70·4
Chemicals (excluding fibres)	1	2·1	6·55	39·7	8·38	77·9
	2	45·9	5·86	54·1	7·69	76·2
	3	52·0	5·34	6·2	6·47	82·5
Overall average			5·60		7·88	71·1
Electrical engineering	1	1·9	5·60	53·9	7·47	75·0
	2	34·6	5·22	32·2	6·51	80·2
	3	63·5	5·15	18·9	6·12	84·2
Overall average			5·18		6·98	74·8
Precision engineering, optics and watch making	1	2·4	5·72	53·6	7·26	78·8
	2	38·0	5·17	33·9	6·46	80·0
	3	59·6	5·27	12·5	6·03	87·4
Overall average			5·24		6·84	76·6
Paper and associated products	1	3·7	5·03	35·9	7·53	66·8
	2	48·2	4·81	38·1	6·46	74·5
	3	41·1	4·49	26·0	5·79	77·5
Overall average			4·66		6·68	69·8
Footwear	1	28·6	5·55	49·2	6·75	82·2
	2	36·8	4·99	37·2	6·04	82·6
	3	34·6	4·26	13·6	4·61	92·4
Overall average			4·90		6·20	79·0
Clothing	1	13·2	5·42	50·3	6·99	77·5
	2	70·4	5·05	35·6	6·33	79·8
	3	16·4	4·43	14·1	5·59	79·2
Overall average			5·00		6·55	76·3
Foodstuffs and luxuries	1	3·5	4·74	52·8	7·38	64·2
	2	22·1	4·82	25·9	6·52	73·9
	3	74·4	4·62	21·3	6·07	76·1
Overall average			4·67		6·88	67·9

Source: Statistisches Bundesamt: *Preise, Löhne, Wirtschaftsrechnungen.* 1971.

Table XV. Wage Structure and Gross Monthly Earnings of Commercial Employees in Industry, Commerce, Banking and Insurance, by Sex, October 1971

Sector	Performance Group*	Females Distribution (%)	Females Absolute monthly earnings value (DM)	Males Distribution (%)	Males Absolute monthly earnings value (DM)	Female hourly earnings as a percentage of male monthly earnings (%)
Industry, commerce, banking and insurance	II	4·4	1·692	27·4	2·116	80·0
	III	28·3	1·295	46·1	1·591	81·4
	IV	53·9	·934	22·5	1·184	78·9
	V	13·4	·802	4·0	1·059	75·7
Overall average			1·052		1·622	64·9
Industry (including construction)	II	4·6	1·780	30·4	2·202	80·8
	III	35·2	1·362	50·0	1·643	82·9
	IV	49·7	1·023	17·6	1·244	82·2
	V	10·5	·811	2·0	1·030	78·7
Overall average			1·155		1·730	66·8
Wholesale trade	II	5·8	1·590	24·1	2·027	78·4
	III	32·3	1·232	47·2	1·553	79·3
	IV	50·6	·919	25·3	1·154	79·6
	V	11·3	·758	3·4	·923	82·1
Overall average			1·040		1·545	67·3
Retail trade	II	4·1	1·626	23·0	2·004	81·1
	III	16·1	1·127	38·9	1·491	75·6
	IV	68·9	·799	34·2	1·092	73·2
	V	10·9	·642	3·9	·867	74·0
Overall average			·868		1·448	59·9
Banking and other financial institutions	II	3·1	1·751	25·3	2·121	82·6
	III	23·0	1·404	39·2	1·626	86·3
	IV	40·4	1·143	23·4	1·250	91·4
	V	33·5	·937	12·1	1·218	76·9
Overall average			1·153		1·614	71·4
Insurance	II	4·3	1·681	34·5	1·973	85·2
	III	51·2	1·260	46·4	1·453	86·7
	IV	38·7	1·016	16·9	1·129	90·0
	V	5·8	·839	2·2	1·003	83·6
Overall average			1·159		1·568	73·9

Source: Statistisches Bundesamt: *Preise, Löhne, Wirtschaftsrechnungen*, 1971.

the Statistical Office of the European Communities made an attempt to examine residual female disparities after correcting for skill composition and a variety of individual characteristics of wage earners[57]. The study, which related to manual workers alone, considered the following independent variables: sex, qualifications, age, length of service, size of company, wage system and overtime. The five country analysis indicated that the crude gap between the average hourly earnings of male and female industrial workers dropped considerably when distinguishing between a comparison of all the manufacturing industries with no differentiation between structural repercussions and a comparison of each of four branches of industry (textiles, food, ready made clothing and electrical engineering) which took account of individual criteria or other structural factors. The findings of the study with respect to the Federal Republic might usefully be briefly adumbrated.

For all four industries identified within the study, age would appear to play a fairly limited role in assisting the explanation of wage differences between male and female manual workers. If we examine female wage disparity[58] by qualification and age group (distinguishing between those aged 21-29 years and those aged 30-44 years) the observed level of wage disparity is of much the same order of magnitude. The wage disparity of the older age group per qualification category is, however, never less than the corresponding disparity of the younger age group. The small differences that do emerge are plotted in Table XVI. The results mirror the age/earnings profiles of the sexes mentioned above.

Establishment size would, on the other hand, appear to significantly influence female earnings disparity. In all industries identified, with the possible exception of

Table XVI.   Percentage Deficiency of Female Hourly Earnings* within Selected Industries, by Qualification and Age Group, October 1966

Industry (NICE)	21—29 Years 1†	2	3	4	30—44 Years 1	2	3	4
Food and luxuries (20B)	−30	−26	−24	−32	−31	−26	−25	−32
Textiles (23)	−16	−14	−16	−19	−16	−15	−17	−21
Footwear, clothing and bedding (24)	−22	−22	−20	−24	−24	−24	−21	−27
Electrical engineering (37)	−25	−22	−14	−25	−27	−25	−16	−28
Manufacturing industry (2/3)	−24	−24	−22	−28	−27	−27	−23	−31

*Difference between appropriate male earnings (=100) and corresponding female earnings.
†Code 1=Qualified; 2=Semi-Qualified; 3=Non-Qualified; 4=Total.
Source: Office Statistique des Communautés Européennes: *Statistiques Sociales*, Annuaire 1972, Table IV/15, pp. 246-247.

the food sector, a plant size in excess of 500 units would appear optimal from the point of view of reduced female earnings disparity. In the food industry the optimal plant size would appear to be in the region of 100-499 employees. In manufacturing industry the female earnings/plant size function is of greater slope than that of males[59]. The extent to which female earnings disparity may be reduced is illustrated in Table XVII, which relates to the textile industry.

Finally, with respect to length of service no clear wage disparity pattern emerges after standardisation for occupation and age. The regression of earnings on length of service for manufacturing industry as a whole indicates that the length of service variable is more important for male workers than for females. This association is, however, significantly affected by the transformation of unskilled workers to semi-skilled and skilled occupations through time and after correction for this the male earnings/length of service function is dramatically reduced in slope[60].

To summarise then: after standardisation for age, establishment size and skill composition the statistical wage discrimination observed at broad industry level is reduced. Without such correction, wage discrimination within food, textile, footwear and electrical engineering industries stood at approximately — 33%, — 20%, — 26% and — 27%, respectively. After standardisation the corresponding values, as at 1966, appear as — 23%, — 19%, — 20% and — 22%, respectively. Two cautionary observations should however be made in parenthesis. Firstly, the occupational classifications used in the study are broad in the extreme and encompass considerable skill differences within each skill classification. Secondly, the residual earnings disparity observed after standardisation cannot necessarily be regarded as indicating the degree of pure discrimination. As intimated earlier, wage disparities may have an economic rationale from a demand point of view.

Table XVII

Textile Industry

Percentage Deficiency* of Female Manual Worker Standard Hourly Earnings by Broad Qualification Group, Age and Size of Establishment Unit, October 1966

Establishment Size (No. of employees)	Age Group							
	21—29 Years				30—44 Years			
	1†	2	3	4	1	2	3	4
10—99	−24	−24	−23	−27	−24	−23	−24	−27
100—499	−16	−18	−17	−21	−17	−16	−18	−21
> 500		−13	−14	−19	−17	−13	−16	−20

*Difference between the appropriate male earnings value (=100) and the corresponding female earnings value.

†Code 1=Qualified; 2=Semi-Qualified; 3=Non-Qualified; 4=All Groups.

Source: Office Statistique des Communautés Européennes: *Statistiques Sociales. Structure et répartition des salaires* 1966, Série Speciale, Table 8/2300, pp. 158-159.

Finally, we crudely address the question of the relative importance of unequal earnings opportunity (the male/female earnings differential) and unequal employment opportunity (different industrial distributions of the sexes). The analysis relates to October 1971 earnings and employment data and covers manual workers only. The method adopted is as follows.

Firstly, we grant females within each industry the appropriate mean male earnings value but leave the industrial distribution of females unchanged. We then obtain a weighted average of female earnings across industry (B). Secondly, we industrially re-distribute females to accord with the "expected" females distribution, which is computed on the basis of the proportion of female manual workers within the total manual labour force (here, 27·6%). We then obtain a weighted average of female earnings across industry after this re-distribution and after having again granted female workers the appropriate mean male earnings value (C). The two resultant weighted averages may then be compared with the weighted average of actual female earnings across industry (A). The results of this exercise are contained in Table XVIII.

Whilst this test is crude in the extreme it indicates that redistributing females keeping earnings constant makes little difference to average earnings in comparison with granting females male earnings in their existing industries. This result must qualify the negative association that one observes between male earnings by industry and the proportion of female workers within the corresponding industry labour force[61]. The policy conclusions may well be that the inequality of wages is more crucial than the unequal industrial distribution of manpower by sex.

Table XVIII.   The Effect on Female Earnings of Industrial Re-distribution, October 1971

Sector/Effect	Average hourly earnings (Dm)
Manufacturing	
A	5·12
B	6·94
C	7·16
All Industries	
A	5·12
B	6·95
C	7·09

Sources: *Statistiques Sociales*, Annuaire 1972, Statistical Office of the European Communities Table 4, pp. 196-197.
   Statistiques Sociales, No. 1, 1973, Table 23, pp. 156-159.

IV. CONCLUSIONS

The Federal Republic is one example of a country in which guarantees against discrimination on grounds of sex have been built into the constitution. Constitutional rights have been augmented by legislation—such as the Equal Rights Law (Gleichberechtigungsgesetz) of 1957 which forbade separate wage groupings in collective agreements—and jurisprudence. Despite jurisprudence "equal pay" in practice has meant that men and women in the same job category should be paid the same basic rate, whilst the phrase "equal work" has tended to become defined for industrial workers in terms of the extent to which the work is physically demanding (measured in terms of caloric consumption). This is not necessarily to say that where jobs are regarded as equal that rates are unequal. A more accurate assessment would be that equality in jobs is still interpreted with some partiality in various sectors of German industry. Light-work groups still exist in a number of branches and their specification often indicates an overemphasis on brute strength and a corresponding under-emphasis on other job characteristics to include dexterity, responsibility, precision, resilience and monotonous concentration. Evidence of a similar down-grading of females is perhaps more difficult to cite within the salaried sector. A study by Vogelman, conducted in 1972, would appear to suggest that a university-education is too high for employment at a commensurate level. A female graduate in chemistry evidently earns far less and is offered comparatively less interesting positions involving responsibility and promotion potential than are male applicants. And, again, while 47% of all female employees at the various ministries in Bonn have Mittlere Reife (intermediate school leaving certificate) or Abitur (higher school leaving certificate) compared with 36% of all male employees, only 8·9% of such females are classified as upper-level employees as opposed to 24% of males[62].

Even in such cases it is difficult to determine the extent to which sex wage differentials are the outcome of social (conventional or prejudicial) forces rather than economic ones. The German situation clearly illustrates the existence of two labour markets—delineated by sex and reflecting differing demand and supply considerations[63]—with an apparently low elasticity of substitution. On the demand side, a variety of factors (legal, conventional and natural) act to favour the employment of males. And on the supply side, the "split loyalties"[64] of married females which tend to reduce women's work to the level of a sideline would indicate lower supply prices. From both their own and the employer's point of view women offer poor investment prospects and are therefore concentrated in lower skilled occupations which result may in turn act to further depress the female wage rate.

The statistical discrimination observed in Sections II and III may, then, take several forms and may have causes that are economic rather than discriminatory *per se*. Two main areas of statistical discrimination have been identified; namely, wage discrimination (post-entry) and employment discrimination or segregation (pre-entry). In the case of the former, part of the wage difference may reflect a "life-time" productivity differential. Lower female wages may be seen both as a means of raising the rate of return on training investment and as compensation for the higher costs resulting from the shorter expected duration of employment. As intimated earlier, the classic interruption of working life and the higher turnover of female labour will imply different rates of investment in human capital and hence a different industrial and occupational distribution.

Equally, however, both forms of discrimination may reflect tastes for discrimination and conventional attitudes concerning the nature of the woman's role and ability. Even after correction for skill and a variety of individual characteristics it has been shown that the female earnings disparity is still in the order of — 20%. Again, the acquisition of human capital by females may be reduced by biases in the educational system. Alternatively, if female earnings are depressed by post-entry discrimination then females will invest less in their own human capital for this reason—even lower female earnings which have an economic cause may well act to reduce such investment. While lower supply prices may suggest that sex wage differences are not indicative of pure discrimination, since women are prepared to work at similar jobs to males at lower wages, it is also possible that the lower transfer earnings of females reflect active sex discrimination throughout the labour market. For the above reasons, then, it is reasonable to suppose that both supply and demand conditions may be at least conventionally as well as economically determined. The policy prescription area is therefore complicated. A strengthening and extension of equal rights legislation may well be grounded on social rather than economic arguments. There is some evidence to indicate that inequality of wages is more crucial than the unequal industrial distribution of manpower by sex and to this extent a tighter application of equal pay legislation may have greater potential than anti-discrimination moves. Whilst the removal of discrimination and the creation of equal opportunities for women may be important as an objective of social policy it does not necessarily follow that women will be prepared to increase the investment in themselves. Under the Employment Promotion Act (Arbeitsförderungsgesetz) of June 1969 and the Vocational Education Act (Berufsbildungsgesetz) of August 1969 training has been availabile to females for many occupations which in practice were hitherto almost closed to them. Surveys made of the training facilities indicate, however, that most females are still being trained for only a few careers while the training of male apprentices covers a full activity spectrum. The consensus would appear to be that this disproportion is not due to the lesser physical aptitude of females but rather to traditional prejudices concerning "manly" occupations. From an economic point of view, then, the problem of female employment and labour market policy in Germany has to take account of deep-rooted ideas entertained by both men and women regarding woman's role in society. As long as household duties take precedence over a career an optimal allocation of manpower may require substantial differences between male and female occupational structures or, alternatively, substantial intra-occupational wage differentials.

References

1. *Statistischen Jahrbach der BRD*, 1970, p. 120.
2. Over the course of 1961-71 the number of gainfully employed females declined from 9·9 millions to 9·6 millions. *Die Frau in Beruf, Familie und Gesellschaft*, Report of the Federal Government, Printed matter V, 1909, Bonn, 1964, p. 67.
3. Kohler, H., and Reyer, L., "Erwerbstätigkeitsphasen der Frauen", *Institut für Arbeitsmarkt— und Berufsforschung*, 3/1970, p. 89 *et seq*.
4. *Wirtschaft und Statistik*, Book 6, 1967, p. 362.
5. This accords with the so called 3-phase theorem. See:—Myrdal, A., and Klein, V., *Die Doppelrolle der Frauen in Familie und Beruf*, Köln/Berlin, 1971.
6. Weltz, F., *Bestimmungsgrossen der Frauenerwerbstätigkeit*, München, 1970, p. 32.
7. *Statistisches Jahrbuch*, 1971, p. 128.
8. *Wirtschaft und Statistik*, 7/1971, p. 416.
9. These figures relate to April 1970. *Wirtschaft und Statistik, ibid*.
10. *Arbeits-und Sozialstatistik*, 1971, p. 24.
11. Over the period 1950-71, in contrast, the numbers of females in gainful employment increased by 30·6%. Employment within the primary sector declined by — 58·4%, whereas increases of 73·9% and 93·4% occurred within the secondary and tertiary sectors. See—*Arbeits-und Sozialstatistik*, 1971, p. 24.
12. *Arbeits-und Sozialstatistik*, 1971, p. 30.
13. *Arbeits-und sozialstatistische Mitteilungen*, Book 5, Bonn, 1968, p. 130.
14. *Bundesanstalt für Arbeit*, 19. Jg, Special No., July 1971, p. 112.
15. *Arbeits-und Sozialstatistik*, 1971, p. 30, *et seq*.
16. For a longer-term perspective see:—Joppe, L., "Struktur und Entwicklung der Frauenerwerb- stätigkeit in der BRD", Research Conference: *Die Frau in der Sozialen Sicherheit*, Vienna, 1972.
17. *Arbeits-und Sozialstatistische Mitteilungen*, 5/1972, p. 162.
18. Statistical Office of the European Community, *Statistiques Sociales*, No. 1, 1973, p. 156.
19. *Arbeits-und Sozialstatistische Mitteilungen*, 3/1973, p. 74.
20. For a definition of the 8 Berufsbereiche see:—*Materialien aus der Arbeitsmarkt-und Berufsfor- schung*, MatAB, 1/1972, p. 17.
21. Altogether, some 59 occupational groups can be demonstrated to have a female employment share of more than 33%. MatAB *ibid*. 13/1972. Datensammlung zum Wandel der Beruf.
22. The Leistungsgruppen can only yield crude guidance as to skill structure since they are primarily activity-specific and not purely qualification-specific. For definition and comment see:— *Frauenarbeit und Technischer Wandel*, Soziologisches Forschungsinstitut, Göttingen, Footnote 20, pp. A4-A6.
23. Statistisches Bundesamt, *Wirtschaft und Statistik*, Vol. 3, 1969, p. 144.
24. In the order of a 1 percentage point improvement or deterioration in the proportion of skilled females.
25. Statistisches Bundesamt, *Preise, Löhne, Wirtschaftsrechnungen*, 1967 and 1971.
26. *Arbeits-und Sozialstatistische Mitteilungen*, 5/1972, p. 30.
27. Statistisches Bundesamt, *Wirtschaft und Statistik*, Vol. 6, 1969, p. 309.
28. In 1961 females constituted 40% of all secondary school pupils and 36% of all matriculated students. *Report of the Federal Government on Measures to Improve the Situation of Women*, Printed Matter VI/3869, Bonn, 1972, p. 92.
29. The figures cited relate to 1968. Statistisches Bundesamt, *Jahrbuch für die BRD*, 1970, pp. 72-73.
30. Statistisches Bundesamt, *Bevölkerung und Kultur*, Series 10, Mainz, 1971, p. 24.
31. Report of the Federal Government, *op. cit*., p. 93.
32. Bundesministerium für Arbeit und Sozialordnung, *Arbeits-und sozialstatistischen Mitteilungen*, 12/1967, pp. 10-21.
33. *Jahresstatistik der Berufsberatung*, 1968/69.
34. For a detailed account of these activities, see:—Hofbauer, H., "Potentialle Berufsfelder für Frauen", in *Mittellungen aus der Arbeitsmarkt-und Berufsforschung*, W. Kohlhammer, Stuttgart, 4/1971, p. 339.

35. *Berufsministerium für Arbeit, op. cit.*, pp. 10-21.
36. *Bundesanstalt für Arbeit: Amtliche Nachrichten*, 11/1970, p. 827.
37. viz: Baden (Art. 37, section 5); Bayern (Art. 168, section 1); Bremen (Art. 53); Hessen (Art. 33, section 2); Rheinland-Pfalz (Art. 56, section 2); Württemberg-Baden (Art. 20, section 2); and Württemberg-Hohenzollern (Art. 90, section 2).
38. *Entscheidungen des Bundesarbeitsgerichts*, Vol. 1, Walter de Gruyter & Co, 1965, pp. 258 and 348.
39. Knapp, B., *L'Egalité de Rémunération des Travailleurs Masculins et Féminins dans la Communauté Economique Européennes et en Suisse*, Centre d'Etudes Juridiques Européennes, Geneva, 1968, pp. 24-27; and Isele, H. G., "Le Principe de Non-Discrimination dans la République Fédérale d'Allemagne", *Revue Internationale de Droit Comparé*, Vol. 21 No. 1, January/March 1969, pp. 11-17.
40. Namely, Recommendation 123, which deals with women having family responsibilities. It urges that such women who work outside their homes should have the right to do so without discrimination.
41. For example, rates which came into force on 1st September 1969 still differentiated between the sexes. In the case of leather workers employed on the right bank of the Rhine the main differences were as follows:

Hourly Rates (Dm), by Sex, September 1969

Skill classification	Males	Females
Skilled workers	3·38—3·69	
Semi-skilled workers	3·22—3·31	2·82—2·87
Unskilled workers	3·08—3·17	2·72—2·77

Source: *Report of the Commission of European Communities*, SEC(70) 2338, Brussels, 18th June 1970.

42. See, for example: Radke, O., and Rathert, W., *Gleichberechtigung?* Europäische Verlagsanstalt, Frankfurt am Main, 1964.
43. European Parliament. *Working Documents.* 1974-75. *Document* 21/74/rev. Report drawn up on behalf of the Committee on Social Affairs and Employment, 22 April 1974, Rapporteur: Härzschel, K. p. 11.
44. Moreover, there is the suggestion that many employers favour an Article 119 interpretation of equal pay; that is, equal pay for the *same* work and not equal pay for *equivalent* work.
45. For a detailed analysis of the variables affecting female participation, see Bowen, W. G., and Finegan, T. E., *The Economics of Labour Force Participation*, Princeton, New Jersey, 1969.
46. Becker, G., *Human Capital*, New York, National Bureau of Economic Research, 1964, pp. 7-36.
47. Although, of course, discrimination in so far as it exists will limit higher earnings potential.
48. Joppe, L., *Aufgaben der Bundesanstalt für Arbeit in unserer Zeit*, 29th July 1971, p. 9.
49. Bosanquet, N., and Doeringer, P. B., "Is there a Dual Labour Market in Great Britain?" *Economic Journal*, June 1973.
50. *Statistiques Sociales: Structure et répartition des salaires*, 1966, Special Series 8, Statistical Office of the European Communities.
51. *ibid.*, pp. 62-63.
52. *ibid.*, pp. 58-59.
53. *ibid.*, pp. 66-67.
54. Perlman, R., *Labour Theory*, Wiley, New York, 1969, pp. 58-62.
55. *Statistiques Sociales*, No. 1, 1973, Statistical Office of the European Communities, pp. 36-41.
56. There are, however, important limitations attaching to the performance grade classification system. The Federal Statistical Office cites a three-fold manual worker grade structure yet German collective agreements specify considerably more than 3 wage groups (see:—Radke, O., and Rathert, W., op. cit. pp. 116-118) with considerable emphasis being placed upon training and effort (calorie consumption) inputs. On this account, the performance group classification is far too broad to permit accurate comparison of like with like within semi-skilled and unskilled grades 2 and 3. Again, in the skilled worker context, collective agreements may typically stipulate 3 or more skilled rates and not merely a basic skilled rate or *Ecklohn*. There exist, then, qualified-

skilled-worker rates which yield up to 133% of the basic skilled rate. Significant numbers of male workers receive such rates whereas the vast majority of skilled females earn the basic skilled rate. This is not to confirm or deny the efficacy of job evaluation procedures adopted in German collective agreements (see:—Weber, M., "Programmatische Forderungen des DGB im Jahr der Arbeitnehmerin", *Gewerkschaftliche Monatshefte*, 11/1972, p. 681) but, rather, to emphasise the limitations of intra-group comparison.

57. *Statistiques Sociales: Structure et répartition des salaires*, 1966, *op. cit.*

58. Wage disparity is defined as the absolute earnings difference between males and females of equal skill, age, etc. expressed as a percentage of the absolute male earnings value.

59. The regression equations of earnings on plant size were as follows:—

$ym = 3 \cdot 281 logx + 90 \cdot 0$ $(r^2 = 0 \cdot 99)$
$yf = 6 \cdot 95 logx + 81 \cdot 9$ $(r^2 = 0 \cdot 98)$

where m and f refer to males and females.
Source: Statistiques Sociales: Structure et repartition des Salaires, 1966. *op. cit. x*p. 40-52.

60. *ibid.*, pp. 64-76.

61. The rank correlation coefficient between male earnings and percentage female employment by industry is — 0·52, which is significant at the 5% level. This association suggests evidence to favour a "crowding hypothesis" interpretation of female earnings disparity, namely that females are unfavourably distributed by industry which acts to depress their relative wage levels. (Edgeworth, F. Y., "Equal Pay to Men and Women for Equal Work", *Economic Journal*, Vol 31, 1922.)

62. Quoted in:—*European Parliament. Working Documents*, 1974-75, *op. cit.*

63. That is, male and female labour is non-homogenous. The observed behaviour of the sexes will clearly differ under conditions of unequal opportunity and where tasks, abilities, social pressures and physical and psychological attributes diverge.

64. Pross, H., *Gleichberechtigung im Beruf*, Frankfurt, Athenäum Verlag, 1973.

Equal Pay in Canada: History, Progress and Problems

M. Gunderson

As in most industrialised countries, women have come to play an increased role in the Canadian labour market. This increased role has drawn attention to the inequities that exist between the labour market status of men and women. The response has included anti-sex discrimination legislation as well as the appointment of various commissions including the Royal Commission on the Status of Women in Canada. This in turn has led to a proliferation of agencies, committees and bureaux to deal with sex discrimination in employment. An abundance of written material—much of it polemic—has also emerged.

The purpose of this paper is to discuss the history, progress and problems associated with the equal pay issue in Canada. Since equal pay and equal employment opportunity are closely related, the paper deals with the whole issue of sex discrimination in employment.

By way of background, a basic description of the Canadian labour market is first provided along with a brief description of the labour force participation, occupational distribution, union status and wage and earnings position of Canadian females. In a more detailed fashion, evidence of sex discrimination in the Canadian labour market is then presented, based on a number of empirical studies of wage and earnings differences. This is followed by a discussion of Canadian legislation pertaining to the employment of women, with particular reference to equal pay, fair employment, maternity leaves, "protective" legislation and international conventions. Some court cases are discussed so as to give an indication of the actual interpretation of the law. The paper concludes with a discussion of various unanswered questions, research needs and unresolved problems.

Basic Description of Women in the Canadian Labour Force

The industrial relations setting of the Canadian labour market is one of fairly decentralised collective bargaining with a minimum of government interference either in the wage setting procedure or in the bargaining structure. Although only about one-third of the eligible labour force is unionised, the impact of unions is believed to extend beyond their own jurisdiction as they set wage patterns that influence all sectors. Although the magnitude and desirability is of considerable debate, American influence on the Canadian labour market is believed to exist in the form of wage spillovers, international unions and multinational corporations. The immense size of

Table I.   Labour Force Participation Rates for Males and Females
Census Years 1901-1971

Year	Males	Females	Year	Males	Females
1901	88	16	1941	86	23
1911	91	19	1951	84	24
1921	90	20	1961	81	29
1931	87	22	1971	76	37

Source: S. Ostry and F. Denton. *Historical Estimates of the Canadian Labour Force.* 1961 Census Monograph. Ottawa: Dominion Bureau of Statistics, 1967 for the years 1901-1961. *The Labour Force* (Jan. 1972), Information Canada No. 71-001, p. 14 for 1971.

Canada, with its natural lines of communication often running south into the US rather than east and west across the country, has also tended to separate the various labour markets into distinct fragments. This is compounded by the cultural differences that prevail because of the large waves of immigrants and the prevalence of the French language and culture in the province of Quebec. These background factors should be kept in mind when discussing Canadian labour market phenomena.

As Table I indicates, the Canadian female labour force participation rate exhibited a steady upward growth from 1970-1971, accentuated in the 1950's, 60's and 70's. Most of this increase has come from middle-aged, married women with children, many of whom are re-entering the labour force as their children attain school age. In contrast, the male labour participation rate has generally exhibited a small decline over the period, mainly from the sharp decline in the participation of male teenagers and older men.

Reasons for the increase in the participation rate of women—especially middle-aged, married women—are similar to those of other industrialised countries: an expansion of the white collar sales and service sector; increased education of females (hence increased opportunity cost of household work); improved household technology and availability of substitutes for household production; a shorter work week and more part-time employment making for greater job flexibility; increased urbanisation with its accompanying white collar jobs and attitudes that are more conducive to women working; and a decreased family size. Many of these factors are as much the *result* as they are the *cause* of increased labour force participation of women; the relationship is completely interrelated.

Although exhibiting the same upward growth and twin-peaked participation profile, the labour force participation rate of Canadian women is considerably lower than in most other industrialised countries. In 1970, female participation rates (ages 15-64) were: Canada ·41, Australia ·45, West Germany ·49, USA ·49, UK ·52, Japan ·56, and Sweden ·59[1]. These in turn were considerably lower than Eastern European rates of ·77 in the Soviet Union (1959), ·69 in East Germany (1964), ·66 in Poland (1960) and ·63 in Czechoslovakia (1961)[2]. The low participation rates in Canada may reflect a variety of factors including differences in labour force definition, part-time participation, tax structure, family size, education, attitude, race, unemployment insurance benefits, and agricultural employment.

In the occupations in Canada, females tend to be over-represented in the generally low-wage clerical and service occupations and under-represented in the high-wage managerial, durable manufacturing and professional (except for teaching and nursing) occupations. Since the early 1900's female occupational growth has occurred mainly in the clerical and sales occupations; female occupational decline has occurred in the professions and in blue-collar manufacturing[3]. Apparently, few significant inroads into traditionally male jobs have been made by females over the past 70 years in Canada. Their increased labour force participation has occurred in the growing female sector of the labour force.

In Canada, approximately one third of the total eligible labour force is unionised, with approximately 23% of women workers and 40% of men workers being union members[4]. Although women constitute about 24% of all union members, they hold only about 11% of the executive board positions within the trade union movement[5]. Clearly, women are less likely than men to be members of a union; and when they are members they are less likely to hold influential jobs within the union.

Women are less likely than men to be in a union partly because they tend to pre-dominate in the relatively unorganised sector of the labour force—namely, white collar clerical, sales and service occupations. In recent years, however, there has been a growth of union activity in these areas. Even within these occupations, women are less likely than males to be unionised. This may reflect their traditional secondary attachment to the labour force; women may not expect to be in the labour force or at the same job long enough to reap the full benefits of joining a union. Perhaps this will change over time as women become more permanently attached to the labour force. The lack of female unionisation may also reflect a neglect on the part of the labour movement in general, especially to the extent that males predominate in the decision making bodies of the unions.

Union attitudes towards women have been mixed[6]. At the centralised level, as evidenced by union charters, conventions, platforms, president's reports and policy statements, there is considerable support for the principles of equal pay and equal employment opportunities. At the local level and with the rank and file, this support generally diminishes. Traditional views prevail, whereby the women's place is deemed to be in the home and female income is regarded merely as additional income while male income is used to support the family. Male concern for their own job security may partially account for their attitudes.

The basic picture of women in Canada's trade union is one where they are un-represented especially at the higher decision making levels. Whether the growth of unions in predominantly female areas of employment and the growing militancy of women in general, will overcome traditional male attitudes in the rank and file is an open question.

As in most industrialised countries, males tend to have considerably higher annual earnings than females. In 1967, for example, the ratio of female to male earnings was ·46 for all workers[7]. Much of this differential however comes about because women work fewer weeks per year than men as well as engage in more part-time employment (fewer days per week or hours per day). Adjusting for the differences in weeks worked raised the ratio of female to male earnings to ·54 for full-year workers (50-52 weeks per year). Adjusting for differences in part-time employment raises the ratio to ·58 for full-time workers. It is notable that the ratio of female to male earnings is smallest in sales occupations (·38 for full year sales persons in 1967), suggesting the importance of customer discrimination.

Much of the difference between the annual earnings of males and females occurs because females tend to be crowded[8] into low-wage "female-type" occupations (particularly clerical, service and sales), and within these occupations they tend to hold the low-pay job. However, even when we look at extremely narrowly-defined occupations with identical job descriptions the wage gap is still considerable. For nine occupations for which continuous data existed from 1946-1971, the average ratio of female to male wages was ·75[9]. The average ratio of female to male wages within the same establishments for some 2,600 jobs in Ontario during 1968 and 1969 was ·82[10]. This is an unweighted average; to the extent that proportionately more females were clustered in low-wage establishments or low-wage occupations, a ratio that was weighted by the number of males and number of females in each job would be lower. Table II gives the ratio of female to male wages in 29 narrowly defined occupations with identical job descriptions in Canada during 1971. The unweighted average ratio of female to male wages is ·85. Again, if this were weighted by the number of males and females in each occupation, the ratio would presumably be lower, reflecting the larger proportion of females in the low-wage occupations.

Although these wage gaps are large, they are considerably smaller than the gross earnings differentials cited earlier. Clearly, the more homogeneous the group within which comparisons are made, the smaller the wage gap. This does not imply that comparisons of gross earnings differentials overestimates the degree of sex discrimination; females may well receive lower earnings because they are involuntarily segregated into low-wage establishments and occupations as well as into part-time work. Nor do comparisons within narrowly defined occupations, even within the same establishment, imply that the wage gap is all due to sex discrimination. Productivity differences, as well as differences in absenteeism and turnover, could account for some of the difference, although the narrowly defined occupations suggest that the work is substantially similar.

The previously cited figures simply give an indication of the magnitude of the income and wage gap that exists between males and females in Canada. In order to find out how much of the gap is attributable to discrimination and to determine the factors influencing the wage gap we must look to empirical studies that have attempted to control for the influence of various wage determining factors.

**Table II.   Male-Female Wages in Select Narrowly-defined Occupations
with Identical Job Descriptions, Canada, 1971**

Occupation	Male wage	Female wage	Female/Male wage ratio
1. Fitter, men's clothing	2·67	1·73	·65
2. Inspector, electrical equipment	3·42	2·23	·65
3. Machine operator	3·54	2·43	·69
4. Inspector, rubber products	2·76	1·94	·70
5. Assembly wirer	2·93	2·14	·73
6. Circular knitter	2·36	1·87	·79
7. Bundler	2·86	2·28	·80
8. Knitter	2·19	1·75	·80
9. Machinery operator	3·23	2·58	·80
10. Assembler, small appliances	2·51	2·03	·81
11. Bakery wrapping machine operator	3·00	2·50	·83
12. General bakery helper	2·70	2·32	·86
13. Sewer, men's clothing	2·16	1·88	·87
14. Selector, glass products	3·25	2·83	·87
15. Twister, wool and yarn	2·24	1·96	·87
16. General helper, biscuits	2·85	2·54	·89
17. Electrical receiver inspector	3·23	2·89	·89
18. Labourer	3·81	3·44	·90
19. Assembler, simple	2·59	2·34	·90
20. Warper and beamer	2·29	2·07	·90
21. Wet and dry operator	2·37	2·15	·91
22. Filler and packager	2·57	2·33	·91
23. Aligner	3·00	2·76	·92
24. Assembler, office machinery	3·30	3·09	·94
25. Operator	4·24	4·02	·95
26. Dishwasher, small hotel	1·72	1·65	·96
27. Veneer patcher	3·61	3·53	·98
28. Dishwasher, large hotel	1·82	1·80	·99
29. Grader, textiles	2·14	2·49	1·16

Source: Neville, E., and Eastham, K., "Employment Status of Women in Ontario", paper for 1972 meeting of American Statistical Association. Montreal, Canada, 1972, p. 15. Based on data from Canada Department of Labour, 1971 Survey of Wage Rates, Salaries and Hours of Labour.

Evidence of Male-Female Pay Differentials

Various Canadian empirical studies have attempted to analyse the factors explaining male-female wage and earnings differentials with a view towards determining how much of the gap is due to productivity related differences and how much of it to sex discrimination.

Based on the 1961 Canadian census, Ostry[11] computes the ratio of female to male annual earnings as ·54 for all workers and ·59 for full-year workers, leaving an "unexplained" gap of 41 percentage points. Adjusting for the differences in the occupational distribution of males and females would raise this ratio to about ·66[12].

That is, if males and females had the same occupational distribution, females would earn about 66% of what males earn. This suggests that occupational segregation, whereby females are crowded into low-wage jobs, accounts for about 7 percentage points or about 17% of the original 41 percentage point earnings gap. Adjustments for male-female differences in education and age (as a proxy for experience) raised the ratio of female to male earnings a further 16 percentage points to ·81 suggesting that differences between education and age of males and females accounts for about 37% of their annual earnings differential. Based on these crude adjustments, slightly over half of the male-female earnings gap is explained by differences in the occupational distribution and the age and education of the sexes. Ostry concludes (p. 42): "The adjustments which were made were very rough—distributional differences other than occupational were not taken into account nor were a number of important 'quality' factors such as those stemming from male-female differences in turnover, work experience, absenteeism, etc. More detailed adjustments would no doubt have reduced the 'unexplained' gap even further. However, it seems clear that some portion of the residual differential stemmed from 'discrimination', i.e. from the fact that women were paid less than men for comparable work."

Ostry also computes the unadjusted and adjusted ratios of female to male earnings by major occupational groups. As Table III indicates, after adjusting for differences in age and experience as well as differences in the proportion of females at the low end of the wage structure within each occupation (i.e. assuming the same proportion of females as males were at each wage level within the occupation), the wage gap was reduced considerably in manual jobs, namely craft and production worker and labourers. If sex discrimination exists in manual occupations, it would occur in the form of employment segregation whereby females are crowded into the low-wage

Table III. Ratio of Female to Male Full-time, Full-year Earnings by Major Occupational Group, 1961

Occupation	Unadjusted	Adjusted	Adjustment increase
All occupations	·59	·81	+ ·22
Managerial	·52	·65	+ ·13
Professional and technical	·61	·71	+ ·10
Clerical	·74	·89	+ ·15
Sales	·45	·69	+ ·24
Service and recreation	·47	·69	+ ·22
Farmers	·60	·52	— ·08
Craft and production	·56	1·10	+ ·54
Labour	·67	·92	+ ·25

Source: Adopted from S. Ostry, *The Female Worker in Canada*, Ottawa, Dominion Bureau of Statistics, 1968, p. 44. The adjusted ratio is simply an average of Ostry's two ratios based on the female and male weights.

jobs within each broad occupation grouping[13]. Wage differences within more narrowly defined sub-occupations appear not to be an important phenomena in manual occupations when differences between the sexes in age and education are controlled for.

In contrast, the adjustment factors do little to raise the ratio of female to male earnings in the higher-status managerial, professional and technical occupations. Most of the small increase in the adjusted earnings ratio comes from the adjustment for differences in the distribution of males and females among sub-occupations; age and education differences were not important in accounting for the wage gap[14]. This suggests wage discrimination (unequal wages within occupational sub-groups even after age and education are controlled for) to be more important than occupational segregation in the high status jobs.

Although the adjustment factors are admittedly incomplete, the following tentative conclusions emerge from the Ostry study. Even after allowing for differences in such factors as the work year, the occupational distributions, as well as age and education, sizeable pay differences remain between male and female workers in Canada. Discrimination appears to be greater in the high-status managerial and professional occupations, with wage discrimination being more predominant than the segregation of females into the low-wage end of the salary structure. Discrimination appears to be smaller in manual occupations and what does exist is mainly a result of the crowding of females into the low-wage jobs within the manual sector.

Utilising data from the 1967 Survey of Consumer Finances (which is based on the Labour Force Survey), Holmes estimates the ratio of expected lifetime earnings of females relative to males to be ·41 tending to be slightly higher for higher education levels and lower for lower education levels[15]. This ratio is ·49 when only full-time workers are considered. Adjusting[16] for differences in such factors as weeks worked, occupation, marital status (to reflect absenteeism and turnover), class of worker, region, residence and immigration status raises the ratio of female to male earnings to about ·56. Adjustments for region, residence, immigration status and class of worker had a negligible impact on the ratio because the distribution of males and females was fairly similar across these characteristics. Adjustments for occupational distribution and weeks worked had a very large impact reflecting the fact that females tend to predominate in the low-wage occupations and they tend to work fewer weeks per year than men. The productivity adjusted ratios of female to male earnings tend to be smallest for the less educated worker and largest for more educated workers leading Holmes to conclude (p. 17) that "females are better able to compete with males for the better jobs, and are less likely to be forced into overcrowded occupations where their productivity and rate of pay is low".

When differences in male-female productivity related variables are taken into account, the ratio of female to male earnings increased by 15 percentage points, from ·41 to ·56. Thus, differences in productivity related characteristics account for about one-fourth of the original 59 percentage points earnings gap. Holmes speculates that differences in turnover and experience would account for an additional one-quarter of the earnings gap with the remaining one-half of the gap attributable to sex discrimination.

Using aggregate data, as in the Ostry and Holmes studies, necessitates that one control for the effect of productivity related factors so as to compare male-female earnings of similar workers. Data limitations preclude anything more than relatively crude adjustments in the attempt to control for the effect of productivity related factors. Partly to overcome the problems inherent in the use of such aggregate data, Gunderson[17] compares male-female wages within the same narrowly-defined occupations, within the same establishment. Only those occupations with identical job descriptions for males and females were selected; consequently, the study concentrates on wage discrimination within an occupation rather than the question of occupational segregation whereby females may be crowded into low-wage jobs with no male counterparts.

The study found that the ratio of female to male wages within the same narrowly defined occupation within the same establishment averaged. ·82. Unionised establishments had a much smaller wage gap of slightly less than ·90 suggesting that unions were effective in raising the wages of females relative to males. This may occur because unions rationalise and formalise the pay structure of establishment or because they tend to bargain for equal absolute wage increments which implies larger relative gains for low-wage females. Unions may bargain for equal pay out of a concern for the (usual) minority position of females within the union; or they may be attempting to protect male jobs from low-wage female competition.

Having an incentive pay system in the occupation tended to raise the ratio of female to male wages by about 6 percentage points from ·82 to ·88, suggesting that an incentive pay system closes about one-third of the wage gap. To the extent that wages are paid according to productivity under an incentive pay system, then the earnings ratio of ·88 could be taken to reflect the true productivity of females relative to males. If this were the case then wage discrimination (unequal pay for equal work) would account for one-third of the wage gap and productivity related differences the remaining two thirds. This is probably a conservative measure of the extent of wage discrimination however, since females may still receive a lower guaranteed wage than males and since women may be given job assignments that make it more difficult to earn production bonuses.

Although not as important as a union or an incentive pay system, other factors were found to influence male-female wage differentials. The gap was smaller in larger companies and in the low-wage "dead-end" occupations. Presumably, reflecting customer discrimination, the male-female wage gap was large in the trade sector where customer interface is important. Surprisingly, the impact of recent changes in equal pay legislation was found to have little impact on narrowing male-female wage differentials. This conclusion should be regarded as tentative however since establishments may not have had sufficient time to adjust to the equal pay legislation.

Other Canadian studies have tended to document male-female earnings differentials without really analysing the factors that influence these differentials. Judek documents male-female earnings differentials in the public service and concludes[18]: "Almost invariably men were earning more than women with similar education and experience." The differential widened with work experience and narrowed with higher education. Based on 1966 and 1967 data in 34 mixed occupations in the public service, Archibold[19] found that women were clustered at the lower end of the salary scale in most of the occupations. In a study of 1965/66 academic salaries, Robson and Lapointe[20] compute female salaries to be about 80% of male salaries. Adjusting for differences in age, field, rank, degree, region and university size raised this ratio to about ·90. Thus, they attribute about half of the male-female wage gap to sex discrimination in wage payments. It is noteworthy to point out that sex discrimination could still be responsible for differences in some of the adjustment factors: females may be discriminated against in obtaining a higher degree; they may be segregated into lower-pay "female-type" fields; and they may be excluded from the higher ranks in the academic profession.

Clearly the various empirical studies of earnings differentials in Canada indicate considerable pay gaps between men and women. Even after adjusting for differences in productivity related variables—differences which themselves may reflect discrimination—sizeable pay gaps remain. The ratio of female to male earnings, after adjusting for productivity related variables, tends to be in the rough neighbourhood of ·75 to ·90. Wage discrimination appears to account for the remaining 10 to 25 percentage points. Employment discrimination, whereby females are segregated into low-wage, dead-end jobs, would further widen the male-female wage gap due to sex discrimination.

Time Pattern of Male-Female Pay Differentials

Can we expect the male-female wage gap to disappear, or at least narrow, over time? Would a tight labour market narrow the differential? Most important, has the differential narrowed in recent years with the increased attention to equal pay legislation and the employment position of women in general?

As with most other countries, little analysis has been done on the time pattern of male-female wage differentials in Canada. Theory generally provides us with ambiguous answers as to the expected trend and cyclical pattern of the wage gap.

In the long-run over time, the forces of competition should serve to reduce, if not eradicate, any discriminatory wage gaps. Profit maximising employers would hire the low-wage females who are as productive as high-wage males. This increased demand for female labour would increase their wages; the process would stop only when relative wages were equal to relative marginal productivities. Certainly, adjustment costs and non-competitive, non-profit maximising forces would work against this trend[21]; yet these basic forces would be at work to reduce discrimination in wages and employment over time. Increased education and knowledge may also reduce discrimination over time, partly because they are determinants of tastes and prejudice and partly because discrimination may arise out of erroneous information. The large growth of the female labour force may also serve to break down sex stereotypes and other barriers to female employment. Due to urbanisation and improved transportation and communications, the forces of monopsony have also probably declined over time. In monopsonistic labour markets[22] females do not have the effective threat of mobility necessary to command a competitive wage. Their immobility results from their traditional ties to the household and to their husbands' places of employment. On the demand side, the decline in importance of heavy manual jobs and the rapid growth of white collar jobs, especially in the clerical and service sectors, should also increase female wages and employment.

Working against these forces are a variety of factors that would tend to depress female wages relative to male wages over time. To the extent that segments of society have a taste or preference for discrimination, then as income grows over time more of everything will be "purchased", including discrimination. In addition, the rapid increase in the labour force participation rate of females may depress female wages both because of the augmented supply of female labour and because prejudice may increase as the larger number of females constitute more of a threat to male job security.

In recent years, equal pay and equal employment laws, as well as pressure from the women's rights movement in general, may have narrowed male-female wage differentials. On the other hand, equal pay laws may actually widen the wage gap by reducing training options for females who would accept lower wages in order to acquire training in order to raise their future wages. In addition, equal pay laws may create unemployment amongst females and crowd them further into low-productivity jobs.

The business cycle may also alter male-female wage differentials over time, again in an undetermined manner. At the peak of a business cycle firms may be unable to expand their male workforce; consequently, they hire additional females with the result that female wages are increased. This may be augmented by the fact that during prosperity many females may withdraw from the labour force because they no longer need to supplement the family income. On the other hand, during periods of prosperity, females who were previously discouraged from looking for work because of the high unemployment rate, may now enter the labour force to look for work, thereby depressing female wages.

Since theory does not tell us unambiguously what will happen to male-female wage differences in the long-run and over the business cycle, we must appeal to the facts. Unfortunately, in Canada, as in other countries, little empirical work has been done on the subject. In comparing the 1951 and 1961 census years, Ostry[23] concludes: "From these data one might conclude that the "sex differential" was unchanged over the decade, but an examination of more detailed occupational information for the two census years suggests that the gap between male and female earnings may have widened between 1951 and 1961. However, the data are too fragmentary to sustain any intensive analysis and a study of trends must await further developmental work in the construction of historical series." Data from the Survey of Consumer Finance also indicate that between 1962 and 1967, "the overall female/male earnings differential has not narrowed"[24]. The salary gap between male and female academics was also reported to have widened between 1956 and 1964[25]. A study using narrowly defined occupations also finds that the male-female wage differential appears to be growing slightly over time and the gap does not narrow at the peak of the business cycle when the unemployment rate is low[26]. The study is confined to the province of Ontario, however, and it is based only on nine occupations that had continual data on male-female wages from 1946 to 1971.

Although the Canadian empirical evidence on the time pattern of male-female wage differentials is scant, the tentative conclusion that emerges is that we cannot hope for the passage of time to remove the wage differential. In fact the gap may well be widening over time. If this is the case, then legislation designed to combat sex discrimination in the labour market takes on an even more prominent role.

Sex Discrimination Legislation in the Labour Market

Labour legislation in Canada is complicated by the fact that under the Canadian constitution, legislation pertaining to labour and civil rights are under provincial jurisdiction[27]. The Federal government has jurisdiction only in specific industries of an inter-provincial or international nature: inter-provincial transportation and telephone communication, air transport, radio and television broadcasting, shipping and banks, fall under federal jurisdiction. Amendments to the constitution have extended the Federal government jurisdiction to certain areas of national concern, namely, unemployment. This has led to the development of a Federal unemployment insurance scheme as well as Federal manpower and training programmes. In spite of the limited jurisdiction of the Federal labour laws—they apply to less than 10% of the Canadian workforce—they often serve as a model for provincial legislation.

Ontario was the first province to introduce equal pay legislation in 1951. Subsequently, the Federal government (in 1956) and all other provinces with the exception of Quebec[28], have adopted equal pay legislation. Although there are important differences in the laws of each province they basically require equal pay for substantially similar work within the same establishment. Clearly the legislation is restricted in that job comparisons can only be made within the same establishment. In addition, action is usually taken only when an individual complains. And although most acts prevent reprisals from employers, this may not provide sufficient protection in the minds of most employees. Besides, there may be a reluctance to carry out an action that would involve considerable time and effort on the part of one, or a few, individuals, when the benefits may accrue to many workers. Partly to overcome these problems, in some provinces (e.g. Manitoba and Nova Scotia), the director of the appropriate government agency can initiate action. However, only in Ontario and the Federal government are investigations carried out on a routine basis, usually at the same time as inspections for violation of minimum wage laws.

Since there have been so few court cases involving equal pay laws in Canada, it is difficult to establish any pattern concerning interpretation of the law. The judge's statements in the case of Beckett v. Sault St. Marie Police Commission[29] are noteworthy: "He being a married man with a family to maintain and support, was paid at a rate somewhat higher than (the plaintiff) who was single and has no family obligations whatever (p. 635) . . . (The plaintiff) was fully aware of the salary she had agreed on (p. 640) . . . She is not being discriminated against by the fact that she receives a different wage, different from male constables, for that fact of difference is in accord with every rule of economics, civilisation, family life and common sense (p. 641) . . . It would appear from the evidence, both written and verbal, that this female member of the force is undermining the morale of the force. She is a menace to its esprit de corps (p. 641)". Needless to say, the judge ruled that the plaintiff, a female constable, was not entitled to the wages of a male constable.

Both the tone and interpretation of this case are in sharp contrast to some later interpretations. In the Greenacres Nursing Home Case[30] (Regina v. Howard), a court of appeals reversed an initial court interpretation that the same work meant identical work. The appeal court (p. 557) interpreted the same work to mean "work in fact being performed for an employer in the same establishment by females and males which is of the same nature or kind and the performance of which requires equal skill, effort and responsibility and which is performed under similar working conditions". The appeal court also determined that comparisons for equal work should be made on the basis of the work actually performed rather than on the nature of the job description or terms of employment.

In the Riverdale Hospital Case[31] the following interpretations emerge: different job titles do not indicate different work; differences in education or training requirements do not make the work unequal especially when such requirements are not relevant to the nature of the work performed; within an occupation, as long as some males do the same work as females then equal pay is justifiable for the whole occupation; slightly different job assignments do not make the work unequal; work can be essentially the same even if males and females are not interchangeable in that females, for physical reasons or reasons of conventional decency, do not perform certain tasks (e.g. heavy lifting, patient care of a personal nature).

In the case of Bell Canada v. Palmer[32] the Federal Court of Appeal upheld a lower court decision that equal pay procedures in progress could continue under a repealed statute even though an entirely new procedure is in operation. This is an important precedence in the equal pay area where laws and procedures are rapidly being changed.

Although it is difficult to generalise from so few court cases, it appears that equal pay laws are generally being interpreted rather broadly, especially with regards to what constitutes equal work. Inconsequential differences in qualifications or even in the tasks performed do not constitute grounds for pay differences between the sexes.

Having a law in the statute books and having it effectively enforced can be quite different. The following gives an indication of the differing enforcement efforts of the various jurisdictions[33]: Federal government, July 1971 to July 1973, 6 cases with settlements totalling $25,000 for 42 employees; Ontario, January 1969 to June 1973, 150 cases totalling $1,000,000 for 4,000 employees (Ontario stepped up its investigations in August 1973 with the result that $38,000 was awarded to 86 employees by the end of October); Newfoundland, September 1971 to September 1973, 10 cases totalling $813,500 for 2,312 employees; British Columbia, 1969 to 1973, settlement of $30,000 to 24 employees as well as $5,000,000 retroactive pay to 9,000 hospital workers. In other provinces, the number of cases has been minimal and the awards small. Clearly there is considerable variation in the attempts to enforce equal pay throughout the various labour jurisdictions of Canada.

In addition to equal pay laws, all provinces except Prince Edward Island have fair employment practices legislation designed to ensure equal opportunities between males and females in recruiting hiring and promotion. In most cases, the sex category was added by recent amendment to existing fair employment laws. Prince Edward Island and the Federal Government do have legislation prohibiting employment on the basis of race, national origin, colour or religion, but no explicit reference is made to sex. During 1972, 1973 and 1974 the Federal Government's Canada Labour Code was to be amended specifically to include a sex category; however in each case the amendment never went past first reading. As of August 1974 the Federal Labour Code still does not explicitly prohibit discrimination in employment opportunities on the basis of sex.

In most provinces, fair employment laws are part of the Provincial Human Rights Code. Although important differences exist in the procedures of each province, the basic process starts out from a complaint from an individual party to the provincial Human Rights Commission. An officer of the Commission tries to reach a settlement, usually by informal means out of court. If this is unsuccessful, a board of inquiry investigates and makes a decision or the employer is taken to court. Court cases are rare, however, and settlements are usually arrived at outside of court. In most cases, the Commission regards its role as a persuader rather than enforcer of the law. Efforts are often made to prevail upon employers to more actively recruit, hire and promote females.

Since court cases are rare and persuasive tactics important, little formal evidence exists of the enforcement activities or effectiveness of fair employment laws as they pertain to sex in Canada. Also, since most provinces have only just recently added the sex category to their fair employment laws, such an evaluation may be premature at this time.

In contrast to equal pay laws which are likely to have an adverse employment effect on females[34], fair employment practice legislation may increase both female wages and employment. This occurs because fair employment laws increase the demand for female labour at the recruiting, hiring and promotion stages[35]. Through the impersonal forces of the market this would serve to increase female wages.

In addition to equal pay and fair employment laws, other labour laws pertain specifically to female workers. As of January 1973, maternity leave provisions exist in the federal jurisdiction and in some provincial jurisdictions—namely British Columbia, Alberta, Manitoba, Ontario, New Brunswick and Nova Scotia[36]. To the extent that maternity leave provisions are regarded by employers as an additional cost, they would make employers reluctant to hire females unless they would accept a wage reduction to offset this cost. Of course, neither of these policies—reluctance to hire females or wage reduction by virtue of being a female—are permitted under fair employment or equal pay laws. Nevertheless, the pressure is there, and whether the laws can thwart such pressure is an open question.

The most controversial legislation pertaining to women are the "protective" labour laws. In addition to the usual labour standards laws that apply to both men and women, most jurisdictions[37] have legislation requiring the employer to provide free transportation to women on a midnight shift as well as legislation prohibiting the employment of women in some specified occupations. Although the intent of such legislation may be well meaning, there is the belief that it perpetrates the stereotype of women as the weaker sex and, in the words of Canada's Royal Commission on the Status of Women[38]: "Protective legislation for women has the effect of restricting their job opportunities."

Because of the divided labour jurisdiction in Canada, ratification of International Labour Conventions has been difficult. In 1964 Canada did ratify the International Labour Organisation Discrimination in Employment and Occupation Convention No. 111; and in 1972 Canada ratified the International Labour Organisation Equal Remuneration Convention No. 100. Adherence to the later convention will be difficult however partly because it requires equal *remuneration* for work of equal *value*. Most Canadian jurisdictions only require equal wages (not all forms of re-muneration) and they have shied away from the nation of "equal value", partly because of difficulties of practical application[39]. In order to comply with the ILO convention, most Canadian jurisdictions will have to remove exceptions to their law, step up enforcement activities, broaden the notion of pay to include all remuneration, specifically include males as well as females as entitled to equal pay, and attempt some form of job evaluation so as to determine work of equal value.

Unresolved Problems

Clearly there remain a variety of problems associated with the existing Canadian legislation on sex discrimination in the labour market. Coverage is not always complete; pay differences in the form of fringe benefits and other non-wage aspects of employment are not usually dealt with; wage comparisons are limited to the same establishment; and enforcement efforts are often negligible. We know precious little about the impact of such legislation on the relative wages and employment of females.

Nor do we know its aggregate impact on inflation, unemployment or income distribution.

Our knowledge of the basic trend and cyclical patterns of male-female wage differentials and occupational distributions, is also scant. Is the problem disappearing or worsening over time? Do full employment policies improve the wage and occupational position of females relative to males? What has happened in recent years with the advent of equal pay and fair employment laws and the women's movement in general? What will the picture look like in the future, given certain basic trends in occupational and industrial demand? What will be the future impact of various changes in labour supply such as fertility, immigration, labour force participation and hours of work? Even partial answers to these questions would help in our understanding of the time dimension of the issue of sex discrimination in the labour market.

Although somewhat more academic in nature, other questions pose dilemmas to researchers in the area. Can sex discrimination persist in a competitive economy in the long run, or would profit maximising firms eradicate such discrimination? More controversial: is sex discrimination more likely to persist in free enterprise, capitalist economies or in socialist-communist economies? Is discrimination more likely to prevail under decentralised collective bargaining or centralised bargaining or mixed systems? What are the main sources of discrimination—employers, customers, co-workers, unions or governments? Who gains and who loses from discrimination? What theories of discrimination are most applicable: those that emphasise the tastes and preferences of discriminators or those that emphasise occupational crowding, segmented labour markets and market imperfection? Answers to these questions have obvious policy implications.

Support of the union movement is generally regarded as extremely important in the move towards equal pay and equal employment opportunity. Unions can provide the vehicles for complaints (e.g. shop steward, grievance procedure) as well as the formal collective agreement to ensure equal pay and employment opportunities. In addition, they provide a mechanism to formalise job descriptions so as to determine work that is of equal value or substantially similar. Finally, the internal trade-offs within the union determine the size of the package they will bargain for and how their gains are distributed within the union. Only if women are well represented will they have a say in these union objectives. The unresolved issue then is how to involve women more in the union movement, especially at the decision making levels. Although there is no single answer, two observations have repeatedly been voiced: union leaders must press upon the rank and file that issues of equal employment opportunity and equal pay for equal work are fundamental union objectives; and women must look primarily to themselves to make progress within the rank and file and leadership of the unions.

Perhaps the potentially most important unresolved issues lie outside of the labour market. Pre-labour market discrimination and years of conditioning in female roles may give women a perception of themselves that leads them to perform below their potential in the labour market. Can, and should, these factors be changed? If they are changed, will the labour market change to accommodate the rising expectations of females? How can the attitudes of employers, customers, co-workers and unions be altered to provide an environment that is conducive to removing sex discrimination in the labour market? Until such basic attitudes change, it is not clear that legislation or any other form of market intervention can have much of an impact.

References
1. *Women in the Labour Force: Facts and Figures*, Ottawa, Information Canada, 1974, p. 281.
2. Galenson, M., *Women and Work: An International Comparison*, Ithaca, New York State School of Industrial and Labor Relations, Cornell University, 1973, p. 85.
3. For a discussion of the time pattern of the occupational distribution of females in Canada see Ostry, S., *The Occupational Composition of the Canadian Labour Force*, Ottawa, Information Canada, 1971, especially pp. 27-29.
4. *Women in the Labour Force, op. cit.*, p. 265.
5. Gelber, S., "Organised Labour and the Working Woman", in *Woman's Bureau* 1973, Ottawa, Information Canada, 1974, p. 18.
6. For a discussion of these attitudes see, Geoffroy, R., and Sainte-Marie, P., *Attitude of Union Workers to Women in Industry*, Study No. 9 for the Royal Commission on the Status of Women in Canada, Ottawa, Information Canada, 1971.
7. All figures in this paragraph are from *Earnings and Work Experience of the 1967 Labour Force* No. 13-535, Ottawa, Information Canada, 1971, p. 15. The data base is the Survey of Consumer Finance.
8. The crowding hypothesis was first advanced in Fawcett, M., "Equal Pay for Equal Work", *Economic Journal*, 28 (March 1918), pp. 1-6, and Edgeworth, F., "Equal Pay to Men and Women for Equal Work", *Economic Journal*, 32 (December 1922), pp. 431-57. It has subsequently been formalised in Bergmann, B., "The Effect on White Incomes of Discrimination in Employment", *Journal of Political Economy*, 79 (March/April 1971), pp. 294-313.
9. This is the average ratio of female to male earnings for the period 1946-1971 for the nine occupations in the province of Ontario which had identical job descriptions for males and females. See Gunderson, M., *Time Pattern of Male-Female Wage Differentials: Ontario 1946-71*. University of Toronto, Centre for Industrial Relations, 1974, p. 13. Data is from the Canada Department of Labour Survey of Wage Rates, Salaries and Hours of Labour. The female to male average wage ratio, w_f/w_m, of ·75 is calculated from the average proportionate wage differential, $(w_m-w_f)/w_f$, of ·33.
10. Gunderson, M., "Male-Female Wage Differentials and the Impact of Equal Pay Legislation, *Review of Economics and Statistics*, forthcoming.
11. Ostry, S., *The Female Worker in Canada*, 1961 Census Monograph, Ottawa, Dominion Bureau of Statistics, 1968, p. 43.
12. Actually the ratio of female to male earnings is ·672 based on female weights (i.e. assuming males were represented in the occupation in the same proportion as females), and ·656 based on male weights (i.e. assuming females were represented in the occupation in the same proportion as males). This is akin to the familiar index number problem. For ease of exposition, a simple average of the two figures is presented for all the adjustment factors; the true figures are given in the Ostry text.
13. Ostry does not give the occupational breakdown of the contribution of each adjustment factor in closing the male-female wage gap; consequently, we do not know whether it was the adjustment for age and education or for the distribution of males and females within each occupation that was responsible for closing the wage gap.
14. *Ibid.*, p. 44.
15. Holmes, R. A., "Male-Female Earnings Differentials in Canada", Simon Fraser University, Department of Economics and Commerce, Discussion Paper 74-5-2, p. 9.
16. To adjust for differences in male-female characteristics, male earnings are first regressed against the male characteristics variables (e.g. occupation, marital states, etc.); the regression coefficients indicate the effect on male earnings of changes in their characteristics. Multiplying the regression

coefficients for the male wage equation with the average value of the corresponding explanatory variables for females, gives the expected female wage if females were paid according to the male pay structure. Since the pay structures are the same for both sexes, differences in expected earnings reflect differences in the characteristics of males and females. The earnings differential would be purged of the effects of wage discrimination (different pay for the same characteristics); however it may still reflect discrimination to the extent that males and females are distributed differently across different characteristics (e.g. occupation). Similar adjustment techniques have been used in Blinder, A., "Wage Discrimination: Reduced Form and Structural Estimates", *Journal of Human Resources*, 8 (Fall 1973), pp. 436-55; Malkiel, B. and J., "Male-Female Pay Differentials in Professional Employment", *American Economic Review*, 63 (September 1973) pp. 693-705; and Oaxaca, R., "Male-Female Wage Differentials in Urban Labour Markets", *International Economic Review*, 14 (October 1973), pp. 693-709.

17. Gunderson, M., "Male-Female Wage Differentials and the Impact of Equal Pay Legislation", *Review of Economics and Statistics* (forthcoming). Data are from the Canada Department of Labour Survey of Wage and Salary Rates for the years 1968 and 1969 for the province of Ontario only.

18. Judek, S., *Women in the Public Service*, Economics and Research Branch, Canada Department of Labour, Ottawa, Information Canada, 1967, p. 49.

19. Archibald, K., *Sex and the Public Service*, Study for the Public Service Commission of Canada, Ottawa, Information Canada, 1970, pp. 24-27.

20. Robson, R., and Lapointe, M., *A Comparison of Mens' and Women's Salaries and Employment Fringe Benefits in the Academic Profession*, Study No. 1 of the Royal Commission on the Status of Women in Canada, Ottawa, Information Canada, 1971.

21. For a discussion of these factors and their implications for the persistence of discriminatory wage payments see: Arrow, K., "The Theory of Discrimination", in *Discrimination in Labour Markets*, edited by O. Ashenfetter and A. Rees, Princeton, Princeton University Press, 1973, pp. 20-23; Stiglitz, J., "Approaches to the Economics of Discrimination", *American Economic Review Papers and Proceedings*, Vol. 63 (May 1973), pp. 287-96; and Freeman, R., "Decline of Labour Market Discrimination and Economic Analysis", *American Economic Review Papers and Proceedings*, Vo. 63 (May 1973), pp. 280-87.

22. For a discussion of sex discrimination and monopsony see Madden, J., *The Economics of Sex Discrimination*, Lexington, Mass., Lexington Books, 1972, pp. 69-85.

23. Ostry, S., *op. cit.*, p. 39.

24. *Earnings and Work Experience of the 1967 Labour Force*. Publication No. 13-535, Ottawa, Dominion Bureau of Statistics, 1971, p. 14.

25. Robson, R., and Lapointe, M., *op. cit.*, p. 11.

26. Gunderson, M., *Time Pattern of Male-Female Wage Differentials: Ontario 1946-71*, University of Toronto, Centre for Industrial Relations, 1974.

27. For a discussion of these jurisdictional issues see Gelber, S., "Women and Work in Canada: A Study of Legislation", 23rd Annual Conference, Industrial Relations Centre, McGill University, 1974.

28. Quebec's Employment Discrimination Act does prohibit any distinction, exclusion or preference made on the basis of sex which has the basis of nullifying or impairing equality of opportunity of treatment. No explicit reference is made to equal pay however.

29. *Ontario Reports*, 1968, Vol. 1, pp. 633-642.

30. *Ontario Reports*, 1970, Vol. 3, pp. 555-57.

31. *Ontario Reports*, 1973, Vol. 2, pp. 441-447.

32. *Dominion Law Reports*, 1974, Vol. 42 (3d.), pp. 1-7.

33. *Women at Work*, Vol. 1 No. 2 (December 1973), Women's Bureau, Canada Department of Labour, p. 3.

34. The magnitude of the adverse employment effect of equal pay laws depends on the elasticity of derived demand for female labour. The demand for female labour will be inelastic and the adverse employment effect small if: female labour costs are a small proportion of total cost; few good substitute factors (including male labour) are available; substitute factors are in inelastic supply so that an increase in their utilisation raises their price; and the demand for the product produced by females is inelastic so that cost increase can be passed on to the consumer in the form of price increases without there being much of a reduction in the demand for the product and hence in the derived demand for females.

35. This statement may not be entirely true. Faced with the prospect of having to promote females once hired, employers may be reluctant to hire them. Or faced with the prospect of having to hire females once they are screened, employers may be reluctant to recruit them. In this way the demand for female labour might be reduced at the recruiting and hiring stages. Of course, an effective fair employment law would prevent such actions. Nevertheless, the possibility remains that employers may be reluctant to recruit females for fear of being accused of discrimination at the hiring and promotion stages.
36. For a discussion of eligibility, length of leave time and reinstatement provisions in the various jurisdictions see *International Instruments and Canadian Federal and Provincial Legislation Relating to the Status of Women in Employment*, Ottawa, Labour Canada, Women's Bureau, 1972, pp. 14-16.
37. *Ibid*, pp. 17-25.
38. *Report of the Royal Commission on the Status of Women in Canada*, Ottawa, Information Canada, 1970, p. 89.
39. *Equal Remuneration for Work of Equal Value*, Ottawa, International Labour Affairs Branch, Canada Department of Labour, 1970, pp. 6-7.

The Equal Pay Question in Japan

by E. & K. Thurley

I. Japan as a Special Case?

On the face of it there are a number of reasons for expecting the equal pay question in Japan to have some special features. The most obvious reason is the extent and severity of distinctions based on sex (and age) criteria in traditional Japanese culture and society. The Japanese language itself has different inflections according to the sex of the speaker. The roles of women were prescribed particularly under the Tokugawa Shogunate in the 17th, 18th and 19th centuries, to a very precise degree. In some areas there was total segregation enforced for Samurai families for eating and even for washing clothes, where male and female garments had to be kept completely apart.

"Every house of noble class, in those days, was divided into the home department, ruled by the mistress, where there were only women attendants and the lord's department, where every branch was done by men. For delicate and artistic duties, such as tea-serving and flower arranging, graceful youths were chosen who dressed in gay garments with swinging sleeves like girls and wore their hair in an artistic crown-queue with fluffy sides"[1].

At all levels of society, family roles showed clear distinctions in the demands placed on boys and girls after they grew beyond the stage of infancy. As Geoffrey Gorer puts it:

"The girls must still remain passive, but they are no longer the centre of attention and are no longer so much rewarded for their passivity; instead they are severely punished for any lapse therefrom, for any gesture of self assertion that they may make. As they grow up, the restrictions on their movements, posture and language are constantly increased, reaching their culmination at marriage. There seems to be a conscious fear among Japanese parents that their daughters will grow up inadequately feminine; the greatest praise that can be given a girl or her parents is that she is *onnarashii* (like a girl) or *otonashii* (quiet and inconspicuous); the term *otokorashii* (like a boy) is the worst insult that a girl can receive and the most humiliating that a parent can hear. It is worth noting that the converse is not true of boys; even the most effeminate and cowardly boy is so superior to any women, that there is no equivalent term for 'sissy' "[2].

Gorer goes on to describe the dominance boys exert from an early age over all female relations. In a dispute with a sister, he says both parents will insist on the girl giving way and displays of aggression against the mother and aunts are clearly permitted in the home. Women have to rise earlier than men and have to take their bath later. This picture of traditional sex distinctions is borne out by the evidence from novels of the Meiji period (late 19th century) about the plight of the daughter-in law (yome) in the household of her husband. A newly wedded girl occupied the lowest adult status in the household and was clearly subordinate to the instructions of her mother-in law (shutome). If a girl wanted to remain unmarried, it was certainly difficult to do so against the pressures exerted by family, friends and elders in the community. Even as a widow, the pressures exerted to control behaviour were not relaxed. The stories of nine Second World War widows have been related in a book recently published[3]. They lived in a farming village in the north of Honshu and twenty years after the war had not remarried. Nevertheless they had to serve both children and parents-in law in a situation of almost complete isolation and ridicule from their fellow villagers.

The existence of strict norms about sex roles in society is not unique to Japan, of course. What makes it of interest for international comparisons of the relative rewards and positions of women in advanced societies, is the survival of such belief into a period of rapid and dramatic economic growth. According to Ohkawa and Rosovsky[4], GNP (in 1934-36 prices) increased from Y2,318 m in 1879 to Y40,466 m by 1960, representing a growth of GNP per head of Y63·3 to Y433·3. In real terms, Gross Domestic Product increased further from 1960 to 1971 at the average rate of 9·6% per capita per annum[5]. This growth was only made possible, as we shall see below, by a sharp shift of manpower into manufacturing and related activities. The last ten years in Japan, therefore, provide an opportunity to examine the impact of mounting labour shortage, in a situation of very severe sexual regulations defining the family and work roles of women. The development of labour market pressures, eroding traditional norms and expectations, is thus the main subject of interest in this essay. The effect of changing belief about the equality of women is far more difficult to disentangle in manpower and wage data and in any event can hardly be seen as a major political and social force up to the present. What needs to be stressed, however, is that institutional practices have channelled such labour market pressures in four major directions:

(1) Firstly, migration from country to city has traditionally in Japan been a male migration movement. The sex ratio of Edo and other castle towns in the Tokugawa period (exclusive of warriors and priests) was greatly in favour of men in the eighteenth century, but had become almost equal by the mid-nineteenth century[6]. In recent years, there has been a tendency for men to leave agriculture for seasonal construction work or industrial work and for women to keep the farms going. The small size of most Japanese farms, since the land reforms of 1947-8 is one factor which has allowed this to happen. A further complication here is the rapid decline of rural fertility rates since the late forties. Much occupational mobility in Japan in the last hundred years has been possible due to the existence of much higher fertility rates in rural areas than in the cities, allowing a constant flow of the younger sons of farmers into the cities, followed by some of their daughters.

(2) The prevalence of 'lifetime employment practices' among Japanese industrial and commercial enterprises has been much discussed of late[7]. One of the main policies at the root of this so-called industrial paternalism is the aim of recruiting key workers, white collar staff and managers directly from school or university. Such recruitment has often been deliberately from rural areas, tapping the surplus labour resources discussed above. Recruitment of female school leavers, however, has not been identified traditionally with a life time career. On the contrary, until fairly recently, the typical company would expect to have some responsibility for the education and welfare of young female employees and indeed to help with possible marriage partners, but at the point of marriage, employment ceased. The existence of cadres of life-time committed male staff in Japanese companies, however, dominates the structure of wage differentials. The explosion of Japanese growth in the 1960's has been through institutions which were expanding rapidly but which were based on the provision of life-time careers and therefore of age and seniority related salaries for both blue and white collar staff. In spite of many changes of detailed policy on wages, introducing particularly, job-related wage elements, the wage structure is based on the seniority and career principle. This fact has major implications for the questions of equal pay and equal opportunities for women.

(3) Government legislation since 1945 has tended to follow international practice in defining labour standards, in supporting the principle of equal wages for work of equal value,* in restricting hours of work and night work for women, in providing maternity leave and in promoting measures for protecting the welfare of women. There has, therefore, been some pressure on the public sector at least, to provide formal equality in wage levels for similar jobs.

(4) Finally, Government intervention in the labour market in terms of improved employment services and specialized vocational training centres has become much more important since 1965. The Vocational Training Law which was revised in 1969, has been the main instrument of change here.

Japan, therefore, has some claim to be of special interest for the equal pay debate as it provides a classic case of conflict between the traditional cultural norms of discrimination, and economic necessity, in terms of labour shortages. It is, however, a very complex situation, as one has to assess this conflict in the middle of shifts in demographic structure, migration patterns, educational changes and government intervention, all of which affect the structure of the labour market, traditionally dominated by paternalistic personnel policies. Before examining actual wage data, therefore, it is necessary to look at these factors in a little more detail.

---

*In September 1947, the Labour Standards Bureau defined equal pay as follows: "differentiation of wages by reason of differences in individual efficiency shall not be unlawful, but differentiation by reason of the efficiency of women workers being in general and on the average lower than that of male workers shall be unlawful". In 1967 the Government ratified ILO Convention No. 100, "Equal Remuneration".

II. Political, Demographic, and Educational Changes

Politics

Women received the vote for the first time in Japan after the Second World War and Article 14 of the new Constitution of November 3rd 1946 states:

"All of the people are equal under the law and there shall be no discrimination in political, economic or social relations because of race, creed, sex, social status or family origin."

The effect of liberal and democratic policies was dramatic in many areas of Japanese society, for example, Labour Union Organisation, land reform and local government functions and structure. How should one evaluate the importance of feminism as a political pressure group? The answer to this question can be partially seen in Table I.

Two trends are apparent from the table. The gradual increased interest of women in voting at general elections and the decline in the number of women actually elected. In fact there is a slightly lower proportion elected to municipal and prefectural assemblies although there are also some 30,000 women active in public work (September 1970). Women, for example, form a little over 30% of the mediation committee of Domestic Affairs, Welfare Commissions and Child Counsellors. Two women have been appointed to cabinet positions since the war and several more women have been parliamentary vice-ministers. However, it is clear that, in spite of the existence of some 50 national associations of women (many organised under each political party) and in spite of some active political lobbying for new legislation for women's and children's welfare through women members of the Diet, it would be difficult to argue that the women's movement in Japan has had any really major impact on the political scene. A survey by the Prime Minister's Office noted that women's political consciousness is still very low; only 16% indicated a "high" or "fair" amount of interest in political affairs. Women's Lib or "Ribu" groups do exist now in Japan since 1969 or 1970, but they tend to recruit unmarried girls under twenty five who are mostly ex-students. They only organise into autonomous groups or cells locally and there is no national organisation, no central head-quarters and they have no plan to form one[8]. Students pick up political experience in the student movement,

Table I. Sex differences in post-war voting behaviour in Japan
(Elections for House of Representatives)

Dates of election	Eligible voters (m)		Votes cast (m)		Voting rates (%)		Women elected	Total no. elected
	M	F	M	F	M	F		
April 10 1946	16	21	13	14	78·5	67·0	39	466
Oct. 1 1952	22	24	18	18	80·5	72·8	12	466
Nov. 20 1960	26	28	20	20	76·0	71·2	7	466
Dec. 10 1972	36	38	26	28	71·0	72·5	7	491

(Source: Election Bureau, Ministry of Home Affairs)

but it is notable that there are no courses on politics in women's junior colleges and only five in women's colleges and universities[9]. We should therefore be fairly cautious before attributing any major political importance to feminist groups up to the present.

Demographic changes

We need to turn now to examine some recent changes in family life which clearly are important in affecting labour markets in Japan. Table II summarises the trends in vital statistics between 1933 and 1972.

The drastic decline of the birth rate since 1955 has meant that the average number of children per couple has dropped from more than five in pre-war years to 2·7 in 1970. At the same time, child-bearing ages for the mother have been concentrated particularly during the period from 25 to 29 years of age. The decline in the death rate reflects an increase of life expectancy. In 1972 it had become 70·49 years for men and 75·92 for women, an increase of five years during the last ten years.

The effect of these trends on the age and sex structure of the population is seen in Table III and Figure 1. The decline in the size of the age cohorts under twenty years of age is very marked. It also should be noted that the sex ratio of these groups is different from those over 20, girls now becoming a minority rather than a majority group.

We can summarise the demographic situation, therefore, as leading to the following possibilities:

(1) A greatly increased proportion of women from 35-40 upwards, who are relatively free from looking after children and are therefore potentially available for paid employment;

Table II. Vital Statistics

Year	Births	Deaths	Natural Increase	Infant mortality rate (per 1,000 live births)	Expectation of life at birth* Male	Female
	per 1,000 persons					
Av. 1933—37	30·8	17·4	13·3	115·1	46·92	49·63
1947—49	33·6	12·7	20·9	67·0	50·06	53·96
1950—54	23·7	9·4	14·3	52·1	59·57	62·97
1955—59	18·1	7·8	10·3	37·7	63·60	67·75
1960—64	17·2	7·3	9·9	25·9	65·32	70·19
1965	18·6	7·1	11·4	18·5	67·74	72·92
1968	18·6	6·8	11·8	15·3	69·05	74·30
1969	18·5	6·8	11·7	14·2	69·18	74·67
1970	18·8	6·9	11·8	13·1	69·33	74·71
1971	19·2	6·6	12·6	12·4	70·17	75·58
1972	19·3	6·5	12·8	11·7	70·49	75·92

*For 1933—37 and 1950—54, averages of 1935 to 36 and 1950 to 52, respectively. For 1947—49, 1955—59 and 1960—64, at the first year of the period.
(Source: Ministry of Health and Welfare)

Table III. Population by Age and Sex (1973)

(1,000 persons)

Age	Total	Male	Female	Age	Total	Male	Female
All ages	108,710	53,331	55,379	45—49	6,864	3,346	3,518
0—4	9,866	5,072	4,793	50—54	5,265	2,306	2,959
5—9	8,573	4,386	4,187	55—59	4,537	2,051	2,485
10—14	8,007	4,087	3,921	60—64	4,110	1,879	2,231
15—19	8,166	4,149	4,017	65—69	3,149	1,460	1,690
20—24	10,296	5,136	5,160	70—74	2,441	1,093	1,348
25—29	9,561	4,737	4,824	75—79	1,488	624	864
30—34	8,940	4,440	4,500	80—84	735	276	459
35—39	8,434	4,210	4,224	85 years	347	107	239
40—44	7,931	3,972	3,959	and over			

(Source: Bureau of Statistics, Office of the Prime Minister)

Figure 1. Population by age and sex (1973)

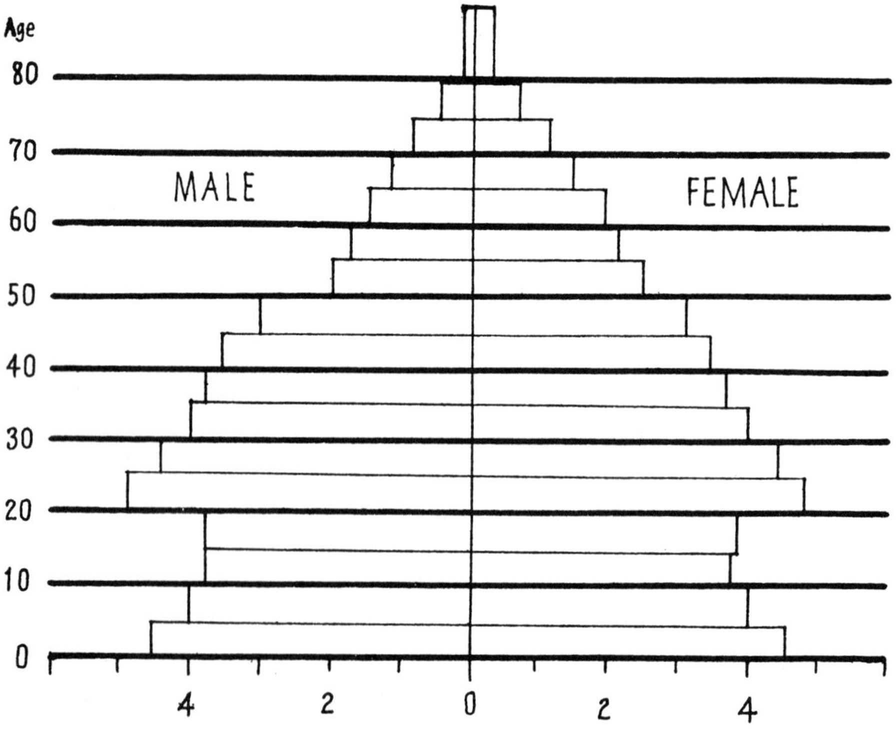

(2) A greatly decreased number of young girls available for employment, especially over the next ten to fifteen years;

(3) A smaller proportion of girls leaving school compared with boys, which will increase their scarcity value.

Education

The other main factors affecting these predictions are trends in secondary and higher education. Table IV shows the percentage of the age groups 15-18 and 18-20 in 1955, 1970 and 1973 entering secondary and higher education.

The drastic changes in education over this period are brought out by this table. Virtually the whole of the 15-18 age group is now in full or part-time education and nearly a third continues on with their education after this age.

Table V shows that there has been a rise in the proportion of girls continuing on after their high school education from 1950 to 1972. By comparison, the proportion of boys was larger to start with; it fell in the 1960's, but is now climbing again.

Table VI shows the popularity of 'tankidaigaku' (2 year colleges) for women and shows that in spite of nearly equal proportions between the sexes of the age group going to all higher education, two thirds of the full-time institutions are still occupied by males. It also demonstrates the small number of girls studying natural science and social science. From all these tables we can conclude: (a) that the growth of higher education has further reduced the numbers of unmarried girl school leavers under 20

Table IV. Percentage of age group entering senior high schools (15-18) and all types of higher education (universities and colleges) (including those attending whilst in employment) (18-20)

	Senior high schools		Higher education	
	M	F	M	F
1955	55·5	47·4	20·9	14·9
1970	81·6	82·7	25·0	23·5
1973	88·3	90·6	31·6	30·8

(Source: Report on school statistics, Ministry of Education)

Table V. Percentage of senior high school graduates entering higher education (including those attending whilst in employment)

	M	F	Total
1950	34·6	17·2	30·3
1960	19·7	14·2	17·2
1970	25·0	23·5	24·3
1972	30·0	28·4	29·2

(Source: Report on school statistics, Ministry of Education)

Table VI. Types of student employment in higher education (1972)

| | Numbers of students ('000s) | | |
	M	F	% of women
2 years course colleges	45	239	84
Universities	1,182	278	19
State	255	71	22
Private	926	206	18
Main subjects studied at universities			
Literature	87	102	54
Social Science	576	36	6
Nat. Science	38	6	14
Teachers Training	46	54	54

(Source: Report on school statistics, Ministry of Education)

available as new entrants to companies; (b) that much of this higher education is of a non-vocational character and does not necessarily lead to the growth of a professional female labour force.

Changes in family structure

There remains the effect of changing pattern of family structure on the female labour force. The census data from 1920 showed the average farm household contained 5·4 members compared with 4·40 for manufacturing, 4·16 for professional and public service occupations and 4·60 for commerce. 42% of such families had three or more generations living together compared with 17% of the families occupied in commerce, manufacturing, public service and professional work[10]. The changes in this situation after the Second World War can be seen by examining Tables VII and VIII.

The growth of nuclear families can be hypothesised as having the effect of weakening the traditional duties of wives to parents in law and of (potentially) allowing such wives to return to employment when their children were over primary school age. The

Table VII. Average household size and proportion of rural in total population, 1946-60

| | No. of persons per household | | Population in farm households as % of total population |
	All Japanese households	Rural households	
1946	4·9	6·0	46·8
1950	5·0	6·1	45·4
1955	5·0	6·0	40·8
1960	4·6	5·7	37·0

(Source: Fukutake Tadashi[11])

Table VIII. Type of household by region, 1920 and 1960

	Type of family	All Japan	6 large cities	Smaller cities	Towns & villages
1920	Nuclear	60·0%	73·5%	72·6%	56·9%
	Extended	40·0%	26·5%	27·4%	43·1%
1960	Nuclear	65·1%	78·2%	67·8%	55·0%
	Extended	34·9%	21·8%	32·2%	45·0%

(Source: Fukutake Tadashi[12])

reduction of the rural population does not necessarily release female labour (as argued above) but if the number of households are reduced in the long run this will also lead to a potential rise in the participation rates of women in the labour force.

III. Women in the Labour Force

We can now briefly explain the actual trends in the employment of women in Japan, reflecting the factors noted above. Table IX summarises the nature of the labour force in Japan and shows the extent to which it increased from 1960 to 1973.

The growth of the male employed labour force was much greater than that of the female labour force in this period. Table X makes this clearer by showing the labour force participation rates for each sex.

Table IX. Labour force status (1,000 persons)

	Pop. 15 yrs+		Employed L/force		Wholly unemployed		Not in L/force	
	M	F	M	F	M	F	M	F
1960	31,450	33,700	26,290	18,070	440	310	4,720	15,260
1970	38,250	40,600	30,910	20,030	380	210	6,910	20,320
1973	39,690	42,390	32,110	20,210	430	240	7,040	21,830

(Source: Bureau of Statistics, Prime Minister's Office)

Table X. Labour force participation rates for each sex

	Male	Female
1960	84·8	54·5
1965	81·7	50·6
1970	81·8	49·9
1973	82·0	48·3

(Source: Bureau of Statistics, Prime Minister's Office)

Table XI. Women in the Labour Force by Age Group (1,000 persons)

	Number		Participation rate	
	1968	1972	1968	1972
Total	20,030	19,810	50·7%	47·8%
15—19 year olds	1,990	1,170	38·1	28·5
20—24	3,320	3,670	70·1	67·4
25—29	2,120	1,910	48·0	43·0
30—34	2,090	1,990	49·6	45·7
35—39	2,320	2,310	58·5	55·4
40—54	5,610	6,080	62·1	60·7
55—64	1,850	2,000	45·1	43·7
65 and over	730	680	18·9	15·6

(Source: *Labour Force Survey*, Statistics Bureau, Office of the Prime Minister)

The impact of the expansion of higher education can be clearly seen in these figures. The decline in the female participation rate is particularly marked. An analysis of employment participation rates by age group shows different rates of decline (Table XI).

The age groups, 20-24, and 40-64 expanded in numbers in the labour force, although participation rates declined slightly. Sharper falls in participation rates were seen in the under 20 group and the 25-40 group. Where were these women employed? Table XII shows the shifts that have taken place in these thirteen years between different sectors of the economy.

The increase in the tertiary sector is largely due to increase in services and commerce and finance. Just over a quarter of women in the labour force are in manufacturing, compared with 49% in services, wholesale and retail trade, finance, insurance and real estate. Figures for 1972, show that women in agriculture and forestry only represent 19% of total female employment, but they were 52% of the labour force in those industries. In manufacturing, women were 37% of the labour force, in wholesale, retail trade, finance, insurance, real estate 46% and services 49%.

Women in the labour force can be classified into paid employees, family workers and self-employed. Figure 2 shows how quickly paid employees are replacing unpaid family workers.

Table XII. Female labour force by sector of economy (1,000 persons)

	Primary	Secondary	Tertiary
1960	7,160	3,490	7,410
1970	5,070	5,180	9,500
1973	4,180	5,420	10,250

(Source: Bureau of Statistics, Office of Prime Minister)

Figure 2. Trend of Employed Women

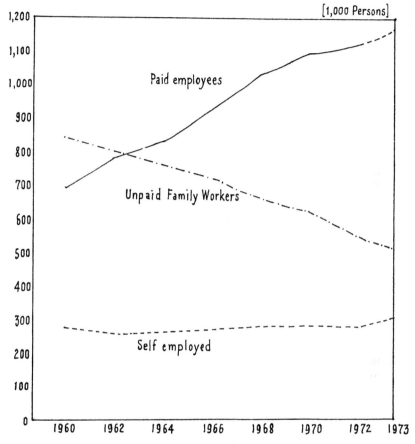

(Source: *Labour Force Survey*, Statistics Bureau, Office of the Prime Minister)

If we examine paid employees alone, they numbered 11·2 millions in 1972, (32% of all paid employees). 28% were between 20-24, 29% between 25-39 and 32% between 40-64. Participation rates for paid employees vary considerably from those shown for all women in the labour force in Table XI.

The figures in Table XIII make it clear that the majority of family workers and self-employed workers are in the older age groups. Apart from the sector of activity, it is useful to examine the distribution of women workers by occupation. Figure 3 shows the relative proportion of women employees in various occupations. Clerical work accounts for nearly one third, operative (in manufacturing) another 27%.

Table XIII. Participation rates of all women in the labour force by age group compared with paid employees (1972)

Age group	Participation rates	
	All labour force	Paid employees
15—19	28·5	26·1
20—24	67·4	57·6
25—29	43·0	27·0
30—34	45·7	22·2
35—39	55·4	26·9
40—54	60·7	28·6
55—64	43·7	15·1
65 over	15·6	3·1
Total	47·8%	27·0%

(Source: *Labour Force Survey*, Office of Prime Minister)

Figure 3. Women Employees by Occupation—1972

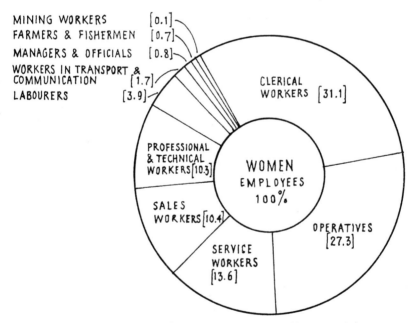

MINING WORKERS [0.1]
FARMERS & FISHERMEN [0.7]
MANAGERS & OFFICIALS [0.8]
WORKERS IN TRANSPORT & COMMUNICATION [1.7]
LABOURERS [3.9]

CLERICAL WORKERS [31.1]

PROFESSIONAL & TECHNICAL WORKERS [10.3]

WOMEN EMPLOYEES 100%.

SALES WORKERS [10.4]

OPERATIVES [27.3]

SERVICE WORKERS [13.6]

(Source: *Labour Force Survey*, Statistics Bureau, Office of the Prime Minister)

The proportion of women to men in each occupational strata is also worth noting. Table XIV gives some overall proportion for 1972. Table XV shows the changes between 1965 and 1970 for a selection of more precise occupational groups.

Table XIV. Proportion of paid women employees to men in occupational strata (1972)

	%
Service workers	53·0
Clerical and related	46·8
Professional and technical	41·8
Labourers	31·9
Sales workers	31·7
Operatives	25·6
Farmers and fishermen	20·0
Workers in transport and communications	8·6
Managers and officials	5·2

(Source: *Labour Force Survey*, Statistics Bureau, Office of Prime Minister)

Table XV. Women in Selected Occupations

Selected occupation	Number (Persons)		As per cent of total employed	
	1965	1970	1965	1970
			%	%
Technicians	2,700	9,795	0·6	1·4
Teachers	304,100	379,375	35·5	37·9
Physicians	10,500	11,245	9·9	9·5
Pharmacists	15,300	24,170	60·9	48·2
Nurses	230,500	306,780	98·3	97·6
Artists	37,000	30,445	35·5	25·7
Scientists	4,900	5,160	7·0	5·2
Judges, Prosecutors, Lawyers	200	300	0·5	2·4
Nursery nurses	64,800	95,845	100·0	100·0
Social workers	8,600	16,140	39·5	44·8
Managerial workers	79,200	97,590	5·6	4·8
Clerks	1,666,100	2,240,265	39·4	45·2
Stenographers, Typists	85,200	86,930	96·6	96·9
Operatives (electric machinery)	228,900	488,740	42·1	52·2
Operatives (yarn, thread and fabric mills)	858,200	788,745	71·9	71·0
Service workers (except household)	1,814,600	1,877,665	67·8	66·8
Household workers	185,500	138,810	100·0	98·3
Civil servants in managerial posts	900	1,060	1·1	1·0
Telephone operatives	161,400	145,110	96·6	97·0
Farmers	5,790,000	5,078,185	54·4	56·1

(Source: Population Census)

The concentration on service occupations is very striking as well as the relatively small proportions of women in professional and technical jobs. Figure 4 shows the contrast with male employment in each occupation.

Figure 4. Employed Persons by Occupation (1972)

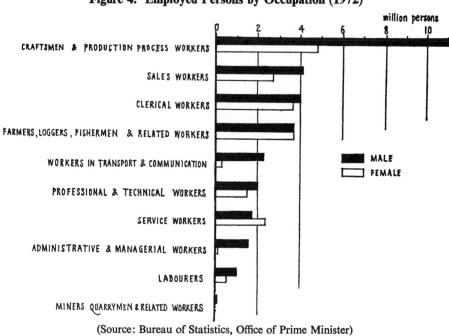

(Source: Bureau of Statistics, Office of Prime Minister)

We have argued above that the shortage of young school leavers has begun to force employers to consider employing older women. The significance of this change can be tested by examining the proportion of married women workers to single, widowed or divorced. Taking the non-agricultural sector, in 1960 25% of all women workers were married and 62% were single. By 1972, 46% were married, 43% single and 10% widowed or divorced[13]. The three million extra employees that joined in the labour force in the 1960s were mostly married women. One in five married women are now working in the non-agricultural sector of the economy. As would be expected, this is associated with an increase in the proportion of part-time women workers (in 1969 11·5%, in 1973 14·4% of all women workers).

What implications can be drawn from this data for the equal pay question?

Firstly, it is clear that the labour market is structured by the dual economy of Japan[14], so that the shifts to paid employee status and the increases in employment of women in services, wholesale and retail, finance, insurance and real estate are particularly important. It is only in the "modernised" sector of the economy that the equal pay question is even relevant.

Secondly, economic expansion has coincided with a growing shortage of school leaver recruits to employment (for demographic and educational reasons) and demand for labour has therefore grown for older married women. 53·9% of paid women employees were over 30 in 1973 and 47·2% were married. Figure 5 shows that about a third of each main age group of married women are working (in the non-agricultural sector) with a drop between 20-35 for child rearing.

The rate of inflation and pressures for keeping up high standards of living now increasingly persuade married women to take up employment. Such a tendency conflicts with paternalistic personnel policies and wage systems based on seniority, but it is possible to adjust the system to employ married women in relatively marginal positions.

Thirdly, shortages of female labour and the practice of recruitment of older married women (in the medium and long run) has an effect on wage levels because such recruits are in a position to make comparisons of pay and conditions, i.e. a true labour market starts to develop. It is therefore, important to note that in 1973 of all women taking employment, (1·4 million), 41% were coming from another job, 32% were school leavers and 27% were coming to work with no recent employment experience.

Figure 5. Rates of women's employment according to age and marital status

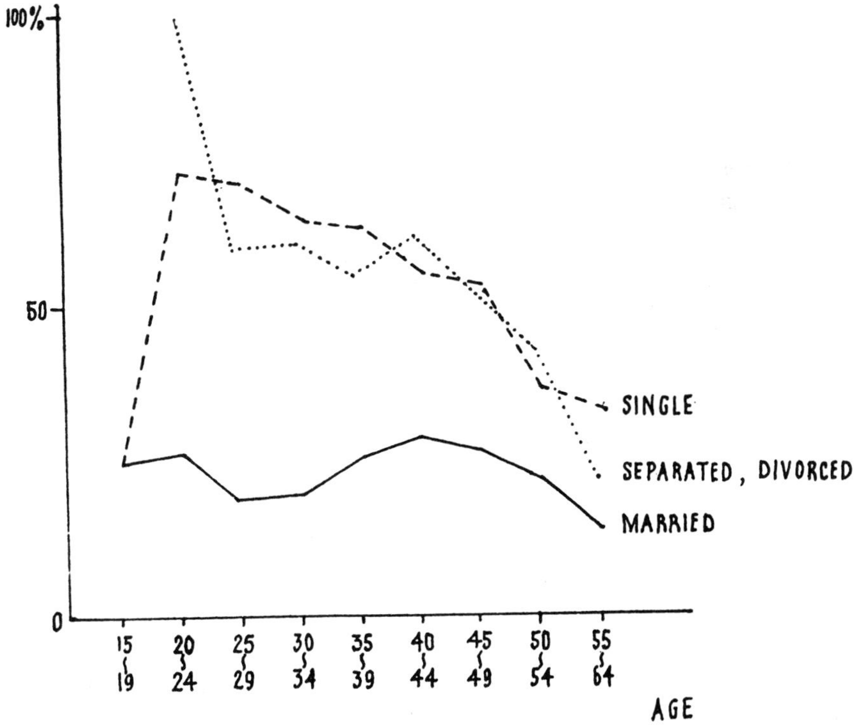

(Source: *Investigation of labour force*, Prime Minister's office)

Table XVI. Rate of Entrance and Separation by Age Group (1966)

				Age Group					
		Total	19–	20–24	25–29	30–34	35–39	40–49	50+
Entrance rate	Male	17·1	61·2	22·3	12·8	9·7	7·9	7·4	9·4
	Female	31·2	14·3	20·9	24·0	24·3	22·7	21·2	14·8
Separation rate	Male	15·9	31·3	22·1	15·1	11·5	9·1	8·7	16·7
	Female	29·4	27·1	36·5	39·5	24·7	21·2	20·5	18·1

(Source: Ministry of Labour, *Koyō dōkō chōsa* [Survey on employment trends], Tokyo, 1967, pp. 30, 68)

Note: Entrance rate $= \dfrac{\text{Number of those who got a job}}{\text{Number of employees (as of January 1)}} \times 100$

Separation rate $= \dfrac{\text{Number of those who quit a job}}{\text{Number of employees (as of January 1)}} \times 100$

Fourthly, the distinction between small and large enterprises persists in a number of ways. For example, although the average age of women employees has risen from 29·5 years in 1969 to 32·3 in 1973, the average age of women employees in 1973 in enterprises employing over 1,000 has risen from 27·1 to 29·2, whereas the average age in enterprises of between 10 and 99 employees has risen from 32·7 to 36·6 years, i.e. younger girls are still seen as better and smaller enterprises have to make up their numbers with proportionally more older women. Wage differentials between enterprises are therefore likely to have become highly critical.

Lastly, the evidence on leavers shows that 42% of all women leavers are quitting between the ages of 20-24 and a further 17% between 25 and 29. Family reasons are quoted for leaving in 25% of cases, dissatisfaction with the job is quoted as important in 90% of cases. The length of service of such leavers shows a slow increase over the last few years. 80%, however, of all women leavers have less than 5 years service[15]. This seems to bear out the persistence of the traditional pattern of short spells of employment for women. Table XVI shows that even by 1966 there was a striking contrast in this respect with male employment patterns.

IV. Wage Structure and Differentials

We are now in a position to describe and assess the relative rewards of women workers in Japan, bearing in mind the complexities of the trends in employment related above. Average monthly cash earnings have increased sharply in the last eleven years.

Wages have increased slightly faster for women than men. The nominal wage index for women (1970 = 100) increased from 73·9 (1969) to 166·6 (1974) whereas the index for men went from 74·1 to 159·7. For women on average in this period, cash earnings

Table XVII. Wage index of regular workers' cash earnings* (1970 = 100)

	All industries Nominal	Real	Manufacturing Nominal	Real
1960	32·1	56·7	31·1	54·9
1965	52·5	68·4	50·3	65·6
1971	114·7	108·1	113·9	107·4
1973	161·7	130·5	162·8	131·4

(Source: Ministry of Labour)
*(Cash earnings include standard & overtime pay and bonus)

have risen annually between 14·8% to 21·4% and for men between 13·5% and 21·9% (all this is before the inflationary wage settlements of 1974 at an average of 31%). The actual average cash earnings of women in 1973 were Y76·324 per month compared with Y143·614 per month for men[17].

The actual composition of Japanese wages is formed from a personal base rate (calculated from seniority, age, job rank etc.), incentive element, allowances, overtime and bonuses (Table XVIII).

Table XVIII. Composition of Wages, 1963-1965 (by percent) (a)

		1963(b)		1964(b)		1965(b)
A. Regular wages						
Base rate:		81·5		82·3		83·6
Type I(c)	7·5		8·8		9·4	
Type II(d)	8·7		7·2		9·0	
Type III(e)	65·3		66·3		65·2	
Incentive rate		8·0		7·1		6·1
Allowances:						
Job-duty		2·9		3·1		3·1
Living		5·5		5·7		5·8
Encouragement		1·5		1·4		1·2
Others		0·6		0·4		0·2
Total		100·0		100·0		100·0
B. Total wages						
Regular wages(b)		87·5		87·9		89·1
Overtime pay		11·8		11·5		10·3
Other payments		0·7		0·6		0·6
Total		100·0		100·0		100·0

(Source: Ministry of Labor, *Kyūyo kōsei chōsa-hōkoku* [Survey Report on Wage Components] (Tokyo: Ministry of Labor, 1965))
(a) Regular wages exclude overtime wages and non-contractual wage payments.
(b) As of September.
(c) Based on age, length-of-service, education, and/or job experience.
(d) Based on job rank, job skills, and job type.
(e) Based on a comprehensive determination including factors in Types I and II.

Figure 6. Composition of Wages by Industry (1972)

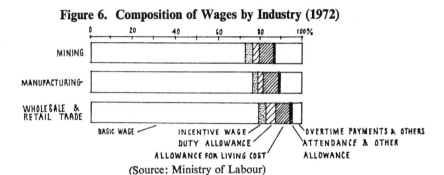

(Source: Ministry of Labour)

In 1973, the proportion of total cash earnings provided by the standard or basic wage was 73% for women and 72% for men. This has declined since 1969 when the proportions were 77% and 76% respectively[19]. The difficulty lies in making accurate comparisons with other data. The terms "standard" wage or "regular" wage have different meanings in different enterprises and in different surveys. In the case of the data given for overall earnings of women they include overtime but exclude bonus, marriage presents or adhoc payments. We can, however, certainly conclude that female wage settlements have tended to be more favourable to men than increases in supplementary wages, especially the twice annual bonus, over the last five years.

Figure 7. Average Monthly Cash Earnings, 1972

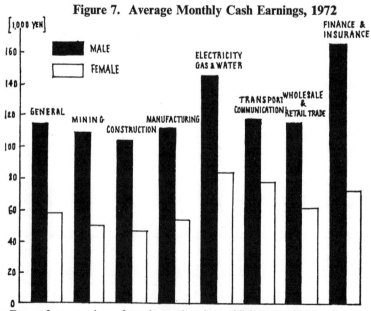

Note: Data refer to earnings of regular workers in establishments with 30 or more regular workers
(Source: Ministry of Labour)

If we analyse the distribution of earnings by men and women by industry type, there are large variations.

Such differentials have moved in favour of women over this period of 12 years, but not equally so in each industry (Table XIX).

Manufacturing, wholesale and retail trades and transport and communications have improved considerably, but other industries have a constant ratio (the utilities) and others show a worsening ratio (finance, and insurance, construction). The reasons for this clearly reflect a conbination of different factors, especially the age and service composition of the labour force, its educational make-up, the relative size of enterprises, etc.

The difference made by age to the earnings of men and women is shown in Figure 8. The separation of the two reward systems is demonstrated clearly in this figure. There is little or no career progression to be found in the age profile for women's earnings, whereas the earnings of men are dominated by the age (and seniority) factors.

This, however, is a feature of the aggregated gross average earnings for all women working in paid employment. Directly, this data is shown according to the size of the enterprise, then it becomes clear that the larger enterprises are paying more according to age, particularly for the age-group 40-55 (Figure 9).

We have already seen that the average age of women employees is lower in these larger enterprises, which indicates that they employ younger workers when they can get them. Three explanations are thus possible, none of which are exclusive and all may be true.

(1) The larger enterprises have grown so fast and require so much labour that they are prepared to pay higher rates for married women to re-enter employment than the smaller firms.

(2) The larger enterprises have greater possibilities for specialisation and therefore are beginning to provide more senior positions at higher salaries than smaller firms (for example, librarians, technicians and English typists).

Table XIX. Rates of women's earnings to men's by industry group (%)

	1960	1965	1970	1972
Mining	42	41	44	46
Construction	46	45	43	44
Manufacturing	39	45	45	47
Wholesale and retail trade	44	50	53	54
Finance and insurance	47	48	45	45
Transport and communications	56	60	63	66
Electricity, gas and water	58	58	58	58
Total	43	48	48	50

Note: Establishments with over 30 regular workers.
(Source: Ministry of Labour)

Figure 8. Workers' regular wage according to age, 1973

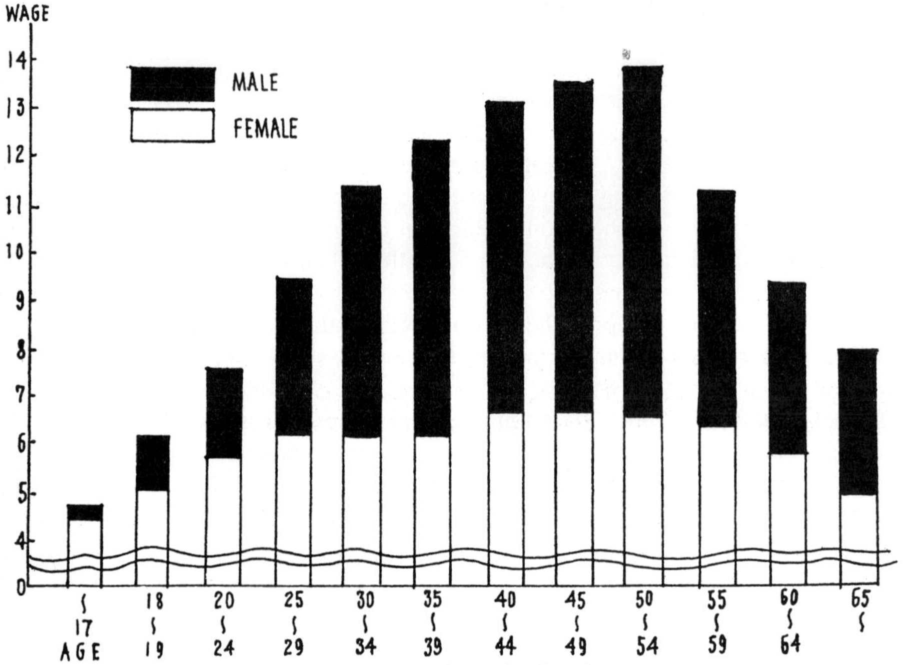

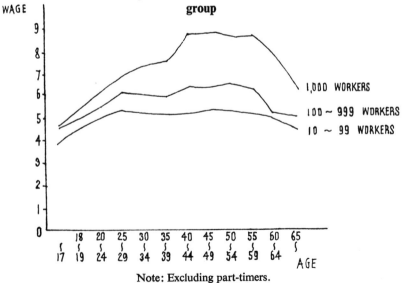

(Source: Ministry of Labour)

Figure 9. Women workers' regular wage according to the size of enterprise and age group

Note: Excluding part-timers.
(Source: Ministry of Labour)

(3)   The larger enterprises have greater stability of employment and therefore in spite of the overall trend of short spells of employment for women workers, the "Japanese system" of seniority base pay can be seen to be working here for women as for men.

Whatever the explanation, the data itself is of very considerable importance as it shows the importance of the "dual economy" for female as for male labour. Figure 10 shows the percentage that women's contractual cash earnings are of men's, for the same age and length of service groups in 1972. The contrast with Figure 9 could not be greater.

Overall, the largest differences between men's and women's earnings lie between the ages of 30-50. In the probationary stages of employment, the differences are very much less. One must conclude that the effect that employment in larger enterprises has on the level of earnings for women is discounted overall by the general tendency for men to be paid on a "life-time" career basis and for women to be paid on a more short-time service basis.

Other factors besides service and seniority do have to be taken into account, of course. Education, for example, might be thought to be a factor of considerable importance, bearing in mind the numbers of women recruited from higher education. Table XX shows the regular wages of women workers in 1973, according to age group and contrasting university graduates and middle school leavers.

Figure 10.   Women's wages as a proportion of men's by age groups (male = 100)

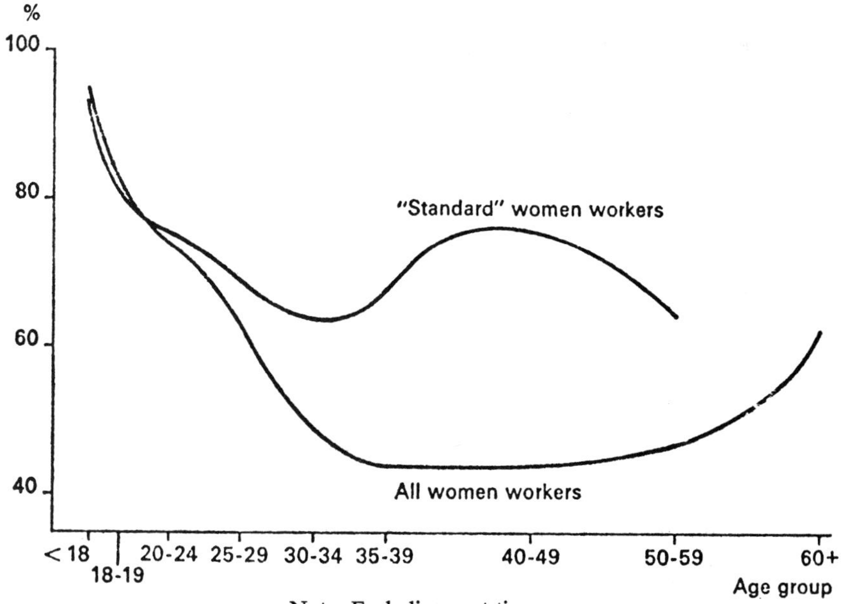

Note: Excluding part-timers.
(Source: Ministry of Labour)

Table XX. Regular wages per month by age and qualification
Monthly earnings

	A Primary & Middle school education only	B University education	% A as proportion of equivalent male earnings	% B as proportion of equivalent male earnings
20–24	44·3	59·4	61·1	94·6
25–29	43·9	67·1	57·4	87·7
30–34	40·8	74·4	50·3	71·4
35–39	42·5	70·8	42·5	55·3
40–44	41·5	89·7	49·8	58·1
45–49	41·9	71·3	50·9	47·6
50–54	42·5	77·2	50·1	55·2

(Source: Ministry of Labour)

The contrast between the university-trained pattern of rewards and the ordinary school leaver is clear enough. The former has a peak at the ages of 40-44, presumably to encourage re-entry to employment; the latter declines from the starting wage and is more or less constant throughout the age range. When compared with male wages, however, the ratio worsens for women who are ordinary school leavers from 20 to 40, but improves after that age. The university girl, apart from the age group 40-44, suffers a worsening ratio from 20 to 50, when it improves again. In general terms, therefore, education is clearly a factor distinguishing the occupation and company and therefore the overall level and career pattern of rewards. University education, however, seems to be less important with age (apart from the mid-forties age group) as a factor equalising rewards with men.

Figure 11. Variations in sex wage ratios over time (Male = 100)

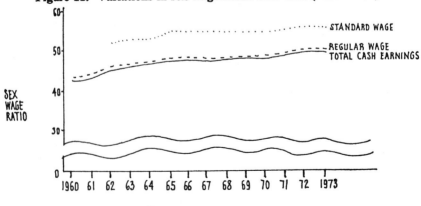

YEARS 1960 - 1973
(Source: Ministry of Labour)

Two other factors can be discussed briefly. The effect of changes in the composition of wages on the question of equal pay does not according to Figure 11, appear to be very important.

Figure 11 shows a long term stability for the proportion of the "shotenai kyuyo" (standard wage) of women, compared with men. There is a slight tendency for the regular wage (including allowances and regular bonus) of women to become a larger proportion and this is also true for overall cash earnings (including overtime). But the effect of these non-standard earnings is extremely small.

Secondly, the effect of hours of work on the problem is equally very limited. Actual hours of work in Japan have been reduced in recent years. In 1960, for all workers (male and female combined) the average hours worked per month was 202·7; by 1972 this was reduced to 184·7. However, comparing hours worked by men and women, in 1969 men worked on average 198·6 hours in the month and women 178·8. By 1973, the hours had been reduced to 187·8 and 169·2. The proportion of women's to men's

Figure 12. Actual hours worked per month by male and female workers according to the size of enterprise

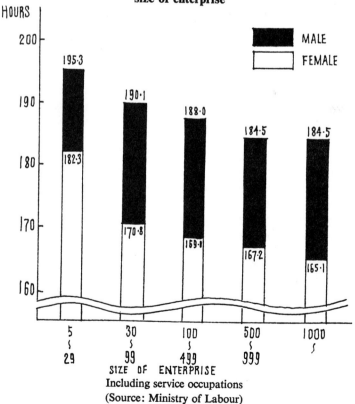

Including service occupations
(Source: Ministry of Labour)

hours, however, remained approximately at 90%[20]. Figure 12 shows the large differences which exist for hours of work between sizes of enterprise. It will be noted that the difference in actual hours of work between men and women is greater for larger enterprises than smaller enterprises. If overtime is paid, therefore, this ought to mean that women's cash earnings are proportionately less for larger enterprises than smaller enterprises. However, much of the "overtime" for staff of larger enterprises may be voluntary (and unpaid); there is little evidence that overtime is important in determining cash earnings as this Figure might suggest. Occupational differences are probably more important here, e.g. typists have high wages proportionately and short hours, and dress-making is the reverse. Part-time wages have generally been left out of the data presented. There is little variation with age and part-timers are paid on average Y246 per hour, (increased year by year proportionately with general wage increases).

V. Government Intervention and Labour Market Pressures
The evidence presented here can be summarised in these propositions:
  (1) Japan is a society with a strong traditional culture in which women had specialised and distinct roles and behaved in a distinct manner compared with men.
  (2) Occupationally, women have been clearly segregated from men and the effect of mass higher education for women has been surprisingly small on such segregation.
  (3) Since 1956, however, the structure of the economy has been transformed, under the influence of a 9% annual real growth rate. This has created an enormous demand for labour in the secondary and tertiary sectors of the economy and the proportion of women in paid employment has increased, even though the overall participation rate (in the labour force) has declined.
  (4) The bulk of this expansion has been in the employment of married women, which is a clear break with traditional personnel practice. Nevertheless, there are grounds for believing that this extra labour has been absorbed without making much impact on female career opportunities.
  (5) It has also been possible to re-employ women without challenging the life-time career principle for key male staff, although (i) the rewards in larger enterprises for women over 40 have had to be increased fairly sharply, (ii) the ratio of women's earnings to men has risen from 43% to 50% overall since 1960 (in manufacturing from 39% to 47%), (iii) the earnings of young female university graduates (under 30) are now over 87% of male equivalents on average.
  (6) The demographic situation is such as to suggest that demand for employing married women will expand much further. Inflationary pressures are likely to support pressures on wives to re-enter employment after their children have entered middle school, if not before. Part-time employment, now about 15% of total female employment, is also likely to increase.

From a comparative point of view, therefore, there is some interesting evidence here, (i) that economic expansion can have a marked effect in lessening inequalities of wages, especially in the modernising sector although (ii) the basic personnel policy and practice of using a "life-time" career reward system for men has not been dis- continued (and in many respects has been expanded). Therefore, (iii) the practice of operating separate labour markets for men and women has continued.

We have placed little emphasis to date on government intervention, as this has not been a major factor in the situation. There are grounds now for thinking that in the next decade this situation will change.

In the first place, whilst public attention was focused on young employees, it has been assumed in Japan that "good and progressive employers" would provide dormitories, high school education, flower arrangement classes, help with family problems and with marriage etc. Large department stores and enterprises such as Sony and Matsushita have placed a large emphasis on the protection and welfare of young female workers. Specially assigned older workers were asked to take care of individuals (the so-called "Elder Sister" scheme). The employment of married women raises quite new problems for employers and these are often issues with which the community and the State are vitally concerned. The Working Women's Welfare Law of 1972 makes it clear that the protection of the welfare of working women is vital because of their role in bringing up children. "Article 2" states:

"In view of the fact that working women are the persons who have an important role in nursing children who are the support and driving force of the future world and who are contributing to the development of economy and society, they shall deserve to receive appropriate consideration which will help them secure harmony between working life and home life and to secure a working life with a sense of fulfilment, by making best use of their abilities, with their maternity respected and yet without discriminatory treatment by sex."

This argument, no matter how vague sounding it appears, is then used to justify government intervention, particularly over health guidance, vocational guidance, vocational training, child care and the establishment of welfare centres. Crèches for children are already growing in numbers. (There were 242,000 children eligible for nurseries in 1972 and 130,000 actually attending.) Hours are already being reduced for women and this process of protection seems likely to continue. The effect on the price of female labour is surely going to be seen in the near future.

Secondly, the Vocational Training Law of 1969 has already resulted in specialised training being offered for women in a limited number of occupations, e.g. garment and textile fabric work, sewing and knitting machine operation, clerical work, typing and beauty care. There is no inherent political or social reason blocking the development of these training courses into a wider range of occupations. Japan does not have a highly developed set of unions based on occupations, determined to preserve job rights. Enterprise unionism is much less interested in job demarcations or the boundaries of occupations than unions in the British context. Directly economic pressures are more explicit, then the government could (and no doubt will) expand its output of trained women in specialist occupations. Such a development could easily lead to pressure for higher job grades for experienced workers and this fact alone, if agreed by employers, would certainly alter the sex-wage ratio.

Thirdly, as Japan is only at the beginning of the expansion of the employed labour force to include married women, their service rights are at present rather low. In five years time, given no major economic depression, then it is reasonable to predict that wage curves will show the effect of increasing seniority among women workers.

Lastly, there is the impact of world wide agitation over equal pay and anti-discriminatory legislation. At the very least, such international trends give government officials a strong motivation to justify intervention. It seems possible that, in Japan, there may be further legislation in the seventies on the lines of the British and American models. The Japanese case, therefore, has many aspects and characteristics which are familiar to those studying the equal pay question in other societies. Chiplin and Sloane suggest that sexual wage discrimination "may most usefully be regarded as a demand side phenomenon in which employers (and employees) obtain satisfaction from various types of exclusion and wage discrimination"[21]. This conclusion would not be untrue in Japan. When circumstances shifted, personnel policies were changed. If necessary, women will be paid at very much higher rates and the sex-wage ratio will be changed. The increase in the employment of married women has so far been achieved with some changes in the sex-wage ratio, but this process may speed up. Again the relative importance of political pressure groups on the equal pay question is not unique to Japan. The relationship shown between demographic changes, economic expansion and labour market changes is certainly familiar to development specialists.

However, there is one aspect of special interest in the data and that relates to the form of wage discrimination. Comparing the age earnings profiles of Japanese and English workers does show the extent to which Japanese males equate with the profiles shown for male non-manual workers in the United Kingdom; the manual curves and the curves for females are flatter as are the aggregate curves for women in Japan[22]. We have seen that in the modernised sector this situation is changed and this evidence suggests that Japanese employers are employing a special rationality in utilising "life time commitment" as a personnel strategy, as argued by Dore[23]. If this is so, then large companies would presumably try in the future to recruit women who could give such commitment and will be paid accordingly for it. In this respect, discrimination would then flow primarily through the "dual structure" of the economy. This possibility brings employers into potential conflict with public policy and if it were realised, would add a new dimension to the problem of sexual wage and employment discrimination in Japan.

References

1. Sugimoto, E. I., *A Daugher of the Samurai*, New York, Doubleday Doran & Co., 1935, p. 276.
2. Gorer, G., "Themes in Japanese Culture" in Silberman, B. S. (ed.), *Japanese Character and Culture*, Arizona, University of Arizona Press, 1962, p. 314.
3. Kikuchi, K., and Omura, R. (eds.), *Anohito wa Kaette Konakatta (He Never Returned)* Tokyo, Iwanami, 1964.
4. Ohkawa, K., and Rosovosky, H., "A Century of Japanese Economic Growth" in Lockwood, W. W. (ed.), *The State and Economic Enterprise in Japan*, Princeton, New Jersey, Princeton University Press, 1965, p. 89.
5. Economic Affairs Bureau, Ministry of Foreign Affairs, *Statistical Survey of Japan's Economy*, 1973, p. 71.
6. Yazaki, T., *Social Change and the City in Japan*, Japan Publications, Inc., 1968, pp. 141-2.
7. Abegglen, J., *The Japanese Factory*, Glencoe, The Free Press, 1957.
8. Dore, R., *British Factory—Japanese Factory*, London, Allen and Unwin, 1973.
8. Baldwin, F., "The Idioms of Contemporary Japan v. Urran Ribu", *Japan Interpreter*, Vol. 8, Spring, 1973, pp. 237-244.
9. Yamaguchi, M., "The Status of Women in Japan: A JAUW Seminar", *IFUW/FIFDU Newsletter*, January, 1974.
10. Fukutake, T., *Japanese Rural Society*, Ithaca, Cornell University Press, 1967, p. 35.
11. Fukutake, *op. cit.*, Table IX, p. 35.
12. Fukutake, *op. cit.*, Table XII, p. 38.
13. Women's and Minor's Bureau, Ministry of Labour, *The Status of Women In Japan*, 1973, p. 13.
14. Broadbridge, S. A., Japan's Dual Economy, 1967.
15. Fujin sho-nen Kyoku, Rodo-sho (Women's and Minors' Bureau, Ministry of Labour), *Fujin rodo-no Jitsujo (The State of Women Workers)*, 1973, pp. 10-27.
16. Quoted in Okochi, K. *et al.*, *Workers and Employers in Japan*, University of Tokyo Press, 1973, p. 159.
17. *Fujin rodo-no jitsujo, op. cit.*, pp. 28-29.
18. Quoted in Okochi, K., *op. cit.*, p. 363.
19. *Fujin rodo-no jitsujo, op. cit.*, p. 28.
20. *Fujin rodo-no jitsujo, op. cit.*, p. 47.
21. Chiplin, B., and Sloane, P. J., "Sexual Discrimination in the Labour Market", *BJIR*, Vol. XII No. 3, Nov. 1974, p. 400.
22. Chiplin, B., and Sloane, P. J., *op. cit.*, Figure 2, p. 376.
23. Dore, R., *op. cit.*

Index